INTRODUCING

ASIAN AMERICAN THEOLOGIES

INTRODUCING

ASIAN AMERICAN THEOLOGIES

Jonathan Y. Tan

ORBIS BOOKS

Maryknoll, New York 10545

Founded in 1970, Orbis Books endeavors to publish works that enlighten the mind, nourish the spirit, and challenge the conscience. The publishing arm of the Maryknoll Fathers and Brothers, Orbis seeks to explore the global dimensions of the Christian faith and mission, to invite dialogue with diverse cultures and religious traditions, and to serve the cause of reconciliation and peace. The books published reflect the views of their authors and do not represent the official position of the Society. To learn more about Maryknoll and Orbis Books, please visit our website at www.maryknoll.org.

Library of Congress Cataloging-in-Publication Data

Tan, Jonathan Y.
    Introducing Asian American theologies / Jonathan Y. Tan.
        p. cm.
    Includes bibliographical references (p.   ) and index.
    ISBN 978-1-57075-768-6
    1. Asian Americans – Religion. 2. Theology, Doctrinal. I. Title.
BR563.A82T36 2008
230.089′95073 – dc22
                                                    2007032622

To
Vân and Ky Ky

Contents

Preface xi

1. Introducing Asian America 1
   A Snapshot of Asian American Demographics   3

2. Asian Immigration to the United States 20
   Early Chinese Immigration to the United States   20
   *Early Japanese and Korean Immigration to the
      United States*   28
   *Twentieth-Century Anti-Asian Hysteria:
      From Exclusion to Internment*   29
   Post–World War II Developments   32
   Hart-Celler Act (1965)   33
   Indochinese Immigration to the United States   34

3. The Asian American Presence in the Present-Day
      United States: Contemporary Experiences
      and Challenges 36
   Asian Americans as the "Model Minority"?   37
   Asian Americans as the "Middle Minority"?   39
   *Asian Americans as "Forever Foreigners" or
      "Honorary Whites"?*   41
   Asian American Experiences of Racism   45
   *Shaping Asian American Identities in the Twenty-first-
      Century United States*   49

4. Understanding Asian American Christianity 57
   Emergence of Asian American Christianity   58
   Why Asian American Churches?   59

Korean American Christianity   61
Chinese American Christianity   62
Asian American Catholicism   64
Conclusion: The Future of Asian American Churches   74

5. What Are Asian American Theologies? 77
Asian American Theologies as Contextual Theologies   78
Sources and Goals of Asian American Theological
    Reflections   80
Asian American Systematic Theologies   82
Theologizing beyond the Asian American World   83

6. Who Are the Asian American Theologians? 85
The Historical Backdrop of the 1950s and 1960s   86
Emerging Asian American Consciousness   87
The First Generation of Asian American Theologians   90
The Second Generation of Asian American Theologians   99
Asian American Feminist Theologians   102
Asian American Catholic Theologians   105
Asian American Evangelical Theologians   106

7. Reading the Bible in Asian America 108
The Dilemma of Asian American Biblical Scholars   109
Defining Asian American Biblical Hermeneutics   110
From Historical-Critical Hermeneutics to Contextual
    Hermeneutics   112
Hermeneutics and the Implications of Diasporic and
    Postcolonial Experiences   114
Hermeneutics and Identity Constructions   115

8. Race and Race Relations in Asian American
Theologies 121
Understanding Race   121
Asian Americans and the "Race" Problematic   125
Asian Americans as Unassimilable?   127

Continuing Prejudice and Stereotyping 131
Asian American Theological Responses to Racism 133
Theologies of Marginality 134
Theologies of Reconciliation and Healing 138

9. **Asian American Evangelical Theologies:**
   Emerging Trends and Challenges 143
   *Rapid Growth of Asian American Evangelical
      Christianity* 144
   Korean American Evangelicalism 145
   Chinese American Evangelicalism 146
   Asian American Evangelical Identity Construction 148
   "The 'Scandal' of the 'Model Minority' Mind?" 149
   Emergence of Asian American Evangelical Theologies 154
   Constructing Asian American Evangelical Theologies 157

10. **The Future of Asian American Theologies** 162
    *Toward a Common Asian American Theological
       Method* 164

References 177

Index 201

Preface

Ask any person in the street about "Asian American Christians" and more often than not, one would get hesitant pauses, blank looks, or stereotypings (e.g., "Asian American Christians are Filipinos, are they not?"). As a result of the deeply entrenched Orientalism in the mainstream United States that is promoted in part by prominent academics, politicians, popular writers, and the mass media, most Americans tend to view Asian Americans in romanticized terms. They associate Asian Americans with the exotic "Oriental" religions of Islam, Buddhism, Daoism, Hinduism, and so forth. In their minds, Caucasians, blacks, and Hispanic Latino/as are Christians, while Asian Americans are the exotic "Other" whose quaint and colorful religious traditions and practices coexist somewhat disconcertingly with Christianity. As far as they are concerned, the phrase "Asian American Christian" seems incongruous and oxymoronic.

Hence, it comes as a surprise to many that Asian American Christians are not only the most diverse group of Christians in the United States, they are also the second-fastest-growing group after Latino/a Christians. As early as 1991, the acclaimed *New York Times* religion reporter Ari L. Goldman, citing the recently released results of the National Survey of Religious Identification commissioned by the Graduate School of the City University of New York, expressed surprise that contrary to popular expectations, "most Asian Americans and most Arab-Americans are Christian, rather than Buddhist, Hindu or Muslim." Goldman went on to explain that "Christians from Arab and Asian countries are more likely to emigrate to the United States" (Goldman 1991). Hence, it is most unfortunate that Asian American Christians are often invisible in the public eye.

On the one hand, it is true that Asian American Christians, whether mainline Protestant, Catholic, Pentecostal, or Evangelical, are but numerically small compared to their Caucasian, black, and Latino/a American cousins. But on the other hand, the fact remains that most Asian Americans are Christians, and their theologies deserve to be better known and studied in the same manner as their black and Latino/a counterparts. It is therefore regrettable that very little has been written about Asian American theologies, in comparison with studies on black and Latino/a theologies. There are no critical surveys or significant studies of Asian American theologies that are easily accessible.

To remedy this shortcoming, this book joins its counterparts, *Introducing Black Theology of Liberation* and *Introducing Latino/a Theologies,* to offer a concise overview and discussion of Asian American Christians and their theologies. In this book, I survey and analyze the historical developments, principal themes, sources, practices, trends, and challenges in Asian American theologies. In addition, I investigate and discuss the historical, legal, and contemporary contexts of Asian American theological reflections, the current issues and challenges raised by these contexts, as well as their implications for the future development of Asian American theologies.

It is my hope that this book would be useful to a wide audience ranging from academics, undergraduates, students preparing for ministry, and those involved in Asian American ministries, to Asian American Christians and others who are interested in this topic. In writing this book as a volume in Orbis Books' "Introducing" series, I have shaped its contents primarily for use in undergraduate and graduate studies, limiting my focus to reviewing, describing, and discussing the major trends and developments rather than proffering my own viewpoint as normative. Nonetheless, I would be delighted if scholars and experts would find the book's extensive bibliography and systematic discussion useful for their further research and in-depth scholarship.

I would like to express my appreciation and thankfulness to everyone who has, in one way or another, assisted me in writing this book. First, my heartfelt love and gratefulness to my parents, especially my mother for instilling in me a love for all things Chinese, Christian, and literary, as well as inculcating in me the desire to expand my horizons through books and writing. My deepest gratitude also goes to John Baldovin, S.J., and Peter Phan for their extensive mentoring throughout my graduate studies at the Jesuit School of Theology and The Catholic University of America. Their scholarly accomplishments have greatly inspired me as I begin my own journey as a scholar of religion, culture, and society.

The legal research, logical reasoning, and intensive writing skills that I acquired during my law studies at the National University of Singapore Law School proved most useful when I explored the legislative and judicial dimensions of Asian American discrimination and exclusion. My decision to integrate a legal analysis of the ramifications of U.S. constitutional and immigration law on Asian American identity constructions with my survey of Asian American theologies may be traced to the enduring influence of Justice Tan Lee Meng, presently judge of the Supreme Court of the Republic of Singapore, who was dean of the National University of Singapore Law School and master of Raffles Hall during my time there. Justice Tan Lee Meng not only taught me the finer points of legal research, debate, and writing over many an afternoon tea in the dining room of Raffles Hall, but also reminded me that we omit all discussions about the legal implications and repercussions of sociocultural, identity, and religious issues to our detriment and peril.

I have also benefited from the many conversations and comments with my colleagues and friends at the Institute for the Study of Asian American Christianity (ISAAC), especially Young Lee Hertig, Timothy Tseng, and Amos Yong, who read and offered incisive critiques and detailed advice on the early draft chapters of this book. They and others at ISAAC have been most enthusiastic about this project, offering prayers and words of inspiration and encouragement, as well as gently inquiring when this book will finally be finished and ready for their use. This book would have accomplished less without their assistance and input.

A generous grant from the Louisville Institute under its First Book Grant for Minority Scholars program enabled me to take a yearlong sabbatical in 2005–6 to research and write this book. The institute's executive director, Jim Lewis, gently ribbed me that nearly all of the Asian American theologians featured in this book are past recipients of grants and fellowships from the Louisville Institute! It is a well-kept secret that many of the major accomplishments of Asian American theologians that are cited in this book are either directly or indirectly funded by grants and fellow-ships from the Louisville Institute. The Asian American theological community is grateful to the Louisville Institute for its role and support in incubating and nurturing the development and growth of Asian American theologies.

A word of thanks to my wonderful colleagues and friends, and an ex-colleague in the case of Paul Knitter, in the Department of Theology at Xavier University, who have also been most supportive and generous with their advice and suggestions. I would also like to express my grateful appreciation to two close friends in California, Kim Loan Le and Khoan Nguyen, for their prayers, support, and advice about family, life, culture, ethnicity, and religious issues. For the successful completion of this book, I am especially indebted to Sue Perry, my editor at Orbis Books, for her wise counsel, in-valuable guidance, and detailed advice as she shepherded the book from its inception to its completion.

Finally, I owe the greatest debt to my beloved wife, Vân, and our vivacious son, Ky Ky, for their gentle presence, unconditional love, and emotional support. Together, they have taught me more about life than anything I could ever learn from books, and to them I have dedicated this book in abiding love and gratitude.

Chapter 1

Introducing Asian America

The term "Asian American" is often used in contemporary discourse as a generic and convenient shorthand to categorize all Americans of Asian ancestry and heritage, with their diverse languages, cultures, and traditions. The U.S. Census Bureau adopts a similar approach in its census reports, defining "Asian" as "those having origins in any of the original peoples of the Far East, Southeast Asia, or the Indian subcontinent including, for example, Cambodia, China, India, Japan, Korea, Malaysia, Pakistan, the Philippine Islands, Thailand, and Vietnam" (U.S. Census Bureau 2003: 1). On their part, many Asian Americans, especially the first generation, tend to identify themselves in practice not only by their ethnicity but also by other distinguishing factors such as caste, region, or dialect, for example, Keralite Indian American, Knanaya Indian American, Taiwanese Chinese American, Hakka Chinese American, Cantonese Chinese American, and so forth.

In the past, the U.S. Census Bureau lumped Asian Americans together with Hawaiians and Pacific Islanders, a category that includes Samoans, Tongans, Tahitians, Fijians, and other ethnicities, despite the fact that Hawaiians and Pacific Islanders have more in common with Native Americans than with Asian Americans in their life experiences, as well as sociocultural and economic-political concerns. Such an arbitrary classification process lends credence to the contention of Michael Omi and Howard Winant that many diverse and unrelated ethnic groups are often aggregated together in a "racially based process" for no other reason than the fact that "the majority of Americans cannot tell the difference between members of these various groups" (Omi and Winant 1994: 23). In Census 2000 the U.S. Census Bureau differentiated Asian Americans and Pacific Islanders into separate statistical categories for the first time.

1

Nonetheless, the term "Asian American" masks distinct racial-ethnic communities under the facade of a homogenous and monolithic pan–Asian American identity that exists more in theory than in reality. Instead of viewing the Asian American identity in rigid and normative terms, perhaps this identity is better understood as diverse and multiple, constantly in flux and being shaped by, as well as shaping, historical social, cultural, and political contexts. Asian American scholar Lisa Lowe explains the implications of Asian American heterogeneity as follows:

> What is referred to as "Asian American" is clearly a heterogeneous entity. From the perspective of the majority culture, Asian Americans may very well be constructed as different from, and other than, Euro-Americans. But from the perspectives of Asian Americans, we are perhaps even more different, more diverse among ourselves.... As with other diasporas in the United States, the Asian immigrant collectivity is unstable and changeable, with its cohesion complicated by inter-generationality, by various degrees of identification and relation to a "homeland," and by different extent of assimilation to and distinction from "majority culture" in the United States. (Lowe 1991: 27)

In truth, the category of "Asian Americans" encompasses groups of peoples of diverse languages, cultures, spiritual traditions, worldviews, socioeconomic classes, and generational levels, such that all attempts at generalizations run a significant risk of error. Indeed, the U.S. Census Bureau has admitted this fact, when it acknowledged that the Asian population in the United States

> is not a homogeneous group; rather, it comprises many groups who differ in language, culture, and length of residence in the United States. Some of the Asian groups, such as the Chinese and Japanese, have been in the United States for several generations. Others, such as the Hmong, Vietnamese, Laotians, and Cambodians, are comparatively recent immigrants. (U.S. Census Bureau 2003: 1)

Interestingly, the diversity and plurality of the Asian American landscape reflects a similar diversity and plurality of the

Asian world, with its immense range of cultures, religions, philosophies, and ways of life. In speaking about Asia, one must bear in mind that there has never been, nor will there be, a normative Asian culture or way of life. Even terms like "Chinese" or "Indian" encompass a colorful mosaic of ethnic groups with their own languages, dialects, cultures, castes, spiritual traditions, histories, customs, and worldviews that dwarf those of Europe. Moreover, this diversity is further accentuated by the presence of large Chinese and Indian diasporic communities all over Asia and throughout the world.

A Snapshot of
Asian American Demographics

Since 1965, Asian Americans collectively constitute the second-fastest-growing and most diverse racial group in the United States. The statistical data from the U.S. Census Bureau's Census 2000 reveals that as of April 1, 2000, Asian Americans make up 4.2 percent (11.9 million) of the total U.S. population of 281.4 million. This figure includes 10.2 million (3.6 percent) who reported only Asian and 1.7 million (0.6 percent) who reported Asian in combination with one or more other races (see Table 1). The largest Asian American ethnic group are the Chinese Americans, comprising 2.7 million who reported either Chinese alone (2.3 million) or in combination with one or more other Asian American ethnic groups or other races (0.4 million) (see Table 2). They are followed closely by the Filipino Americans, Indian Americans, Korean Americans, Vietnamese Americans, and Japanese Americans, respectively. Table 2 also indicates that the three largest Asian American groups — the Chinese Americans, Filipino Americans, and Indian Americans — account for some 58 percent of Asian Americans reporting a single Asian group, and 57 percent of those reporting combination groups. More interestingly, the statistical data in this table reveal that of the six largest Asian American groups, the Japanese Americans are the most likely to outmarry (31 percent in combination with one or more other Asian groups or other races), while the Vietnamese Americans are the least likely to outmarry (only 8.3 percent in combination with one or more other Asian groups or other races).

In general, the statistical data in various categories for the Asian American population as a whole compares favorably with the other races in the United States (see Table 3). To highlight a few key points from this table: as a group, Americans of Asian and Pacific Islander heritage are well-educated compared to the non-Hispanic white American population. As the statistics of the United States Census Bureau show, in the year 2002 some 51 percent of Asian and Pacific Islander men and 44 percent of Asian and Pacific Islander women age twenty-five and older hold at least a bachelor's degree, compared to 32 percent and 27 percent, respectively, for their counterparts in the non-Hispanic white American population. In the American workforce, Asians and Pacific Islanders are concentrated in the managerial and professional specialty occupations: some 41.0 percent of men and 37.2 percent of women in the Asian and Pacific Islander cohort compared to 33.4 percent and 36.9 percent of non-Hispanic white American men and women, respectively. In terms of family income, Asians and Pacific Islanders dominate at both ends of the income spectrum: some 40 percent of all Asian and Pacific Islander households have annual incomes of seventy-five thousand dollars or more, while 10.2 percent of Asians and Pacific Islander households live below the poverty line, compared to 35 percent and 7.8 percent, respectively, of the non-Hispanic white American families.

More significantly, the United States Census Bureau's fifty-year interim statistical projections suggest that, if we exclude all undocumented immigrants, the Asian American population is the fastest-growing segment of the U.S. population by the year 2050. It appears that the projected number of U.S. residents who will identify themselves as Asian alone in the year 2050 is about 33.4 million, comprising some 8 percent of the total population of the United States (see Table 4). In cumulative terms, the projected percentage increase of Asian-only U.S. population between 2000 and 2050 is an astounding 213 percent, compared to 188 percent for Hispanics of any race; a mere 7 percent for the white-only; non-Hispanic U.S. population; and a 49 percent increase in the total population of the United States over this period (see Table 5).

This development should not surprise us, considering that the rise in foreign-born U.S. population since 1970 has continued unabated. Indeed, the U.S. Census Bureau reports that in the thirty-year period between 1970 and 2000, while the percentage of Europe-born U.S. population dropped from 62 percent to 15 percent, the Asian-born U.S. population increased from 9 percent to 26 percent, and the percentage of U.S. population from Latin America has increased from 19 percent to 51 percent (United States Census Bureau 2002b: 17–1). In particular, Census 2000 shows that in the year 2000, about 7.2 million of the United States' foreign-born population were born in Asia, comprising some 26 percent of the foreign-born U.S. population. In terms of numbers, this represents a significant increase from eight hundred thousand in 1970 and 5.0 million in 1990 (United States Census Bureau 2002a: 1). Census 2000 also identifies the top five immigrant-sending Asian countries as China, Philippines, India, Vietnam, and Korea, with the Indian-born U.S. population showing the biggest increase (see Table 6). In absolute numbers, China is the second-largest source of foreign-born United States residents after Mexico. At the same time, the Census Bureau's data paints a generally optimistic profile about the Asian-born U.S. population in comparison with both the native-born U.S. population and the entire cohort of foreign-born U.S. population (see Table 7).

In terms of geographical distribution, most Asian Americans live in the western United States, followed by the Northeast, the South, and the Midwest (see Table 8). About 51 percent of the Asian American population are congregated in three states: California (4.2 million Asian Americans), New York (1.2 million Asian Americans), and Hawaii (0.7 million Asian Americans). The next seven states in terms of Asian American population are Texas, New Jersey, Illinois, Washington, Florida, Virginia, and Massachusetts (see Table 9). The total Asian American population in these ten states aggregates to approximately three-fourths of the total Asian American population for the entire country. Taken as a whole, the statistical data shows that 95 percent of Asian Americans live in metropolitan and urban centers.

A significant percentage of Asian Americans are concentrated in the coastal and urban regions, especially in the large metropolitan regions of the western and northeastern United States, with

New York, Los Angeles, San Jose, San Francisco, and Honolulu being the top five cities in terms of Asian American population (see Table 10). In terms of percentage of Asian Americans, all of the top ten places are in the West: one in Hawaii, nine in California (see Table 11). The city of Honolulu in Hawaii tops the list with Asian Americans comprising some 68 percent of its total population, followed by Daly City in California, with Asian Americans comprising 54 percent of its total population.

TABLES

Table 1
Census 2000: Asian American Population

Race	Number	Percentage of Total United States Population
TOTAL United States POPULATION	281,421,906	100.0
ASIAN ALONE OR IN COMBINATION WITH ONE OR MORE OTHER RACES	11,898,828	4.2
Asian alone	10,242,998	3.6
Asian in combination with one or more other races	1,665,830	0.6
Asian: White	868,395	0.3
Asian: Some other race	249,108	0.1
Asian: Native Hawaiian and other Pacific Islanders	138,802	**
Asian: Black or African American	106,782	**
All other combinations including Asian	292,743	0.1
Not Asian alone or in combination with one or more other races	269,523,078	95.8

**percentage rounds to 0.0
(Source: United States Census Bureau 2002c:3)

Table 2
Census 2000: Asian Population by Detailed Group – List of Top Twelve Groups

Detailed Group	Asian Alone		Asian in combination with one or more other races		Asian detailed group alone or in any combination*
	One Asian group reported	Two or more Asian groups reported*	One Asian group reported	Two or more Asian groups reported*	
TOTAL	**10,019,405**	**223,593**	**1,516,841**	**138,989**	**11,898,828**
Chinese, excl. Taiwanese	2,314,537	130,826	201,688	87,790	2,734,841
Filipino	1,850,314	57,811	385,236	71,454	2,364,815
Indian	1,678,765	40,013	165,437	15,384	1,899,599
Korean	1,076,872	22,550	114,211	14,794	1,228,427
Vietnamese	1,122,528	47,144	48,639	5,425	1,223,736
Japanese	796,700	55,537	241,209	55,486	1,148,932
Cambodian	171,937	11,832	20,830	1,453	206,052
Pakistani	153,533	11,095	37,587	2,094	204,309
Laotian	168,707	10,396	17,914	1,186	198,203
Hmong	169,428	5,284	11,153	445	186,310
Thai	112,989	7,929	27,170	2,195	150,283
Taiwanese	118,048	14,096	11,394	1,257	144,795

*The numbers by detailed Asian group do not add to the total population. This is because the detailed Asian groups are tallies of the number of Asian *responses* rather than the number of Asian *respondents*. Respondents reporting several Asian groups are counted several times. For example, a respondent reporting "Korean and Filipino" would be included in the Korean as well as the Filipino numbers. (Source: abridged from United States Census Bureau 2002c:9)

Table 3
Profile of Asian and Pacific Islander* Population
in the United States (March 2002)

Age Distribution	Twenty-six percent of Asians and Pacific Islanders were under the age of eighteen, compared with 23 percent of non-Hispanic whites. By contrast, only 7 percent of Asians and Pacific Islanders were aged sixty-five and above, compared with 14 percent of the non-Hispanic whites.
Families	Seventy-three percent of Asian and Pacific Islander households were families, compared to 66 for the non-Hispanic white households. In general, Asian and Pacific Islander families were larger than non-Hispanic white families. Some 18 percent of Asian and Pacific Islander families had five or more members, in contrast to 11 percent for the non-Hispanic white families. In addition, 20 percent of Asian and Pacific Islander married-couple families comprise five or more members, compared to 12 percent for the non-Hispanic white families.
Education	On the one hand, Asians and Pacific Islanders have the highest percentage of college graduates, compared to other races in the population of the United States. In the Asian and Pacific Islander cohort age twenty-five and above, 51 percent of the men and 44 percent of the women have at least a bachelor's degree, compared to 32 percent of the men and 27 percent of the women of the corresponding non-Hispanic white cohort. Asians and Pacific Islanders are also high achievers, with 16 percent of those age 25 and over with advanced master's and doctoral degrees, compared with 9 percent for all adults in this age group.
	On the other hand, Asians and Pacific Islanders are also more likely to have *less* than a ninth-grade education (7 percent), compared to non-Hispanic whites (4 percent). In general, some 87 percent of Asians and Pacific Islanders age twenty-five and above have at least a high school diploma, compared to 89 percent for non-Hispanic whites in this age group.
Asian Languages	Chinese is the second-most-widely spoken non-English language in the United States (2.0 million), after Spanish. Tagalog ranks fifth (1.2 million), after French (third) and German (fourth). Vietnamese is the sixth-most-widely spoken non-English language (1.0 million), while Korean is in the eighth position, with 894,000 speakers.

Table 3 (continued)
Profile of Asian and Pacific Islander* Population
in the United States (March 2002)

Income and Poverty	On the one hand, 40 percent of all Asian and Pacific Islander families had income of $75,000 and above, compared with 35 percent of non-Hispanic white families. The 2002 median income of Asian and Pacific Islander households is $52,018, compared with $42,409 for all U.S. households.
	But on the other hand, 17 percent of Asian and Pacific Islander families had incomes less than $25,000, compared with 15 percent of non-Hispanic white families. In this respect, 10.2 percent of Asians and Pacific Islanders lived below the poverty level in 2001, compared to 7.8 percent for non-Hispanic whites.
Employment	In the Asian and Pacific Islander cohort age sixteen and above, about 75 percent of men and 59 percent of women participate in the labor force. Specifically, Asian and Pacific Islanders are concentrated in managerial and professional occupations – some 41.0 percent of men and 37.2 percent of women, compared to 33.4 percent of men and 36.9 percent of women in the corresponding non-Hispanic white cohort. Asians are also well-represented in a variety of professional occupations: 105,300 physicians and surgeons (15 percent of all U.S. physicians and surgeons, compared with 4 percent of the total population); 89,000 postsecondary teachers; 43,000 chief executives; 20,000 lawyers; 3,000 news analysts, reporters, and correspondents; and 200 legislators.

*The data in this table are taken from the United States Census Bureau's Annual Demographic Supplement to the March 2002 Current Population Survey. While Census 2002 differentiates Asians and Pacific Islanders into two separate categories, they are aggregated together as one statistical group in the Current Population Survey data. In Census 2000, the number of respondents who reported Native Hawaiian and other Pacific Islander, either alone or in combination with one or more other races, is 874,000 or 0.3 percent of the total U.S. population. By comparison, Asian Americans comprise 11.9 million or 4.2 per cent of the total U.S. population.

(Source: United States Census Bureau 2003, 2004).

Table 4
Projected Population of the United States by Race and
Hispanic Origin, 2000–2050 (in thousands, resident population)

	2000	2010	2020	2030	2040	2050
Population total	282,125 (100%)	308,936 (100%)	335,805 (100%)	363,584 (100%)	391,946 (100%)	419,854 (100%)
White alone	228,548 (81.0%)	244,995 (79.3%)	260,629 (77.6%)	275,731 (75.8%)	289,690 (73.9%)	302,626 (72.1%)
Black alone	35,818 (12.7%)	40,454 (13.1%)	45,365 (13.5%)	50,442 (13.9%)	55,876 (14.3%)	61,361 (14.6%)
Asian alone	10,684 (3.8%)	14,241 (4.6%)	17,988 (5.4%)	22,580 (6.2%)	27,992 (7.1%)	33,430 (8.0%)
All other races*	7,075 (2.5%)	9,246 (3.0%)	11,822 (3.5%)	14,831 (4.1%)	18,388 (4.7%)	22,437 (5.3%)
Hispanic (of any race)	35,622 (12.6%)	47,756 (15.5%)	59,756 (17.8%)	73,055 (20.1%)	87,585 (22.3%)	102,560 (24.4%)
White alone, not Hispanic	195,729 (69.4%)	201,112 (65.1%)	205,936 (61.3%)	209,176 (57.5%)	210,331 (53.7%)	210,283 (50.1%)

*Includes American Indian and Alaska Native alone, Native Hawaiian and other Pacific Islander alone, and two or more races.

(Source: United States Census Bureau 2004a, Table 1a)

Table 5
Projected Population Change in the United States
by Race and Hispanic Origin: 2000–2050
(in thousands, resident population)

	Cumulative 2000-2050	Breakdown by Decade				
		2000-2010	2010-2020	2020-2030	2030-2040	2040-2050
Total change	**137,729** (48.8%)	**26,811** (9.5%)	**26,869** (8.7%)	**27,779** (8.3%)	**28,362** (7.8%)	**27,908** (7.1%)
White alone	**74,078** (32.4%)	**16,447** (7.2%)	**15,634** (6.4%)	**15,102** (5.8%)	**13,959** (5.1%)	**12,936** (4.5%)
Black alone	**25,543** (71.3%)	**4,636** (12.9%)	**4,911** (12.1%)	**5,077** (11.2%)	**5,434** (10.8%)	**5,485** (9.8%)
Asian alone	**22,746** (212.9%)	**3,557** (33.3%)	**3,747** (26.3%)	**4,592** (25.5%)	**5,412** (24.0%)	**5,438** (19.4%)
All other races*	**15,362** (217.1%)	**2,171** (30.7%)	**2,576** (27.9%)	**3,009** (25.5%)	**3,557** (24.0%)	**4,049** (22.0%)
Hispanic (of any race)	**66,938** (187.9%)	**12,134** (34.1%)	**12,000** (25.1%)	**13,299** (22.3%)	**14,530** (19.9%)	**14,975** (17.1%)
White alone, not Hispanic	**14,554** (7.4%)	**5,383** (2.8%)	**4,824** (2.4%)	**3,240** (1.6%)	**1,155** (0.6%)	**-48** (0.0%)

*Includes American Indian and Alaska Native alone, Native Hawaiian and other Pacific Islander alone, and two or more races.

(Source: United States Census Bureau 2004a, Table 1b)

Table 6
Top Five Countries of Birth of Foreign-Born Population
from Asia: 1990 and 2000

Country	1990	2000
China (includes Taiwan and Hong Kong)	921,000	1,391,000
Philippines	913,000	1,222,000
India	450,000	1,007,000
Vietnam	543,000	863,000
Korea	568,000	701,000

(Source: United States Census Bureau 2002: 1)

Table 7
Profile of Asian-Born U.S. Population

Citizenship	In 2000, about 47 percent of the Asian-born U.S. residents were naturalized U.S. citizens, a rate that is much higher than the percentage for the entire cohort of foreign-born U.S. population (37 percent).
Occupation	Thirty-nine percent of Asian-born U.S. residents were employed in a managerial and professional specialty job, higher than the rate for natives (31 percent) or all foreign-born U.S. residents (25 percent).
Poverty	In 1999, 13 percent of Asian-born U.S. residents were poor, similar to the 11 percent rate for all natives, but much lower than the 17 percent rate for all foreign-born U.S. residents.
Household Income	Households with an Asian-born householder had a median income of $51,400 in 1999 – the highest income of any foreign-born group and higher than the median for all native-born U.S. households ($41,400) and all foreign-born U.S. households ($36,000). The high income levels for the Asian-born U.S. households may be the result of several factors, including a relatively high proportion of workers in managerial and professional specialty occupations (see below).
Education	The percentage of people twenty-five years or older who were born in Asia and had a high school education or higher (84 percent) was slightly less than the percentage for the native-born U.S. population (87 percent), but considerably higher than the percentage for the entire cohort of foreign-born U.S. population (67 percent).
Assistance Programs	In 1999, 17 percent of Asian-born U.S. residents participated in one or more means-tested, noncash programs such as Medicaid. This rate was similar to the rate for natives (15 percent), but less than the 21 percent rate for all foreign-born U.S. residents.

(Source: abridged from U.S. Census Bureau 2002a: 1–2).

Table 8
Census 2000:
Percentage Distribution of Asian Americans by Region

Region	Asian alone	Asian alone or in combination
Northeast	20.7	19.9
Midwest	11.7	11.7
South	18.8	19.1
West	48.8	49.3

(Source: United States Census Bureau 2002c: 4)

Table 9
Census 2000:
Top Ten States in Terms of Asian American Population

State	Total Population	Asian alone or in combination	Asian alone	Asian in combination
United States	281,421,906	11,898,828	10,242,998	1,665,830
California	33,871,648	4,155,785	3,697,513	458,172
New York	18,976,457	1,169,200	1,044,976	124,224
Hawaii	1,211,537	703,232	503,868	199,364
Texas	20,851,820	644,193	562,319	81,874
New Jersey	8,414,350	524,356	480,276	44,080
Illinois	12,419,293	473,649	423,603	50,046
Washington	5,894,121	395,741	322,335	73,406
Florida	15,982,378	333,013	266,256	66,757
Virginia	7,078,515	304,559	261,025	43,534
Massachusetts	6,349,097	264,814	238,124	26,690

(Source: Abridged from United States Census Bureau 2002c: 5)

Table 10
Census 2000:
Top Ten Cities in Terms of Asian American Population

City, State	Total Population	Asian alone or in combination	Asian alone
New York, NY	8,008,278	872,777 (10.9%)	787,047 (9.8%)
Los Angeles, CA	3,694,820	407,444 (11.0%)	369,254 (10.0%)
San Jose, CA	894,943	257,571 (28.8%)	240,375 (26.9%)
San Francisco, CA	776,733	253,477 (32.6%)	239,565 (30.8%)
Honolulu, HI	371,657	251,686 (67.7%)	207,588 (55.9%)
San Diego, CA	1,233,400	189,413 (15.5%)	166,968 (13.6%)
Chicago, IL	2,896,016	140,517 (4.9%)	125,974 (4.3%)
Houston, TX	1,953,631	114,140 (5.8%)	103,694 (5.3%)
Seattle, WA	563,374	84,649 (15.0%)	73,910 (13.1%)
Fremont, CA	203,413	80,979 (39.8%)	75,165 (37.0%)

(Source: adapted with modifications from United States Census Bureau 2002c:7)

Table 11:
**Census 2000: Top Ten Places of 100,000 or More Population
in Terms of Asian American Percentage**

City, State	Percentage of Asian alone or in combination	Percentage of Asian alone
Honolulu, HI	67.7	55.9
Daly City, CA	53.6	50.7
Fremont, CA	39.8	37.0
Sunnyvale, CA	34.2	32.3
San Francisco, CA	32.6	30.8
Irvine, CA	32.3	29.8
Garden Grove, CA	32.2	30.9
Santa Clara, CA	31.4	29.3
Torrance, CA	31.1	28.6
San Jose, CA	28.8	26.9

(Source: Adapted from United States Census Bureau 2002c: 8)

Chapter 2

Asian Immigration to the United States

The Asian American community traces its earliest beginnings to the arrival of Filipino sailors during the Spanish colonial era. The earliest known presence of Asians on U.S. soil occurred in 1587, when Luzon Indians on the Spanish galleon *Nuestra Señora de Buena Esperanza* accompanied Captain Pedro de Unamuno ashore when he landed at Morro Bay on the California coast (Borah 1995/96). More significantly, noted journalist and author Lafcadio Hearn introduced the world to the hitherto unknown Filipino settlement of Saint Malo in Saint Bernard Parish of Louisiana, which was established in 1763 by Filipino sailors who deserted ashore to escape the harsh realities of the Spanish galleon trade (Hearn 1883). Marina Espina has documented the lives of eight generations of the *Manilamen* of Saint Malo (Espina 1988). Although the Saint Malo settlement was destroyed in 1915 by the New Orleans Hurricane, their historical presence on U.S. soil, albeit as a small but thriving community, is an important testimony to the fact that Asians have lived continuously in the United States since the mid-eighteenth century.

Early Chinese Immigration to the United States

1840s–1860s: The California Gold Rush and Chinese Immigration

Large-scale Asian immigration to the United States began with the arrival of boatloads of Chinese in mid-nineteenth-century California. From 1848 until 1882 — that is, from the year when the

California Gold Rush began until the year when the gates of the United States were slammed shut against them — more than three hundred thousand Chinese landed on the shores of California. Compared to the booming economy of the mid-nineteenth-century United States that attracted immigrants from all corners of the world, China was torn apart by natural disasters, as well as civil wars and other uprisings that sought to overthrow an incompetent and corrupt Qing Dynasty in its twilight years. The ensuing turmoil and suffering exacted a heavy toll on the socioeconomic fabric of Chinese society, initiating what would later grow into a mass exodus of Chinese to Southeast Asia, Europe, and the Americas.

Many Chinese braved the high seas and terrible living conditions in a desperate quest for menial jobs in the United States, driven by the hope of building a better future for themselves and their families. To these arriving Chinese, the United States stood out as a land of opportunity and a beacon of hope. They called their adopted country the "Beautiful Land" (*Mei Kuok* in Cantonese, *Meiguo* in Mandarin), and gave California the name "Gold Mountain" (*Kam shan* in Cantonese, *Jinshan* in Mandarin). It is a fitting testimony to these early Chinese immigrants that the names "Beautiful Land" and "Gold Mountain" have persisted until today as contemporary Chinese names for the United States and California. Born in the heady days of the California Gold Rush (1848–55), both of these optimistic names belied the excruciatingly harsh and exploitative reality that awaited them in the gold mines of the Sierra Nevada foothills. In addition to long hours of arduous and backbreaking labor, many Chinese were often cheated by unscrupulous middlemen. The less fortunate ones became victims of anti-Chinese violence when they were beaten, robbed, or killed by rival white American gold prospectors.

When many of the early gold fields became exhausted by the mid-1850s and competition for the remaining gold fields became heated, protectionist legislation and taxes that discriminated against the Chinese gold miners were passed. By a stroke of good fortune, California was experiencing tremendous economic growth during this period, with the burgeoning trade at its ports and expanding farms in its hinterland catering to the emerging markets of the Eastern Seaboard and Europe. As a result, many Chinese left the gold mines to work as unskilled farmhands in the booming farms. Others became coolies, artisans, and tradesmen, while a number opened small businesses that catered to Chinese migrants. In addition, more than ten thousand Chinese laborers toiled on the monumental Central Pacific Railroad that cut across the steep terrain of the Sierra Nevada and the Rockies, until its completion in 1869.

A major development in U.S.-Chinese relations occurred in 1868. In that year, the United States and China signed the Burlingame Treaty, named after Anson Burlingame (1820–70), who signed the treaty on behalf of the Chinese government. This landmark treaty guaranteed, among other things, an open door and favorable treatment to Chinese nationals in the United States and vice versa. Chinese immigration was greatly encouraged, resulting in the number of Chinese immigrants in 1869 almost doubling the numbers for 1868.

1860s–1880s: The Rise of White Nativism and Anti-Chinese Prejudice

The Chinese were not the only immigrant group that flocked to California in search of a new life. A significant number of European immigrants also came during this period. Nevertheless, unlike these European immigrants who were able to blend into the mainstream by virtue of a common skin color, many Chinese immigrants discovered the harsh truth that they could not hide their ethnicity and assimilate easily into the mainstream of the nineteenth-century United States because of their visibly different facial features, skin color, language, clothing, and mannerisms. What made things worse was the fact that even before the first Chinese landed on U.S. soil, many Americans had developed a prejudice against the Chinese as idolatrous, superstitious, filthy, crafty, cruel, dishonest, and intellectually inferior, and as practitioners of intractable vices such as idol worshiping, female footbinding, and female infanticide. This perception came about as a result of the sensationalist eyewitness accounts, negative stereotyping, and racist writings of missionaries, traders, and diplomats that were widely disseminated in the pulpits, newspapers, magazines, and books of that era (Miller 1969).

Moreover, mainstream white America also adopted a racist attitude toward the Chinese immigrants, viewing them as possessing the essence of "racial inferiority" as that of Native Americans, as well as "Negroes and Negro slaves" (Saxton 1971: 19). This overtly racist attitude was clearly evident in the infamous case of *People v. Hall*, 4 Cal. 399 (1854), which concerned the murder of a Chinese man by the accused, George W. Hall. Hall was convicted of the murder of a Chinese man based upon the testimony of Chinese witnesses. Hall did not dispute the fact of the murder. He appealed his conviction on the ground that the only evidence against him — that is, the testimony of Chinese witnesses — was inadmissible under section 14 of the California Criminal Proceedings Act (1850), which provided that "[n]o Black, or Mulatto person, or Indian, shall be allowed to give evidence in favor of, or against a white man." Upon appeal, the California Supreme Court held, among other things, that the Chinese had no *locus standi* to testify in court against whites even in instances of crimes committed by whites against them. Delivering the majority judgment of the court, Chief Justice Murray, with Justice Heydenfeldt concurring but Justice Wells dissenting, held that the terms "Black," "Mulatto," and "Indian" are generic terms referring to "every one who is not of white blood." In Justice Murray's opinion:

> In using the words, "No Black, or Mulatto person, or Indian shall be allowed to give evidence for or against a White person," the Legislature, if any intention can be ascribed to it, adopted the most comprehensive terms to embrace every known class or shade of color, as the apparent design was *to protect the White person from the influence of all testimony other than that of persons of the same caste.* (4 Cal. 399, 403, emphasis added)

The impact of this incredibly racist judgment was clear. White Americans were granted a free pass against Chinese Americans. For all intents and purposes, whites could never be prosecuted for crimes and offenses against Chinese Americans. Moreover, Justice Murray poured oil on the fire when he characterized the Chinese immigrants as

> a race of people whom nature has marked as inferior, and who are incapable of progress or intellectual development beyond a certain point, as their history has shown, differing

in language, customs, color, and physical conformation; *between whom and ourselves nature has placed an impassable difference.* (4 Cal. 399, 405, emphasis added)

Not surprisingly, crimes and violence against Chinese Americans increased significantly in the ensuing decades after this case was decided. Further, in his 1862 inaugural address as governor of California, Leland Stanford stoked the fires of anti-Chinese sentiment when he said:

To my mind it is clear the settlement among us of an inferior race is to be discouraged by every legitimate means. Asia, with her numberless millions, sends to our shores the dregs of her population.... There can be no doubt but that the presence of numbers among us of a degraded and distinct people must exercise a deleterious influence upon the superior race, and, to a certain extent, repel desirable immigration. (Cited in Wu 1971: 109)

This was all the more disingenuous, considering that Stanford would later profit handsomely from the backbreaking contributions of the Chinese laborers on the Central Pacific Railroad, of which he was one of the principal investors.

On the one hand, the Chinese laborers were often prized by their employers for their industrious work ethic, as well as willingness to endure a harsh life and accept low wages. On the other hand, other European immigrants viewed the Chinese as rivals and competitors for the same pool of jobs and other economic opportunities during this period. However, in reality the competition was unequal, with the balance of power in favor of the European immigrants. Working-class European immigrants formed powerful trade unions and lobbied political parties to support their causes. Neither of these avenues was available to their Chinese counterparts.

1880s–1900s: From Discrimination to Exclusion

When jobs were plentiful and labor in short supply, the Chinese presence was tolerated as a necessary evil for California's economic growth. However, the economic growth turned sour by the 1870s, ushering in a period of economic depression and high unemployment known as the Long Depression (1873–96). Before long, the Chinese immigrants found their dreams and hopes dashed by growing antagonistic and racist sentiments. Mindful of the need to protect their members' employment from the influx of a much lower-paid and nonunionized Chinese labor force, many working-class European labor unions indulged in anti-Chinese agitation.

Hungry for the labor vote, politicians were only too happy to use the Chinese immigrants as scapegoats for high unemployment and other economic woes. Political parties that courted the labor union vote soon adopted the anti-Chinese platform to gain a voting advantage. For example, the Workingmen's Party, led by the intractable and fiery Irishman and populist labor leader, Denis Kearney (1847–1907), became a major force in California politics in the 1870s. A skilled orator and rabble-rouser, the vehemently anti-Chinese Kearney rallied his followers on a nativist and racist platform, beginning and ending his speeches with the vitriolic rally cry, "The Chinese must go."

By the 1880s, the question of Chinese immigration had ballooned from a California state issue into an explosive national political issue. Campaigning desperately for the white working-class vote, many politicians seized upon the hapless Chinese immigrants as convenient scapegoats for all of society's ills. In the words of Andrew Gyory:

> By spewing, amplifying, and propagating racist stereotypes of the Chinese and linking the well-being of workers to the exclusion of Chinese immigrants, politicians manipulated the two most volatile issues in American society — race and class — and combined them to produce the first race-based immigration act in American history. (Gyory 1998: 257)

Despite the fact that the Chinese were only a small proportion of the total population in California and elsewhere, they were depicted by these politicians as the "Yellow Peril" that threatened the jobs, incomes, and comfortable way of life of hardworking and God-fearing working-class white families.

Growing hatred against the Chinese fueled increasingly restrictive legislation that excluded them from jobs and barred them from acquiring property, as well as securing permits and licenses.

Lacking the linguistic, communicative, and political skills to fight back, the Chinese became de facto marginalized and disenfranchised in the legal and political spheres. In response to such hostile antagonism, many Chinese immigrants huddled together in close-knit Chinatowns in a spirit of communal support and mutual assistance. These insular ethnic enclaves not only provided a fair measure of protection from the harsh sociopolitical realities of the wider society, but also enabled the Chinese to address their economic, social, cultural, spiritual, and psychological needs on their own terms. Life was harsh in these Chinatowns, and disease and illnesses were rampant in the crowded tenements and backlanes.

Eventually all of these anti-Chinese agitations led to the call being echoed in the chambers of Congress for legislative action to curb Chinese immigration. In 1879, a bill restricting Chinese immigration was passed by the U.S. Congress but was vetoed by President Rutherford B. Hayes. Undaunted, Congress pressed the issue and succeeded on May 6, 1882, with the enactment of the first in a series of Chinese Exclusion Acts. The Chinese Exclusion Act of 1882 suspended Chinese immigration to the United States for a period of ten years, and authorized Congress to extend this prohibition if necessary. In doing so, Congress had brushed aside the feeble protests of an impotent Chinese government and unilaterally terminated the 1868 Burlingame Treaty, which had until now guaranteed an open-door policy on the question of Chinese immigration to, and favorable treatment of all Chinese immigrants in, the United States.

More significantly, the passage of this 1882 legislation meant that for the first time in its history as a nation built by the labor of immigrants, the United States had enacted legislation barring a specific ethnic group from immigrating to the United States solely on the basis of their country of origin. The enactment of this law revealed that anti-Chinese prejudice and discrimination were officially institutionalized at the national level, and this injustice was sanctioned by the highest legislative authority in the United States. In practice, the 1882 legislation also meant that generations of Chinese male immigrants were condemned to a life of perpetual bachelorhood, as few Chinese women had immigrated before the exclusionary restriction was imposed.

It was all the more ironic that on October 28, 1886, a mere four years after the first Chinese Exclusion Act was enacted, the Statue of Liberty was dedicated by President Grover Cleveland with Emma Lazarus's beautiful poem "The New Colossus" inscribed in a memorial plaque at its base. The following lines from this poem rang hollow when the 1882 Exclusion Act against the Chinese was renewed in 1892 and then made permanent in 1902:

> Give me your tired, your poor,
> Your huddled masses yearning to breathe free,
> The wretched refuse of your teeming shore.
> Send these, the homeless, tempest-tost to me,
> I lift my lamp beside the golden door!

Apparently, only the "huddled masses" from Europe were welcomed with open arms. As for the "huddled masses" from Asia, the racist implication was clear. You are not welcome. Please stay home. Moreover, in the words of Japanese American politician Norman Mineta:

> When one hears Americans tell of the immigrants who built the nation, one is often led to believe that all our forbears came from Europe. When one hears stories about the pioneers going West to shape the land, the Asian immigrant is rarely mentioned. (Cited in Takaki 1989: 6)

In 1892, Congress extended the exclusion for an additional ten years by passing the Geary Act. Eventually, the prohibition against Chinese immigration to the United States was made permanent under the Chinese Exclusion Act of 1902. The 1902 Act was eventually repealed by the Chinese Exclusion Repeal Act of 1943 (the Magnuson Act), when the U.S. government sought to extend the hand of friendship to the Chinese in recognition of their importance alliance against the Japanese in the Pacific Front during the Second World War. However, the reality did not match up to the political rhetoric. A limited annual quota of 105 Chinese immigrants to the United States meant that Chinese immigration to the United States was still very tightly restricted.

Early Japanese and Korean Immigration to the United States

Notwithstanding the exclusion of Chinese immigration to the United States, the economic opportunities that resulted from the opening up of the American West necessitated the supply of low-cost labor for their success and profitability. In place of the Chinese, boatloads of immigrant laborers from Japan, Korea, and the Philippines flocked to the United States to fill these jobs in the early part of the twentieth century.

The Japanese formed the second large group of Asians to immigrate to the United States in the late nineteenth century. The first wave of Japanese immigration occurred from the late 1860s to the 1890s. Most of the Japanese who came to the United States during this period were principally diplomats and merchants in search of business opportunities. Beginning from the 1870s onward, an increasing number of Japanese students came to this country. The Meiji Restoration that began in 1868, with its emphasis on the acquisition of modern Western scientific and technological learning, had encouraged many Japanese students to enroll in institutions of higher learning in the United States.

A shift in immigration pattern occurred from the mid-1890s until 1907. During this period, the new arrivals from Japan were increasingly fortune seekers rather than students. Many impoverished farmers and unemployed young men left Japan for Hawaii and California, seeking jobs mainly in the growing agribusinesses in these two states, and opportunities in the fishing, lumber, and construction industries in the western states. The influx of Japanese agricultural laborers during this period was fueled mainly by the loss of Chinese workers after the Chinese Exclusion Act of 1882 went into effect.

The first Korean pioneers were the small number of political refugees and student activists who fled the political turmoil in their homeland in 1883. The first wave of large-scale Korean immigration to the United States took place from 1903 to 1905, with the arrival in Hawaii of boatloads of impoverished Korean farmers who were brought in to work on the island's sugarcane plantations, as well as a smaller number who came to the West Coast of the United States. The Japanese annexation of Korea in 1910 led to many Korean intellectuals, anti-Japanese student activists, and political exiles arriving in the United States in the ensuing years as refugees and asylum seekers. They were followed by a number of Korean women, who came as picture-brides.

Twentieth-Century Anti-Asian Hysteria: From Exclusion to Internment

The Gentlemen's Agreement (1907)

Japanese and Korean laborers also encountered the same racist and discriminatory treatment that the Chinese of an earlier generation had experienced, especially in California. In 1906, the State of California extended its antimiscegenation legislation to outlaw marriages between whites and Asians. At the instigation of the Asiatic Exclusion League, the California Board of Education ordered the segregation of Japanese and Korean schoolchildren from white students in San Francisco's public school system on October 11, 1906. While the Koreans complied, albeit unwillingly, the entire Japanese community refused to follow suit. The resulting school crisis, the San Francisco School Incident of 1906, led to the Gentlemen's Agreement of 1907, comprising a series of six diplomatic notes exchanged between the governments of the United States and Japan in which the Japanese government agreed to a voluntary restraint of Japanese immigration to the United States. In return, the U.S. government persuaded the California Board of Education to rescind the controversial segregation order. As part of this agreement, the United States also adopted a policy of facilitating the reunification of Japanese families, allowing Japanese immigrants residing in the United States to bring in their wives, children, and parents.

In general, the Gentlemen's Agreement, albeit tilted in favor of the United States, had important benefits for the nascent Japanese community. By agreeing voluntarily to restrict future Japanese immigration to family members of existing Japanese families in the United States, the Japanese government hoped to stave off the enactment of wide-ranging exclusionary legislation that paralleled the series of Chinese Exclusion Acts. Unlike the results of draconian

Chinese Exclusion Acts, the Gentlemen's Agreement transformed the Japanese immigrant community from a mainly bachelor-based to a predominantly family-based community.

Asiatic Barred Zone Act (1917)

The 1907 Gentlemen's Agreement was followed by the Immigration Act of 1917 (Asiatic Barred Zone Act). This legislation, among other things, expanded the exclusionary measures previously leveled against China to encompass the "Asiatic Barred Zone," a region comprising the Middle East, South Asia, and Southeast Asia, including Arabia, Afghanistan, British India, Burma, Siam, French Indochina, the Malay states, the East Indian islands, Asiatic Russia, and the Polynesian islands. Congress passed this legislation with an overwhelming majority, overriding its earlier veto by President Woodrow Wilson.

Johnson-Reed Act (1924)

Asian immigration to the United States was eventually curtailed completely under the Immigration Act of 1924 (Johnson-Reed Act). Passed by overwhelming majority in an isolationist Congress, this legislation became popularly known as the National Origins Act, Asian Exclusion Act, or Japanese Exclusion Act. In addition to establishing strict national origin quotas for European immigrants to the United States, the Johnson-Reed Act prohibited all East Asians, Southeast Asians, and South Asians from immigrating to the United States on the basis that they were undesirable. In practice, this legislation put a complete end to the inflow of Japanese immigrants who took advantage of the family reunification provisions of the Gentlemen's Agreement of 1907 to enter the United States. In effect, the Japanese found themselves in the same boat as the Chinese: completely excluded from immigrating to the United States.

Filipino Immigration and the Tydings-McDuffie Act (1934)

Filipinos arrived in the United States in large waves beginning in the early 1900s to work as agricultural workers in the plantations of

Hawaii and produce farms of California. Their numbers increased from the 1920s onward, especially after the passage of the Johnson-Reed Act (1924) that prohibited all Asian immigration to the United States. As residents of a territory controlled by the United States, Filipinos were not subjected to the exclusionary provisions of the Johnson-Reed Act.

However, the passage of the Philippine Independence Act of 1934 (Tydings-McDuffie Act) put a complete halt to Filipinos entering the United States freely. On the one hand, the Tydings-McDuffie Act conferred U.S. commonwealth status on the Philippines and laid the framework for its eventual independence after a transitional period of ten years. On the other hand, this legislation also stripped all U.S. residency rights for Filipinos, reclassifying them as aliens and limiting Filipino immigration to an annual quota of fifty persons.

Executive Order 9066: Internment of Japanese Americans

In the aftermath of the Japanese attack on Pearl Harbor on December 7, 1941, the ensuing public hysteria led to the signing of Executive Order 9066 by President Franklin D. Roosevelt on February 19, 1942, resulting in the forcible seizure of assets, removal, relocation, and incarceration of some 120,000 Japanese without trial in ten concentration camps scattered around the country until the end of the war, including 77,000 who possessed U.S. citizenship from birth. Although practically all the Japanese Americans with U.S. citizenship pledged their unconditional allegiance to the United States of America and indicated their unqualified willingness to serve in the U.S. Armed Forces on combat duty, nonetheless they were still denied their fundamental rights as citizens under the U.S. Constitution and branded as enemy aliens. Thus, the Japanese Americans were the only racial-ethnic group in the United States who suffered the ignominy of mass imprisonment without trial in concentration camps merely on the basis of their ethnicity. By contrast, neither the German American nor the Italian American communities were incarcerated en masse in concentration camps as enemy aliens, despite the fact that the United States also fought against them in the Second World War.

For decades after the war, the lasting and painful memories of an unjust wartime internment spurred generations of Japanese Americans to campaign for redress through organizations such as the National Council for Japanese American Redress (NCJAR). Their persistence in preserving the legacy of internment (e.g., celebrating February 19 as the "Day of Remembrance"), handing down personal stories and experiences, as well as their perseverance in their fight for redress led to the establishment of the Commission on Wartime Relocation and Internment of Civilians (CWRIC). Based upon the recommendations of the CWRIC, Congress passed the Civil Liberties Act of 1988, apologizing for the wartime internment and authorizing the payment of twenty thousand dollars together with a letter of apology to every eligible Japanese American who was interned as reparation for the violation of their freedom and rights that are guaranteed by the U.S. Constitution.

Post–World War II Developments

In the aftermath of the Second World War, legislation was introduced to allow foreign spouses and children of U.S. servicemen to enter the United States (War Brides Act of 1945), relax the absolute restrictions of previous exclusionary legislation against Asian nationals (Luce-Celler Act of 1946), and permit war refugees to enter the United States (Displaced Persons Act of 1948 and 1950). At the height of the Cold War, the Refugee Relief Act of 1953 was passed to accept refugees in the nonquota category. Taken as a whole, these pieces of legislation enabled numerous Chinese refugees fleeing the 1949 communist takeover of China, Korean War refugees, Chinese and Korean war babies and orphans being adopted by American families, as well as Korean wives of U.S. servicemen to enter the United States.

These developments culminated in the passage of the Immigration and Nationality Act of 1952 (McCarran-Walter Act), which reopened the United States to Asian immigration and abolished the category of aliens ineligible for citizenship, thereby affording Asians the opportunity of becoming U.S. citizens through naturalization. However, new restrictive immigration quotas were introduced: each Asian Pacific nation could send up to one hundred quota immigrants annually, with a maximum annual ceiling of two thousand immigrants in total from the entire Asia-Pacific triangle (Hing 1993: 38–39). Not surprisingly, most Asian immigrants admitted between 1945 and 1964 were Asian women married to U.S. servicemen who were admitted as nonquota immigrants.

Hart-Celler Act (1965)

The landmark legislative achievements of the black civil rights movement in the mid-1960s under the administration of President Lyndon B. Johnson paved the way for, among other things, a re-examination of the civil rights of other racial-ethnic minorities in the United States. Of particular significance to the Asian American community is the rethinking of the U.S. immigration legislative framework to eliminate its racist and other discriminatory aspects. With the passage of the landmark Immigration and Nationality Act of 1965 (Hart-Celler Act), a new immigration regime was introduced, transforming the shape and pattern of Asian immigration to the United States. Among other things, the 1965 law abolished the national origins quota system of the McCarran-Walter Act and raised significantly the limits on total annual immigration. The implications of this law were felt in the ensuing decades, as the doors were now flung wide open for new waves of immigrants from Asia, which have continued unabated to this day.

Many factors account for this growing wave of Asian immigration to the United States. First, the preferential treatment given to family reunification is responsible for the big increases in Asian immigration, in addition to immigration from other parts of the world. Second, the population explosion in many Asian countries has compelled many Asians to emigrate, legally or illegally, to escape the lack of jobs or opportunities back home. Third, many well-educated Asians immigrate to the United States for improved job opportunities, while others come to this country with dreams and hopes of better educational prospects for their children. Fourth, there is a significant number of Asians who continue to flee from tightly controlled Asian regimes to enjoy the various freedoms that the United States offers to its people. Fifth, many investors and entrepreneurs, together with their dependents, have immigrated to the United States, hoping to repeat the successes of their nineteenth-century European forebears who struck it rich in the Gilded Age of the United States. Finally, refugees of all stripes and colors are fleeing persecution in various troubled spots throughout Asia, for example, the post-1975 Indochina and post-1989 China. As a result, the previously normative white European facade of American society is being slowly but surely replaced by a multicultural kaleidoscope that encapsulates the vibrant diversity and plurality of contemporary U.S. society.

Indochinese Immigration to the United States

Beginning in the late 1970s and continuing through the 1980s and 1990s, the United States welcomed waves of refugees from Vietnam, Laos, and Cambodia. Collectively, they number about 1.5 million in the year 2000. Most Vietnamese reside in California (especially in and around Orange County and San Jose); Texas (especially in and around Houston, Dallas, and Port Arthur); Louisiana; Florida; as well as in the New York and Washington, DC–Northern Virginia–Maryland metropolitan regions. Many Hmong were resettled in the state of Minnesota.

Of immigrants from the three Indochinese countries, the Vietnamese form the largest group, arriving in the United States in four broad waves. The first exodus of some 130,000 Vietnamese arrived in the United States in the aftermath of the fall of Saigon on April 30, 1975. The second wave comprised mainly ethnic Chinese living in Vietnam who fled the country as a result of the hostilities arising from the Sino-Vietnamese War of 1979. The third wave consisted of more than 300,000 Vietnamese boat people who fled Vietnam in the late 1970s and early 1980s. After being rescued from the high seas and held in transit camps in Hong Kong, Philippines, Thailand, Malaysia, and Singapore, many of them were eventually resettled in the United States. The fourth wave comprised Vietnamese who were mainly relatives and family members of Vietnamese who arrived in the first three waves. These new arrivals were brought into the country under the auspices of the Orderly Departure Program (1979–94) of the United Nations High

Commission for Refugees (UNHCR). After the Orderly Departure Program ended in 1994, many Vietnamese nationals have continued to enter the United States under the Humanitarian Operations program, which was extended by a bilateral treaty that the United States and Vietnam governments signed on November 15, 2005. Additionally, a limited number of Vietnamese continue to immigrate to the United States under current family reunification or employment immigration provisions.

In terms of social and educational background, the first wave of arrivals was predominantly, although not exclusively, Vietnamese employed by U.S. interests who fled in the face of the communist advance — South Vietnamese political, intellectual, and military classes, as well as their dependents. Cosmopolitan in worldview, well-educated, and fluent in English, French, as well as their native Vietnamese tongue, they were generally older and more experienced in life. More often than not, they adjusted readily to life in the United States and are now comfortably ensconced in middle- and upper-class suburban communities in the United States.

By contrast, subsequent arrivals who came by boat or under international refugee resettlement programs from the 1980s onward were largely fishermen, farmers, artisans, unskilled laborers, children sent abroad by families to escape a communist-controlled society, and young men fleeing military conscription. Most of these refugees had merely a rudimentary education. They barely spoke English and often knew next to nothing about life beyond their hamlets or villages. Like the Chinese and Japanese immigrants who came before them, they have congregated around "Little Saigons" that have mushroomed to provide a familiar ethnic-based sociocultural and communal framework for solidarity, collaborative support, and mutual assistance in the face of a fast-paced, competitive, and individualistic U.S. lifestyle. Nonetheless, despite such seemingly insurmountable odds, many children of these Vietnamese immigrants manage to achieve scholastic success and go on to pursue professional careers.

Chapter 3

The Asian American Presence in the Present-Day United States

Contemporary Experiences and Challenges

In the preceding chapter, we saw how Asians have flocked in droves to the United States since the nineteenth century, seeking better opportunities for themselves and their children. These immigrants were emboldened to brave the challenges and travails of life in new and unfamiliar surroundings, leaving behind their homeland and a familiar way of life. On the other hand, they also possessed a deep appreciation for their own cultures, customs, traditions, and values, as could be seen from their efforts to transplant and pass them on to their American-born progeny.

More often than not, the United States they imagined in their dreams turned out to be very different from the United States they entered. Generations of Asian pioneers had to endure not only prejudice, racism, and discriminatory government policies, but also, in many instances, outright anti-Asian hysteria and brazen attacks that were directed at them. Through sheer perseverance, unremitting endurance, and unbounded resourcefulness, many Asian immigrants were able to brave the unrelenting hostility and alienation in the land of their dreams. Inspired by a strong motivation to sacrifice their well-being for the sake of their children, they slaved away at two, three, or more jobs to provide food at the table, and encouraged their children to excel in education in the hope of landing good jobs, thereby getting an opportunity to savor the American Dream.

Asian Americans as the "Model Minority"?

Contemporary Asian Americans are often characterized by white Americans as the "model minority" who have broken through the race ceiling to enjoy the American Dream. Widely propagated by the popular media (e.g., *Newsweek*'s "Success Story: Outwhiting the Whites" and *U.S. News & World Report*'s "Success Story of One Minority Group in the U.S.") and the political establishment, Asian American scholars and community activists contend that this image is more hype than reality, focusing attention on the narrow segment of Asian American achievers who have graduated from prestigious universities, pursued professional or corporate careers, established successful businesses, and thus moved up the socioeconomic rung of the American Dream. The underlying thrust here is that the successes of these Asian Americans testify to the fact that Asian Americans are not victims of discrimination, but prove that the American Dream is open to anyone who is willing to work hard (Osajima 2000).

But is this image accurate? What about those unseen and unglamorous Asian Americans, especially many first-generation immigrants and their children, who struggle to eke out a subsistence living, working long hours in restaurants and factories, or toiling as store clerks, seamstresses, artisans, unskilled laborers, laundry and nail workers, and so on? More often than not, these Asian Americans have to contend with language difficulties and sociocultural adjustment issues, lacking affordable health care, living in ethnic ghettos, struggling with poverty and gangland violence, and wondering whether they would ever break the vicious cycle of destitution and marginalization. What about those Asian American small family businesses that expect their family members to work for long hours under stressful conditions for minimum pay, and with no health benefits or Social Security benefits? And what about the "invisible" Asian American immigrant youth who, because of their inability to cope with their existential angst, continue to experience deep-seated psychological problems in schools, commit suicide, drop out of schools, engage in abusive or violent relationships, turn to drugs or gang membership, or, in the extreme case of Virginia Tech's Seung-hui Cho, commit horrendous mass murder? These are the hidden majority of Asian Americans for whom mainstream U.S. citizens look the other way.

Clearly, the use of the model minority image to characterize Asian Americans is highly problematic and unsupportable by the facts. To begin with, it glamorizes a small minority within the wider Asian American community and essentializes their success stories as normative and applicable to all Asian Americans, thereby excluding alternative perspectives of contemporary Asian American identities and experiences that fall short of the model minority image. In addition, the model minority image presents a rose-tinted superficial view of a problem-free, highly motivated, and super-achieving community with no social, economic, educational, or psychological problems whatsoever (Cheng and Yang 2000). In truth, the reality is far away from this view.

The reality is that Asian Americans often hit a glass ceiling despite being praised as the model minority. While experiencing significant success in the lower rung of management in government, big corporations, and churches, they are often conspicuously absent from the highest decision-making level in these organizations (see discussion in Min and Kim 1999). Similarly, several leading universities in the United States discriminated against Asian Americans in the 1980s. To control their explosive growth on university campuses, Asian American applicants were required by these institutions to score higher than white Americans in order to gain admission. What is important to note here is the fact that Asian American students may often be praised for their high scholastic achievements, but the moment they began to threaten entrenched white interests (e.g., when an increase in Asian American college admissions meant a corresponding reduction in white American admissions), Asian Americans discover that their high achievements were turned around and used as a means of discrimination against them (see discussion in Takagi 1992, Nakanishi 2000).

Two Korean American sociologists, Won Moo Hurh and Kwang Chung Kim, have concluded that the model minority image of Asian Americans is racist, discriminatory, and ultimately anti-Asian. In their opinion, the practical implications of this image are as follows:

(1) exclusion of Asian Americans from social programs supported by public and private agencies (benefit-denying/ fund-saving function); (2) disguise of Asian Americans'

underemployment (institutional racism promoting function); (3) justification of the American open social system (system preserving function); (4) displacement of the system's fault to less-achieving minorities (victim blaming function); and (5) anti-Asian sentiment and activities (*resentment* reinforcing function). (Hurh and Kim 1989: 531)

In other words, the model minority image is often used by the majority in an insidious manner to undermine arguments for affirmative preferences for minorities, thereby maintaining the status quo of institutionalized racism. In truth, the model minority myth is often used to show how some Asian Americans have assimilated into the American way of life without the benefit of affirmative policies or preferential treatment. If other minorities are unable to follow in the same footsteps as the Asian Americans, the problem lies with them and not with the majority white Americans. In this manner, white Americans are able to absolve themselves from all charges of prejudice, discrimination, or racism. This is the point that Korean American theologian Andrew Sung Park makes:

> The media of this country also have conjured up an image of a model Asian American minority, praising these immigrants for having fulfilled the so-called American dream. They have depicted such immigrants as a hard-working, law-abiding, and self-sufficient people. This stereotypical picture of Asian Americans is dangerous when it is used for chiding other groups. The subliminal message says to other ethnic minority groups, especially to African-Americans, "This country is not racist. Look at *this* minority group. Why can't you make it in this great country of equal opportunity like this group? You are basically lazy and inferior to the model minority. You deserve your miserable lot." (Park 1996: 22–23)

Asian Americans as the "Middle Minority"?

Beyond the "model minority" myth, Asian Americans often find themselves experiencing the more insidious phenomenon of being a middle minority or "middle-agent minority" (see Park 1996: 35–37). Specifically, the middle minority group acts as a buffer in turbulent sociopolitical or economic moments between the dominant elite who holds the levers of power on the one side, and the exploited and oppressed groups on the other side. The middle minority finds itself an attractive target for the anger and frustrations of the oppressed, but is itself also discriminated against, and unprotected by the dominant elite. More significantly, the middle minority dilemma illustrates the divide-and-conquer tactics of the dominant elite, namely, pitting one oppressed minority group against another (see discussion in Blalock 1975, Turner and Bonacich 1980, Jensen and Abeyta 1987).

The South Central Los Angeles riots of April 29, 1992, clearly illustrate the unenviable position of Korean American grocery storekeepers as the middle minority caught between the white American dominant elite on the one side, and the poor, angry, and frustrated African Americans on the other. Many Korean American scholars use the term *saigu* (*sai-i-gu* literally means 4–2–9) to express the gut-wrenching pain and suffering that Korean Americans experienced and continue to cope with as a result of the 1992 riots (Sahagun 2007). Again, citing the insights of Korean American theologian Andrew Sung Park:

> Korean-American shops in the Los Angeles area became the targets of looting and arson during the Los Angeles eruptions in part because they represented the face of the dominant group. But in addition they were identified as the oppressors who exploited African-Americans and despised them. ...Korean-American storekeepers effectively functioned as a buffer between Euro-Americans and the oppressed and poorer groups of society. (Park 1996: 36)

Clearly, the angry black rioters viewed the Korean Americans and their properties as symbolic representatives of the dominant white American majority. While the latter's properties were heavily fortified and defended by police, the former's properties were not. This illustrates the fact that notwithstanding the fact that the Korean American minority group possessed economic power, its political impotence had rendered it defenseless and vulnerable to attacks. As a result, the Korean Americans of South Central Los Angeles found themselves instrumentalized by the dominant white establishment as a line of defense to protect its privileges.

Asian Americans as "Forever Foreigners" or "Honorary Whites"?

On the one hand, the model minority image presumes a normative white American way of life into which Asian Americans are supposedly able to assimilate. On the other hand, despite the model minority image, Asian Americans are still subjected to many negative stereotypes, for example, the stereotype as "forever foreigners," notwithstanding the fact that many of them are born in the United States, have English names, and are able to speak good English. This paradox can be explained by differentiating between two kinds of assimilation: "cultural assimilation" and "structural assimilation." Developed by sociologists to explain the phenomenon of the European immigrant, the "straight line" assimilation theory of immigration suggests that a newly arrived immigrant first goes through a period of acculturation or cultural adaptation (that is, "cultural assimilation"), and once this acculturation is complete, that immigrant would be accepted unconditionally by the dominant white American majority as "one of us" (that is, "structural assimilation"). To put it simply, cultural assimilation is assimilation from the perspective of the minority seeking to assimilate (the Asian Americans) into the sociocultural norms of the dominant majority, while structural assimilation is seen from the perspective of the dominant majority who are considering whether to admit the minority into its midst.

The path of Asian American identity from inferior Asiatic to model minority presumes that linear assimilation into the dominant white American sociocultural norm is a path that is open to Asian Americans. Many sociologists uncritically assumed that the straight-line assimilation experience of the European immigrants would be applicable to Asian immigrants. While many Asian Americans are acculturated into the dominant white cultural system, the same cannot be said of structural assimilation. Most Asian Americans have no problems with "cultural assimilation," namely, the *acculturation* into white American cultural norms, so as to enable them to achieve the American Dream in a "white" American society. In particular, Asian Americans who are born in the United States grow up being surrounded by and enculturated into the same sociocultural world as their white American counterparts. Asian American newspapers and magazines are full of advertisements of accent-losing programs ("Learn to speak like an American *without* an accent!") and plastic surgery to "correct" their Asian physiognomic features (e.g., eye slants) to more acceptable (read "superior") white American equivalents.

For Asian Americans to be assimilated structurally means that they are accepted by their white peers as one of them on the same level field, as well as with the same rights, privileges, and opportunities in a color-blind fashion. On the one hand, the dominant white challenge to all immigrants has been "Why can't you be like us?" This represents a call to cultural assimilation. However, cultural assimilation does not automatically imply unconditional acceptance by the dominant white group. The reality is very different. Witness the number of times Asian Americans are asked questions such as: "Where are you from?" "How long have you been in the United States?" and "How is it that you are able to speak English so well?" More often than not, the white questioner is incredulous that the Asian American was born in the United States and not an Asian country, and is very fluent in English on account of having lived in the United States since birth. That Asian American is effectively assimilated culturally in the white American way of life. Nevertheless, structural assimilation remains elusive.

Indeed, a Spanish, Portuguese, or Austrian immigrant to the United States who arrived a week ago and barely speaks English is automatically assumed by white Americans to be "one of us" because of a common skin color, while a fourth- or fifth-generation Asian American who speaks perfect English is automatically assumed to be a "foreigner" or "alien." As a result, while straight-line assimilation is open to European immigrants, this opportunity is not available for Asian immigrants. Korean American sociologist Won Moo Hurh puts it bluntly:

> Non-white immigrants may attain a high degree of cultural assimilation (adoption of American life-style), but structural assimilation (equal life-chances) is virtually impossible unless the immutable independent variable, "race," becomes mutable through miscegenation or cognitive mutation of the WASP. (Hurh 1977: 95)

Thus, Ronald Takaki argues that the theory of linear assimilation into the American way of life is not applicable to Asian Americans because of the racist and discriminatory barriers erected by white Americans that preclude Asian Americans from achieving structural assimilation (Takaki 1989: 73–75). For example, he cites a Filipino immigrant in California who said, "I have been four years in America and I am a stranger. It is not because I want to be. I have tried to be as 'American' as possible. I live like an American, eat like American, and dress the same, and yet everywhere I find Americans who remind me of the fact that I am a stranger" (Takaki 1989: 316). Francis Hsu argues that "complete Americanization to the extent of total similarity with white Americans is impossible" because Chinese Americans are physically different from white Americans; hence, Chinese Americans "in common with other minority groups will have a continuing problem of double identity" (Hsu 1971: 129, 130). Sucheng Chan explains this situation in the following terms: "As immigrants, many of their struggles resemble those that pre-1965 European immigrants have faced, but as people of nonwhite origins bearing distinct physical differences, they have been perceived as 'perpetual foreigners' who can never be completely absorbed into American society" (Chan 1991: 187).

In a similar vein, in an ethnographical study of Korean immigrants in Chicago and Los Angeles, Won Moo Hurh and Kwang Chung Kim conclude that Korean Americans do not attain structural assimilation despite the number of years they have resided in the United States, as well as the impressiveness of their educational, professional, or economic achievements. While factors such as the large number of first-generation Korean immigrants, problems with the English language, and the tendency to congregate in ethnic enclaves play some part, the main reason for their inability to attain structural assimilation is the barrier that the dominant white majority erects to put a distance between the two groups. As Hurh and Kim explain, the "immigrants' perception of such structural limitations and definition of their own limited adaptive capacities and resources would invoke in the immigrants a defense — their desire to maintain and even enhance their ethnic attachment and identity" (Hurh and Kim 1984: 86). More importantly, they also point out that the Korean immigrants' length of stay or acculturation in the United States did not weaken their attachment to the Korean community and the Korean cultural ethos, and therefore they have articulated a new concept, "adhesive or additive assimilation," to describe the process of Korean immigrants "adding" an American acculturation onto their existing attachment to their Korean ethnic culture and ethos (Hurh and Kim 1984: 73–86).

Perhaps the most thought-provoking insights come from Mia Tuan's ethnographical study of third-, fourth-, and fifth-generation Chinese and Japanese in California entitled *Forever Foreigners or Honorary Whites? The Asian Ethnic Experience Today* (1998). In her many conversations with these Chinese and Japanese Americans, Tuan discovered that her informants bemoaned the fact that structural assimilation remains elusive notwithstanding that they have attained a fair measure of cultural assimilation into white American society. Despite being portrayed as model minorities and attaining outstanding educational, economic, and professional achievements, Asian Americans continue to find themselves labeled as "forever foreigners" and therefore viewed as permanent aliens, rather than "honorary whites." It does not help that Asian Americans cannot choose their physical features, unlike second- and third-generation European immigrants, who have no problems assimilating culturally and structurally into mainstream America.

Moreover, Tuan draws our attention to the fact that Asian Americans experience racism differently from blacks: "Blacks may be many things in the minds of whites, but foreign is not one of them" (Tuan 1998: 8). This is because blacks, unlike Asian Americans, do not get asked "Where are you from?" This understanding of being trapped as forever foreigners leads Tuan to assert that unlike European immigrants, Asian Americans do not yet have the same degree of freedom to choose their identities in public (structural assimilation), although they have acquired the freedom to do so at their personal level (cultural assimilation). More importantly, Tuan questions the assumption that Asian American immigrants are being treated in the same manner as European immigrants:

I am skeptical that within a few generations Asian-Americans would automatically be absorbed into the mainstream.

Generations of highly acculturated Asian ethnics who speak without an accent have lived in this country, and yet most white Americans have not heard of or ever really seen them. They are America's invisible citizenry, the accountants who do our taxes, engineers who safeguard our infrastructures, and pharmacists who fill our prescriptions. Nevertheless, over the years they have continued to be treated and seen as other. (Tuan 1998: 159)

Asian American Experiences of Racism

Why do Asian Americans, even the American-born third, fourth, and fifth generations of Mia Tuan's research, all find themselves regarded by the dominant white majority as foreigners who are regarded as "not one of us," but rather, as "the Other"? Why is it that the dominant white majority calls for assimilation, and yet views Asian Americans as forever foreigners? It appears that the white majority's position of power, dominance, and control is predicated upon the unspoken assumption of the *non*-assimilability of minorities such as Asian Americans to threaten their dominance and control. Undoubtedly, this answer is unsettling for many Americans, because it points to the inherent and deep-seated structural racism within the U.S. society.

The black civil rights movement of the 1950s and 1960s has done much to address the issue of structural racism, resulting in landmark court cases and legislation that introduced affirmative-action policies to redress this problem. However, since the early 1990s, the neoconservative ideological movement in the United States has insisted strenuously at every turn that racism is merely a question of personal attitude of one or more individuals, rather than a structural and institutionalized problem that contemporary U.S. society, as a whole, has to confront. In this respect, the neoconservative movement wraps itself in the rhetoric of equality, uniformity, and nondiscrimination, seeking to promote "color-blind" policies (e.g., the 1995 California Civil Rights Initiative [CCRI], popularly known as Proposition 209) in place of affirmative action policies of the 1960s and 1970s. In her critique of Proposition 209, Korean American theologian Young Lee Hertig points out that as far as Proposition 209 is concerned, "uniformity is seen as equality," and therefore, "any deviation from upper- and middle-class white parameters is perceived as a diminishing of quality." She goes on to challenge its underlying premise:

> Does equality mean uniformity? If so, then whose uniform should people wear? While America as a whole is demographically diversifying, the power structure continues to be held mainly by the white power elite.... Ironically, CCRI deceptively claims to reverse discrimination when, in fact, it institutes discrimination. (Hertig 2003: 135–36)

Hertig's contention echoes the foundational assertion of Michael Omi and Howard Winant throughout their groundbreaking work, *Racial Formation in the United States: From the 1960s to the 1990s* (1994), that far from being a color-blind society, the United States is a very color-conscious society that has discriminated against each racially defined minority. In the same vein, Peter McLaren insists: "Racism and the exploitation of peoples considered to be ontologically inferior to Euro-Americans have always been historical allies to the white supremacist, capitalist, and patriarchal hegemony that characterizes the United States" (McLaren 1997: 250). McLaren argues that, in reality, "whiteness" is the norm in contemporary U.S. society, and minorities are compelled to go through the process of *engabachamiento* (whitening) in order to succeed in life. However, the white American majority ensures that a difference is maintained — "white but not quite" — in order to maintain the existing hegemony power arrangement and control structures (McLaren 1997). In other words, Asian Americans are, at best, "white, but not quite."

Hence, Asian Americans, be they first-generation immigrants or subsequent generations of American-born citizens, have never been fully accepted into the mainstream because of the racism of the dominant white American majority that is intent on protecting its privileges. For example, Robert G. Lee believes that Hollywood has produced films that continue to promote the idea of a "Yellow Peril" overwhelming the United States (read: white) way of life (1999: 204–22). Examples of such movies include *Rising Sun*,

Falling Down, Menace II Society, Year of the Dragon, and *Blade Runner.* In particular, he identifies the 1982 film *Blade Runner* as portraying a "Yellow Peril" of the twenty-first century, where Los Angeles is invaded by Asians, and whites have fled into the safety of their own enclaves (Lee 1999: 191–96). Here, Lee highlights the fact that the film's anti-Asian ideology is seen in the designation of the eyes as the difference marker between the white (or right humans) and replicant humans (195). This bears a remarkable similarity to the nineteenth-century anti-Chinese "Yellow Peril" rhetoric that focused, among other things, on the slanted eyes of the Chinese immigrants.

In its most extreme form, anti–Asian American racism takes the form of virulent hate crimes committed against them on the basis of their racial identity. Moreover, it seems that perpetrators of anti-Asian hate crimes appear to hate all Asians without drawing distinctions between immigrant and American-born, or between different ethnic groups. Some of these anti-Asian hate crimes have resulted in murders — for example, the murders of Chinese Americans Vincent Chin in 1982 and Jim Loo in 1989, and the Filipino American postman Joseph Ileto in 1999. Vincent Chin was a Chinese American man who was murdered by two laid-off white auto workers in Detroit who thought that he was a Japanese American. They directed their ire against Japanese car manufacturers against him, blaming him for the loss of their jobs. What was more incredible was the fact that despite the brutality of Chin's murder and unequivocal evidence of the commission of a hate crime, his murderers were allowed "to plead guilty to manslaughter" and subsequently "sentenced to three years' probation and fined $3,780 each" (Takaki 1989: 482). As for the murder of his fellow Filipino Joseph Ileto, the Filipino American theologian Eleazar S. Fernandez has this to say:

> The *Filipinas* magazine calls the year 1999 "a bloody year for Asian Americans... " On August 10, 1999, Joseph Ileto, a Filipino American postman, was pumped with nine bullets by white supremacist Buford Furrow. A few months later, on April 28, 2000, another wave of hate-motivated murders against Asian Americans and other minorities hit Pittsburgh,

Pennsylvania. This shooting rampage claimed the lives of an Asian Indian, a Vietnamese American, a Chinese American, an African American, and a Jewish American woman. . . . In an article about Joseph Ileto, Emil Guillermo painfully reminds us that "hate and ignorance die hard in the land of the free." (Fernandez 2002: 42)

Instead of declining in the twenty-first century, anti-Asian hate crimes have taken on a new dimension in the aftermath of September 11, 2001, especially against the Sikh American community. For example, while seeking refuge after the second terrorist attack on the World Trade Center in New York City, Amrik Singh Chawla, a Sikh American, was chased four blocks by three white males yelling "terrorist" near Broadway and Fifty-second Street (Gerona-Adkins 2001). Four days later, on Saturday, September 15, 2001, Balbir Singh Sodhi, an observant Sikh, was shot to death while planting flowers in front of his gas station in Mesa, Arizona. The accused, Frank Roque, also fired shots at a Lebanese American clerk at a nearby gas station and at a house inhabited by an Afghan family, before he was arrested and subsequently charged for the racially motivated shooting spree (Toteja 2001).

Much to their distress, the five hundred thousand-strong Sikh American community found themselves to be the most visible target of retaliatory attacks, tauntings, and other verbal abuse. This was due to the fact that their beards and turbans often subjected them to being wrongly identified as Muslim Arab sympathizers of Usama bin Laden by many Americans, even though Sikhs are not Muslims. On the one hand, these and other hate crimes committed against Arab Americans and others who were mistaken for Arabs in the wake of the September 11 terrorist attacks reveal the depths of ignorance, prejudice, intolerance, and stereotyping among many Americans, who could not tell the difference between Sikhism and Islam, between Guru Nanak and the Prophet Muhammad. On the other hand, from the perspectives of American Muslims and American Sikhs, their loyalty was called into question, their places of worship were vandalized, their religious faiths were attacked, and all of a sudden, they have become strangers in their own country.

Shaping Asian American Identities
in the Twenty-first-Century United States

In an increasingly global and transnational era, age-old understandings and conceptions of what it means to be Asian American can no longer be assumed to hold true today. This issue has to be reconsidered, investigated, and answered anew. Two questions arise from this issue. First, is the Asian American identity meaningful or relevant in the twenty-first-century United States? Second, what are the implications of transnational networks and ties for the construction of the Asian American identity?

A Postethnic Future?

In his memoir, *The Accidental Asian: Notes of a Native Speaker,* the Chinese American writer Eric Liu contends, among other things, that the Asian American ethnic identity "was but a cocoon: something useful, something to outgrow" (Liu 1988: 83). Indeed, Liu struggles with the dilemma of identifying himself as an American with Asian heritage and ethnicity, wondering aloud the following, which are "the very questions I sometimes ask myself" (196):

> And you — what obligation do you incur? To live not only the life you have — the school bus, the birthday party, the instant memory of the camcorder — but also the [Asian] life you never had? To link yourself to a chain of greater meaning? What duty have you to reconnect the cord — and if not a duty, then what desire? (195–96)

As far as Liu is concerned, he considers himself "an identity libertarian," and wishes "for a society that treats race as an option, the way white people today are able to enjoy ethnicity as an option. As something cost-free, neutral, fluid" (65). In particular, Liu speculates that "the Asian American identity as we now know it may not last another generation" (82).

Liu's viewpoint sums up the perspective of many Asian Americans who have been raised in the comfortable surroundings of American suburbia and find themselves being bombarded with the iconic trappings of the white American lifestyle that have been crafted by diverse multimedia outlets from cable channels, syndicated programs, and lifestyle magazines. These Asian Americans are often ambivalent about identifying with an Asian American ethnic label, which they associate with the unhip, narrow, insular, and clannish ghetto mentality of their immigrant parents or forebears. Liu describes their worldview succinctly when he states that "Asian Americans are only as isolated as they want to be. They — we — do not face the levels of discrimination and hatred that *demand* an enclave mentality, particularly among the second generation" (78).

In short, Liu believes that because Asian Americans have outgrown the need for deliberate Asian American consciousness in the face of overt racist discrimination, the Asian American ethnic identity is a matter of personal *voluntary* choice — not a necessity or imperative, but entirely optional. For him, everyone, Asian American or otherwise, is free to choose the extent, if any, of identification with a specific racial or ethnic group. Liu is not alone in espousing this viewpoint. His conclusion echoes that of the historian David A. Hollinger. In his book *Postethnic America: Beyond Multiculturalism,* Hollinger argues that racial-ethnic relations in the United States are moving toward a postethnic orientation that "favors voluntary over involuntary affiliations, balances an appreciation for communities of descent with a determination to make room for new communities, and promotes solidarities of wide scope that incorporates people with different ethnic and racial backgrounds" (Hollinger 1995: 3).

From our foregoing discussion in this chapter on the issues of Asian Americans as model minority, middle minority, and forever foreigners, as well as Asian American experiences of racism, I would argue that Liu's sentiments are not borne out in the reality of the daily lives of Asian Americans. In truth, middle- and upper-class Asian Americans often find themselves sharing the same experiences of middle- and upper-class black Americans, namely, their nonwhite names and physical features continue to be insurmountable impediments to full integration into the white American mainstream. Moreover, we have also seen how Mia Tuan's groundbreaking ethnographical research reveals that Asian Americans cannot avoid the label of forever foreigners, even if they are the third, fourth, or fifth generations who are born in the United States.

In other words, Hollinger's and Liu's arguments echo the assimilationist advocates with their naive "color-blind" or race-neutral view that everyone has the unfettered choice of assimilating into mainstream U.S. society and enjoying the American Dream regardless of their ethnicities. Hollinger's "postethnic" argument is a restatement of the discredited "assimilationist" argument, that all ethnic minorities can follow the path of European immigrants and their progeny to assimilate fully into the white American mainstream. In reality, Hollinger and Liu have downplayed what minority activists call "white privilege," namely, that white Americans have the unrestricted privilege of pulling all the strings and enjoying a whole range of life options, including the voluntary public determination of their racial and ethnic identification, something that minorities, Asian Americans or otherwise, do not have.

On the one hand, Hollinger and Liu may be correct about cultural assimilation — that is, Asian Americans or other minorities wanting to pursue the American Dream and making the determination to assimilate *culturally* into mainstream America. But on the other hand, they are mistaken about structural assimilation — that is, the dominant white American majority unconditionally accepting ethnic minorities as "one of us." Ethnic minorities have learned the hard way that the white American majority determines the privileges and restrictions of their racial identities, as well as defines the boundaries for interracial interaction in civic settings such as golf courses, country clubs, old-boy networks, university admissions, economic investments, financial borrowing, and so on. Hence, Chinese American New Testament scholar Tat-siong Benny Liew is correct when he explains the issue of Asian American identity in the following terms:

> [Ethnic] identity is complicated because it is not some essentialized thing that just exists inside a person (as the popular expression "simply be myself" or "go find myself" implies), nor is it something that can be freely chosen. Instead, [ethnic] identity is historically motivated as well as sociopolitically particular. One's [ethnic] identity is always already (in)formed and inhibited by myriads of larger existing structures. (Liew 2002: 10)

The Impact of Transnationalism

Since the 1990s, transnationalism has emerged as a social phenomenon that has far-reaching implications for Asian Americans as they discover and define their identities. In their classic work, *Nations Unbound: Transnational Projects, Postcolonial Predicaments, and Deterritorialized Nation States* (1994), Linda Basch, Nina Glick Schiller, and Cristina Szanton-Blanc define transnationalism as follows:

> We define "transnationalism" as the processes by which immigrants forge and sustain multi-stranded social relations that link together their societies of origin and settlement. We call these processes transnationalism to emphasize that many immigrants today build social fields that cross geographic, cultural, and political borders. Immigrants who develop and maintain multiple relationships — familial, economic, social, organizational, religious, and political — span borders we call "transmigrants." An essential element of transnationalism is the multiplicity of involvements that transmigrants sustain in both home and host societies. (Basch et al.: 7)

One year after the publication of *Nations Unbound,* Korean American sociologist John Lie made an impassioned plea to his colleagues in an article entitled "From International Migration to Transnational Diaspora" (1995) to pay more attention to transnationalism and its far-reaching implications. According to Lie, the classic immigration narrative that the "sojourn of immigrants entails a radical, and in many cases a singular, break from the old country to the new nation," leading to their uprooting and "shorn of premigration networks, cultures, and belongings," is no longer tenable or viable in view of a world that is becoming increasingly global and transnational (Lie: 303). As an alternative, he invites his colleagues to focus on transnational movements and networks:

> It is no longer assumed that immigrants make a sharp break from their homelands. Rather, pre-immigration networks, cultures and capital remain salient. The sojourn itself is neither unidirectional nor final. Multiple, circular and return migrations, rather than a singular great journey from one sedentary space to another, occur across transnational spaces.

People's movements, in other words, follow multifarious trajectories and sustain diverse networks. (304)

According to Lie, while it is true that the Hart-Celler Act of 1965 "brought an unprecedented number of people from Asia and the Americas," at the same time "advances in transportation and communication changed the contours of migration in terms of both its origins and its processes. In the history of global diaspora in the late twentieth century, jumbo jets, television, telephone, fax, and e-mail perforce occupy significant roles. These transformations make possible diasporic communities, flung across the globe, that sustain strong social and business ties" (304). More importantly, he argues that these new developments also subvert the "unidirectionality of migrant passage; circles, returns, and multiple movements follow the waxing and waning structures of opportunities and networks" (305). In addition, Lie cites the example of his own Korean American context: "an adequate understanding of the Korean diaspora in the United States requires a consideration not only of its preimmigration crucible, but also of the transnational flows of peoples and ideas across the Pacific" (305).

As a result of these early discussions on transnationalism, many scholars have turned to this paradigm instead of the older paradigm of uprooting and assimilation to explore how immigrants and their progeny construct and negotiate their identities. For example, the Chinese American anthropologist Aihwa Ong made the case for transnationality as a new paradigm for understanding diasporic Chinese communities' identity constructions (1999). Be that as it may, one should not lose sight of the fact that the phenomenon of transnationalism predated the post-1965 immigration surge. Indeed, the pre-1965 immigrants from Europe and Asia also created and nurtured transnational networks, albeit on a much smaller and often primitive scale, as illustrated in the classic work by William Isaac Thomas and Florian Znaniecki, *The Polish Peasant in Europe and America* (1918). However, the pre–Second World War forms of travel (steamships and propeller airplanes) and communication (surface letters and telegraph) could never match the ease of contemporary air travel and the near-instantaneous global communication networks that have intensified the creation and rapid growth of contemporary transnational networks. Peggy Levitt puts it well when she explains why receiving a letter every two weeks is not the same as being able to pick up the phone at any moment of the night or day: "It gives migrants the ability to be involved in the day-to-day decisions of the households they left behind" (2001: 23).

In other words, as a result of the rapid convergence of the forces of globalization, affordable international air travel, advanced telecommunications, and broadband technology, migration is no longer a one-way departure from one's birth country to one's adopted country. Instead of a one-way permanent boundary crossing that ruptures the ties with one's birth country, many immigrants and their descendants are increasingly going back and forth between two or more locations either physically (e.g., by air travel) or virtually (e.g., using cheap international telephone calls, e-mail, instant-messaging, or VOIP technology), initiating and nurturing transnational networks with extended families, clans, business partners, and friends.

Many people often equate transnationalism with education, wealth, and privilege. For example, Aihwa Ong's classic study on the transnationalism of diasporic Chinese communities, *Flexible Citizenship: The Cultural Location of Transnationality* (1999), dealt with middle- and upper-class Chinese who could afford to move back and forth between different locations. However, Kenneth Guest's ethnographical study of Fuzhounese Chinese in New York's Chinatown highlights the fact that many undocumented Fuzhounese, finding themselves "systematically marginalized in the United States, discriminated against because of their economic skills, legal status, language, and even ethnicity," turn to transnational activities in order to "build identities that transcend their dead-end jobs, their transient lifestyles, and their local marginalization" (2005: 159). Guest's groundbreaking study debunks the commonly held view that Chinese transnationalism is characteristic of middle- and upper-class Chinese who possess the economic resources to live, work, and travel in different places (e.g., Ong and Nonini 1997, Ong 1999). In Guest's words:

> For the majority of the Fuzhounese, their transnationalism is much more nascent, grassroots, and fragile; an ocean-borne

transnationalism of the working poor, not the jet-set trans-nationalism of the elite. Unlike the transnational entities so often discussed that transcend the state, most Fuzhounese immigrants mobilize small-scale transnational networks from a position deep within and vulnerable to state structures. As workers, many of them undocumented, they are disciplined by economy and state alike.... Through these [transnational] networks, they seek to transcend regulated national boundaries and construct broader notions of citizenship and participation. They utilize their emerging transnational religious networks to articulate an alternative existence and identity in the fact of the homogenizing influences of global capitalism and the U.S. labor market. Their participation in the life of their home communities — encouraged, facilitated, and rewarded through religious networks — assists in creating and enhancing a transnational identity which may in fact serve as an alternative to immigrant incorporation in the host society. (2005: 160, 161)

As Asian Americans cross the threshold of the twenty-first century, they are increasingly developing transnational networks beyond the United States to their ancestral countries or elsewhere, constructing new identities and maintaining close ties that transcend national boundaries. They are able to build and nurture familial, sociocultural, economic, political, and religious bonds with their ancestral lands with relative ease, rather than breaking away and seeking assimilation into an aspirational lifestyle defined by white Americans. This is true not just of Asian-born Americans, but also third-, fourth-, and fifth-generation American-born Asians who are rejecting uncritical assimilation and searching for identity in the midst of their ancestral roots. This transnational quest is similar to many African Americans rediscovering their pre-slavery African roots and building new networks and ties with Africa. As a result, there is a blurring of boundaries between geographic space on the one hand, and social and experiential space on the other. Instead of a linear Asian American identity, we are now confronted with hybridized, nuanced, and multidimensional transnational Asian American identities that are simultaneously rooted in the United States while reaching out and becoming attached to other social, familial, and religious contexts in Asia.

In turn, these transnational developments mean that Asian Americans are no longer interested or willing to give up their ethnic identity by complete assimilation. Instead, we find Asian Americans becoming creative and adept at negotiating multiple belongings and loyalties, developing a hybridized sense of belonging simultaneously to the United States as well as countries that they or their forebears have left. For example, many Vietnamese Americans display both the Stars and Stripes and the South Vietnamese flags with pride in Little Saigon communities, remit money home to their extended family or clan in Vietnam, as well as travel back and forth between Vietnam and the United States, forging and renewing deep-rooted familial and kinship ties. In a similar vein, Korean Americans joyously celebrate both Korean and U.S. holidays, while an increasing number of third-, fourth-, and fifth-generation Chinese Americans and Japanese Americans are learning their ancestral languages and cultures.

These transnational developments have significant implications for understanding the present situation and future directions of Asian American Christianity. Indeed, contemporary scholars of religion are increasingly emphasizing the important roles that religion plays in shaping and maintaining transnational ties and networks. Kenneth Guest's ethnographic study of undocumented Fuzhounese in New York's Chinatown reveals the deep involvement of Chinese American churches in nurturing transnational networks between China and the United States for undocumented Fuzhounese immigrants (Guest 2003: 201–6). Fenggang Yang's research on Chinese American Evangelical churches reveals how they are forging multiple transnational ties with churches and parachurch organizations in mainland China, Taiwan, and the wider Chinese diaspora (2002a). Thao Ha's study on Vietnamese Catholics and Buddhists in Houston focuses attention on the institutional dimensions of the transnational relations that these Vietnamese temples and churches have forged with their counterparts in Vietnam (2002).

Chapter 4

Understanding
Asian American Christianity

The United States is a mecca of immigration, and its religious diversity began when the first Christian immigrants fleeing persecution in Europe landed on its shores in search of the freedom to practice their own brands of Christianity without interference by state or church officials. Many pre-1965 immigrants from Asia to the United States and their progeny, as well as post-1965 Asian immigrants, came seeking a similar freedom, freedom from communist regimes and other despotic or autocratic governments. Nonetheless, most Americans uncritically assume that American Christians are necessarily Caucasian, black, or Latino/a; Asians are necessarily non-Christians; and religious diversity and pluralism in the United States involves the introduction of diverse non-Christian religions of these immigrants into the United States.

Even academics are not immune to such an uncritical assumption. For example, in her book *A New Religious America: How A "Christian Country" Has Become the World's Most Religiously Diverse Nation* (2001), sociologist Diana Eck describes a new religious landscape pervading the United States, marked by its immense religious diversity, with shrines, meditation centers, gurdwaras, mosques, and temples deep in the American hinterland. As the provocative subtitle of her book makes clear, the United States has become the most religiously diverse nation in the world. While she has done a wonderful job in documenting the rich mosaic of vibrant religious diversity and plurality in the United States, Eck's "New Religious America" suffers nonetheless from a significant shortcoming because she assumes that American Christians are predominantly white Americans who are reaching out to the Asian immigrant newcomers and their non-Christian religions. What Eck and, indeed, many of her fellow academics (e.g., Porterfield 2001) often overlook is the fact that post-1965 Asian immigrants to the United States have contributed to religious diversity and pluralism in the United States not only by bringing their ancient religious faiths to the United States, but also by introducing Asianized forms of Christianity and establishing new Asian American Christian churches that are different from mainstream white Christian churches.

As Raymond Brady Williams explains, immigrants from Asia and elsewhere "precipitate changes in United States Christianity as they develop transnational churches with manifestations in several countries where members and their families maintain associations at the same time as they negotiate new relationships with their American brothers and sisters in Christ" (1996: 3). Writing in the context of Indian American Christianity, he further asserts that the immigration of new Indian Christian immigrants to the United States calls into question dominant modes of analysis, such that the "two models of assimilation and pluralism seem inadequate to deal with the greater complexity of the new immigration," and therefore, "new immigration involves revision of modes of analysis of American society and religion at the same time as it brings acquaintance with new faces and religious groups" (Williams 1996: 3).

Emergence of Asian American Christianity

The two largest groups of Asian immigrants to the United States, the Filipinos and the Koreans, are predominantly Christian, and both groups have contributed significantly to the diversity within Christian churches in the United States. Filipinos, who are predominantly Catholics, make up the largest Asian immigrant group in the United States, while Koreans, the second-largest Asian immigrant community in the United States, are predominantly Protestant (Min and Kim 2002: 4). According to Jung Ha Kim, "sociologists and theologians agree that over 70 percent of Korean Americans are self-claimed Christians" (1999: 202).

Commenting on the growth of Asian Christian churches in the United States in his introduction to *New Spiritual Homes: Religion and Asian Americans,* Asian American historian David Yoo challenges the commonly held assumption that Asian American Christians are more assimilated than their non-Christian counterparts, arguing that Asian American Christians "have consciously forged religious identities in opposition to the discrimination they have encountered" despite the shared Christian faith with other fellow Americans, and observing that "the long-standing presence of independent racial-ethnic denominations attests to how Asian American Christians have created institutions that reflect their concerns and cater to their own needs. Separate racial-ethnic churches, programs, and governing bodies within majority Euro-American religious institutions, moreover, suggest the complex and contested nature of Asian-American Christianity" (1999: 7). In his opinion, "the identification of Christianity with the United States (and the West) has obscured the fact that Asian Christianity is not synonymous with the religion of missionaries," and in reality, Asians and Asian Americans "have made Christianity their own" (Yoo 1999: 9).

Why Asian American Churches?

A significant development that baffles many scholars is the continuing growth and vitality of Asian American churches. Their puzzlement comes about because many Asian American Christians, Protestants and Catholics alike, choose to establish and maintain their own churches or congregations in the United States, rather than assimilating into existing white American churches, notwithstanding that they are fluent in the English language and share common doctrinal and theological positions with their white American counterparts. Here, one should distinguish these post-1965 Asian immigrants to the United States from the pre-1965 European immigrants. Unlike the pre-1965 European immigrants, many of whom were poor, working-class people who spoke no English and consequently withdrew into immigrant enclaves and ghettos, post-1965 Asian immigrants to the United States are mainly highly educated, skilled professionals who are fluent in English. Many of these immigrants are well educated, and their high-paying jobs enable them to lead affluent lives. In view of the foregoing, one would have expected that post-1965 Asian American Christians, unlike their pre-1965 immigrant counterparts from Old Europe, would encounter no problems joining existing American churches since they speak English fluently and are familiar with the American middle- and upper-class lifestyles. But this is not the case.

In reality, Asian American Christian churches thrive even though Asian American Christians could have joined existing American churches, because Asian American churches provide valuable and important social functions that help Asian American ethnic communities define and sustain their unique identity and cultural traditions. It appears that assimilation into existing American congregations is not a viable option for many Asian American Christians not because of differences of language, or theological or doctrinal positions, but primarily because of discrimination and stereotyping arising from their physical inability to blend in with the dominant white American society in the same manner as nineteenth-century and early-twentieth-century European Catholic and Jewish immigrants to the United States were able to do. Sang Hyun Lee explains that the Presbyterian Church and its Korean American members are caught in a dilemma:

> the ethnically particular communal needs of Korean American Presbyterians are not allowed to be fulfilled in other aspects of the denominational life. The heightened ethnic role of Korean American churches is affirmed on the local congregational level and then denied on other levels of the church's life and work. What is expected of the Korean American churches beyond the congregational level is what goes against the very essence of their social function. That, in a nutshell, is the problem. (1991: 326)

This issue is not merely confined to Korean American Christians. In a similar vein, Raymond Brady Williams cites the following unhappy experiences of Indian American Christians at existing American churches: "One faculty member in a theological seminary recalled his treatment when he and his family attended the local congregation of the church of which he was a minister in India: 'We were always treated as guests and not as members of the family.

You cannot survive as a guest in a church. . . .' A layman said that he has been a member of a local congregation for five years, but he will never become an elder because he is 'brown' " (1996: 186). Elsewhere in his study on Indian American Christian churches, Williams cites an unnamed Indian American Christian who says, "I feel at home in God's house when I can pray and sing in my native language," and notes that "this is true even for those who are fully fluent in English and educated from childhood in English-medium schools" (104). Williams further explains the strategy of Indian American Christians as they establish ethnic Indian churches in the United States in the following terms: "Immigrants adapt their traditional genres to new settings and invent new forms for strategic incorporation. Such stability and change is a dynamic interplay of balancing available cultural and religious resources with demands for relevance. Creative flexibility in selecting symbols and in selecting strategies used to relate those symbols to current contexts is the manner in which ethnicity is shaped and transmitted" (194).

Korean American Christianity

In an early study on Korean American Christians, Won Moo Hurh and Kwang Chung Kim note that "among the majority of Korean immigrants, the religious need (meaning), the social need (belonging) and the psychological need (comfort) for attending Korean church are inseparable from each other; they are functionally intertwined under the complex conditions of uprooting, existential marginality, and sociocultural adaptation for rerooting" (1990: 31). In a similar vein, Eui Hang Shin and Hyung Park suggest that immigrant Korean American Christians flock to Korean churches because of their marginalization by the wider American society, such that Korean churches become "the primary sources of comfort and compensation for Korean immigrants" (1988: 235–36). Pyong Gap Min's important study of Korean churches in New York City reveals the significant role that these churches play in promoting Korean culture and ethnic identity, fostering social networks among Korean American Christians. In particular, Min identifies four important social functions that these churches provide to the burgeoning Korean American community: (1) fellowship for Korean immigrants,

(2) maintenance of the Korean cultural tradition, (3) social services for church members and the Korean community as a whole, and (4) social status and social positions for adult immigrants. As he explains at length in a recent essay:

> The major reason Korean immigrants prefer a Korean church is their need for a communal bond. Due to their uprooting experiences, all immigrants seek a communal bond by establishing ethnic organizations. Yet, the need for a communal bond is strong especially for Korean immigrants because of their cultural homogeneity, and the greater language barrier and other adjustment difficulties. Because of their cultural homogeneity, Korean immigrants try to confine their social interactions largely to fellow Koreans and stick to Korean language, customs, and values. Further, most Korean immigrants have severe language barriers and other adjustment difficulties due to cultural differences. (2003: 131)

In addition, Min further thinks that "the Korean church's various social functions alone may not be enough to make approximately two-thirds of all Korean immigrants participate in it weekly," and thinks that because of their great adjustment difficulties in general, and their experiences with downward mobility in social status in particular, "most adult Korean immigrants may turn to religion to find new meaning in their lives" (132). At the same time, many Korean families attend Korean churches because these churches "contribute to maintaining Korean ethnicity by helping to preserve Korean cultural traditions" through Korean language liturgies, Korean language study programs for their American-born children, the celebration of Korean traditional and national holidays, fellowship meetings where members partake in Korean traditional food, and the emphasis of traditional Korean Confucian values such as filial piety, thrift, and perseverance by Korean pastors in sermons (133–34).

Chinese American Christianity

Although Christians might be a minority in China, Hong Kong, and Taiwan, by contrast Chinese Americans are predominantly

Christian. As Pyong Gap Min notes in his introduction to the landmark study *Religions in Asian America: Building Faith Communities,* while only a small proportion of Chinese immigrants are Christians when they enter the United States, many of them turn to Christianity after their arrival, such that 20 percent of Chinese immigrants are Christian, and Chinese American students, together with their Korean American counterparts, constitute a significant proportion of Evangelical Christians on American university campuses (Min and Kim 2002: 4–5). Sociologist Fenggang Yang cites informal surveys of metropolitan areas suggesting that as many as 32 percent of Chinese Americans profess to be Christian, in contrast to the situation in China, where Christians remain a tiny minority of some 5 percent of the total population (1999: 7). He identified 700 Chinese Protestant churches in the United States, compared to less than 150 Chinese Buddhist temples and associations. He notes that in 1995, there were only 3 Chinese Buddhist centers, compared to 20 Chinese churches in Washington, DC (Yang 1999: 7). In a subsequent essay, Yang cites statistics which reveal that in 1952 there were only 66 Chinese Protestant churches; by 1979 the number had shot up to 366; in 1984 the number was 523; in 1994, the number became 700; and by 2000, there were 819 churches (2002b: 88).

With regard to these newly minted Chinese American Christians, Yang observes that despite some tensions and conflicts, Chinese American Christians endeavor to integrate two or more of these three identity constructions, namely, Chinese, American, and Christian (1999: 183–86). According to Yang, those who succeed engage in what he terms "adhesive integration," namely, "adding multiple identities together without necessarily losing any particular one" (185) and becoming bicultural or multicultural in the process. At the same time, Yang argues that when Chinese immigrants embrace Christianity and become American, they do not abandon their Chinese cultural tradition and ethnic identity. Rather, they engage in a creative exercise of selecting, embracing, and integrating what they perceive as nonreligious aspects of the Chinese culture and ethnicity — for example, Chinese language, cultural customs, Confucian ethical values such as humanity (*ren*) and filial piety (*xiao*), as well as festivals such as Chinese New Year and the Mid-Autumn Festival (see discussion at 132–62). In particular, Yang thinks that "the attraction of Evangelical Christianity to Chinese immigrants also comes from its perceived compatibility with Confucian moral values" (94; see extended discussion at 147–56).

At the same time, the endeavors of Chinese American Christians to integrate Evangelical Christianity and Confucianism open them to charges of syncretism. Chinese American Christians take this issue seriously because they want to be faithful Christians and authentically Chinese. In response to the charges of syncretism, Yang explains that for Chinese Christians, Confucianism and Christianity do not compete with each other because the former is "a system of moral values" while the latter "provides transcendent beliefs and spiritual guidance," a dichotomy that allows Chinese Christians to assert: "Worship Jesus Christ as God, revere Confucius as a sage, and honor ancestors as human beings" (154). Despite embracing Christianity, many Chinese Christians continue to maintain a strong sense of ethnic pride and identity as Chinese people (*huaren*), such that they routinely, albeit anachronistically, refer to fellow non–Chinese Americans as *waiguoren* ("foreigners," literally "people of a foreign nation") to differentiate them from fellow Chinese, the boundary being ethnic or racial, rather than political (175–76).

Asian American Catholicism

At its November 2001 General Meeting in Washington, DC, the United States Conference of Catholic Bishops (USCCB) approved a landmark pastoral letter, *Asian and Pacific Presence: Harmony in Faith*. For the first time, the episcopal leadership of the U.S. Catholic Church publicly acknowledged the presence of Asian American Catholics and the rich diversity of cultures, traditions, and gifts that they bring to the church. In this pastoral letter, the U.S. Catholic bishops concede that Asian Americans, be they newly arrived immigrants or native-born whose roots in the United States extend many generations, "have remained, until very recently, nearly invisible in the Church in the United States" (USCCB 2001: 4). This admission echoes an earlier statement in the 1992 position paper of the USCCB's Office for the Pastoral Care of Migrants and Refugees, *The Pastoral Care of Immigrants from the Philippines,* that the "Filipino Catholic community has been one of the least recognized in the country," because their surnames often result in them being mistaken for Latino/as, and since many of them are fluent in English, they are expected to assimilate fully into the "American style" of Catholicism (USCCB-PCMR 1992). More importantly, the U.S. Catholic bishops went on to say in *Asian and Pacific Presence* that the "tremendous increase in Asian and Pacific Catholics across the United States at the beginning of the third millennium is a teaching moment," and hence, "this pastoral statement focuses attention on the little-known Asian and Pacific communities rooted in the United States, as well as new immigrants about whom we should learn more, and whom we should acknowledge as integral parts of the Church in the United States" (USCCB 2001: 4). It is in this context of "learning about" and "acknowledging" the Asian Americans as "integral parts of the Church in the United States" that this section seeks to introduce its readers to the presence of Asian American Catholics, as well as the diversity with which they enrich Asian American Christianity in general, and the U.S. Catholic Church in particular.

Asian American Catholics are not well known within the wider world of Asian American Christianity, which remains predominantly Protestant and Evangelical in character. Nonetheless, their distinctive cultural-religious traditions, deep faith, and devotion, as well as their transnational worldview, help enrich not just the U.S. Catholic Church in particular, but also Asian American Christianity in general. As space does not allow for an extended discussion of each Asian American Catholic community, we focus here on the principal traits that appear to be common, in varying degrees, to the various Asian American Catholic communities, social, cultural, historical, and regional differences notwithstanding.

Varieties of Asian American Catholicism

In the context of U.S. Catholicism, the two major Asian American ethnic communities — the Filipino Americans and the Vietnamese Americans — are heavily Roman Catholic. Indeed, the massive influx of Filipino and Vietnamese immigrants in the past forty years has contributed significantly to the diversity of the U.S. Catholic Church. While accurate statistics are hard to come by, *Asian and Pacific Presence* estimates that some 83.0 percent of Filipino Americans (1.54 million), 29.0 percent of Vietnamese Americans (0.33 million), 17.0 percent of Indian Americans (0.29 million), 12.3 percent of Chinese Americans (0.30 million), 7.0 percent of Korean Americans (0.07 million), and 4.0 percent of Japanese Americans (0.03 million) are Catholic (USCCB 2001: 9).

Asian American Catholic communities may be organized as (1) one of many diverse ethnic communities within a large multicultural parish, (2) a territorial parish, or (3) a personal parish. In the first scenario, a typical multicultural parish often offers special liturgical services and programs for different ethnic communities, including various Asian American communities. This is by far the most common setup in many parts of the United States. Among the Asian American Catholic communities, the territorial parish is common for Vietnamese American Catholic communities in those areas with sufficiently large numbers of Vietnamese American Catholics. As for the third option, many U.S. bishops have established personal parishes for specific Asian American communities. A personal parish is an extraterritorial parish within a diocese that may be erected to minister to the particular needs of a specific community by reason of language, nationality, or liturgical rite. In this regard, many Vietnamese American territorial parishes also function as personal parishes for other Vietnamese living outside their geographical confines. The personal parish setup is common for Vietnamese American, Korean American, and Chinese American Catholic communities, where there is a pastoral need for liturgical services and other programs in the Asian mother tongues, but where the numbers do not justify the establishment of a territorial parish for those groups.

Asian American Catholic Experiences of Migration

Many Asian American Catholics are immigrants, voluntary and involuntary. For example, many Filipino Catholics came to the United States in search of better job opportunities. By contrast, a significant number of Vietnamese American Catholics in the United States fled their homeland because of persecution by the communist regime that seized power in 1975. Writing from both personal experience and academic research, the Vietnamese American Catholic theologian Peter C. Phan writes about the "existential condition of a transnational immigrant and refugee," which includes "violent uprootedness; economic poverty; anxiety about the future; and the loss of national identity, political freedom, and personal dignity" (2003d: 8). He points out that Asian American Catholics often bring with them a form of Catholicism that differs in many areas from contemporary U.S. Catholicism on account of the deep-rooted influence of early missionaries (22–23). He advises theologians and church leaders to pay attention to the deep devotional piety of these Asian American Catholics, as well as the roles that women play in the transmission of spiritual and cultural values in their communities, the lived experiences of navigating betwixt and between conflicting challenges in their daily living, and their openness to engage in a dialogue with the dominant mainstream in the United States (22–25).

Inculturation and Intercultural Theologies

In the case of many first-generation Asian American Catholics who are immigrants themselves, it is inevitable that their various Asian racial-ethnic identities are indelibly imprinted in their lives and brought by them from the "Old World" to the "New World." For them, the age-old sociocultural traditions, religious customs, pious and devotional practices, as well as theological perspectives that they brought with them from the "Old World" are given pride of place and juxtaposed with new traditions, customs, and practices that they would encounter in the "New World." Asian American Catholic theologians sometimes use terms such as "contextualization," "inculturation," "interculturation," and "dialogue" to describe the foregoing process. In doing so, traditional Asian sociocultural, philosophical, and religious understandings are retrieved, revisioned, and reformulated in response to the call to shape emerging Asian American identities.

A good example of an Asian American Catholic theologian who endeavors to construct an intercultural Asian American Catholic theology using Asian and Asian American resources is Vietnamese

American Catholic theologian Peter C. Phan. In his trailblazing essay, "The Dragon and the Eagle: Toward a Vietnamese-American Theology" (2001), Phan endeavors to construct a Vietnamese American theology out of a dialogue between Vietnamese cultural and religious traditions (as symbolized by the dragon) on the one side, and contemporary U.S. Christianity and the pluralistic U.S. society (as represented by the eagle) on the other. His subsequent essays, "Mary in Vietnamese Piety and Theology" (2002) and "Jesus as the Eldest Son and Ancestor" (2003c), seek to construct a contemporary Vietnamese mariology and christology using traditional Vietnamese religious, social, and cultural elements, and in the case of the latter essay, Vietnamese Confucian virtues and practices. Similarly, the Filipino American Catholic woman theologian Rachel A. R. Bundang has engaged in a similar attempt to articulate a contextual theology to explicate Filipino Catholic devotional piety in her paper, " 'May You Storm Heaven with Your Prayers': Devotions to Mary and Jesus in Filipino American Catholic Life" (1998). More importantly, Phan's and Bundang's research reflect the growing interest of second-generation Asian American Catholic theologians to reflect theologically on the deep abiding devotional piety of many Asian American Catholics.

Popular Piety and Devotions

From the preceding paragraph, it becomes clear that one obvious trait of Asian American Catholic communities which they share with Latino/a Catholic communities, and which generally sets them apart from white Catholics and other Asian American Christians, is the prominence that they give to popular devotions. For example, Filipino American Catholics are deeply attached to their favorite devotions — for example, the Black Nazarene, Santo Niño, and *Simbang Gabi* (a novena of masses in the octave before Christmas). In addition, popular devotions to the Blessed Virgin Mary feature prominently in many Asian American Catholic communities — for example, Our Lady of La Vang for the Vietnamese Americans, Our Lady of Vailankanni for the Indian Americans, Our Lady of Antipolo for the Filipino Americans, Our Lady of China, Our Lady of Korea, and so on.

At the same time, Asian American Catholic devotional piety goes beyond mere informal home-based daily or weekly rituals. In several instances, popular devotions also serve important identity formation and maintenance roles. For example, the annual Marian Days (*Ngày Thánh Mẫu*) in Carthage, Missouri, every August since 1978 draws more than seventy thousand Vietnamese American Catholics, making it not only an important Marian festival and pilgrimage, but also a public celebration of Vietnamese American Catholic identity and pride. The dedication of the shrines to Our Lady of Antipolo, Our Lady of Vailankanni, and Our Lady of China in the Basilica of the National Shrine of the Immaculate Conception in Washington, DC, on June 7, 1997; August 16, 1997; and August 3, 2002, respectively, as well as the annual pilgrimages by various Asian American Catholic communities to these shrines bear testimony to the vibrancy of Asian American Catholic devotional piety.

In many instances, these popular devotions have a strong transnational character, originating from the Asian milieu, brought over by the immigrating generations, as well as transplanted and nurtured by subsequent generations. Based on ethnographical studies of various immigrant groups in Houston, Helen Rose Ebaugh and Janet Saltzman Chafetz observe that popular devotions play an important role in maintaining ethnic culture and identity:

> Religious items representing ethnic culture include specific patron saints for Catholics, evidence of traditional ancestor veneration for Vietnamese Catholics, and Hindu saints veneration among some Parsi Zoroastrians, and religiously specific deity statues for Hindus. Home-centered religious devotions and celebrations of life-cycle events are also heavily tinged by the ethnic culture of participants. In these ways, the practice of domestic religion reinforces cultural identity, and women are centrally involved in such practices. (2000: 392–93)

Close Identification between Faith, Ethnicity, and Culture

Another important characteristic of many Asian American Catholic communities is the centrality of the church as a hub for communal fellowship and mutual support, a situation that arises in part because of language barriers, cultural differences, and other adjustment issues. For many Asian American Catholics, the church is the venue for all communal celebrations and traditional cultural festivities (e.g., Lunar New Year, Mid-Autumn Festival, etc.), the preserver of their language and cultural traditions (e.g., classes in the mother tongue and cultural heritage are offered to their American-born children), as well as the provider of social, welfare, and other support services (e.g., English literacy classes are offered to adults, immigration services and citizenship classes are offered to new immigrants, and job opportunities are advertised). While Asian American Catholics consider themselves fully Catholic and part of the worldwide Catholic Church, nonetheless, they also perceive their own distinctive religious worldview, traditions, and practices as integral to their ethnic and sociocultural identities, such that their Catholic faith often becomes the focus of minority ethnic identification, providing the framework for addressing life issues, as well as assisting to preserve, negotiate, and perpetuate their distinctive ethnic identities and cultural traditions in the wider American mainstream.

For example, in many Vietnamese American ethnic communities, a Catholic parish is often the most important ethnic institution, serving various sociocultural roles in addition to the usual religious functions (Zhou and Bankston 1998: 98), and the tendency of the parish church to serve as a community center results in a close connection between the Vietnamese American ethnic community and their Catholic faith (Rutledge 1985: 65–67). As Father Francis Bui, a Vietnamese American Catholic priest in Louisiana, puts it succinctly: "We have the Vietnamese church to preserve Vietnamese culture and to pass on the language. If it wasn't for that, we could just assimilate into other churches for religion" (quoted in Bankston 2000: 44).

Borrowing an insight from sociologist Peggy Levitt, who made this observation in the context of Catholicism and Latino/a and Irish immigrants (2005: 397), one could explain the close identification between faith, ethnicity, and culture by saying that the overlap between ethnicity, culture, and popular religion among Asian American Catholics is so entrenched that when Asian Americans participate in popular devotional practices, they are asserting their religious, cultural, and transnational identities simultaneously. To paraphrase Levitt, one could say that Vietnamese American and Filipino American Catholics would be "hard-pressed to distinguish what is 'national' or 'ethnic' about themselves and what is 'religious,'" and therefore, when they "act out these identities, either privately and informally or collectively and institutionally, they express important parts of who they are and pass these formulations along to their children" (Levitt 2005: 397). In other words, Asian American Catholics continue to maintain these popular devotions in part because they not only nurture faith and spiritual life, but they also enable people to extend and maintain continuous transnational ties with their kinfolk or communities from their ancestral lands in an increasingly globalized world.

Parachurch Organizations

Many Asian American Catholic communities have active parachurch organizations such as lay associations, youth groups, Bible study groups, charismatic prayer groups, RENEW, and Cursillo groups for communal fellowship and empowerment. In addition to the foregoing, they have also established ethnic-based parachurch organizations — for example, the Eucharistic Youth Society of the Vietnamese American Catholics, an organization for young Vietnamese American Catholic boys and girls that is modeled after the Boy Scouts. Interestingly, the most common and prominent lay association in many Vietnamese American, Korean American, Chinese American, and Filipino American Catholic communities is the Legion of Mary. While the Legion of Mary may be moribund in white American suburban Catholic parishes, nevertheless it is thriving and growing in Asian American Catholic communities. The Legion of Mary enables and empowers Asian American Catholic women to take on public leadership and service roles within the context of these traditional patriarchal Asian cultures that have no public space for such roles. Through the Legion of Mary, many Asian American Catholic women who are otherwise marginalized in a traditional patriarchal communal structure and male-oriented clerical parish framework are now able to participate actively in their parish and community life.

Religious Vocations

One silver lining in the declining rate of religious vocations in the U.S. Catholic Church is the significant growth of Asian American priestly and religious vocations in general, and the Vietnamese American Catholic community's significant contribution to priestly and religious vocations in particular. As Vietnamese American theologian Peter C. Phan describes it:

> There are currently some five hundred Vietnamese priests (diocesan and religious), some twenty permanent deacons, and several hundred sisters. Even among the clergy, there are "success stories": a good number of Vietnamese priests are pastors, responsible for not only the Vietnamese but also American parishes; a few of them hold the office of vicar general, and some have even been made monsignors [and recently, one has been made a bishop]! Vietnamese vocations to the priesthood and religious life have been numerous. In some dioceses (e.g., Orange, California, and New Orleans, Louisiana), Vietnamese priests constitute a significant percentage of the clergy; and in some religious societies, e.g., the Society of the Divine Word, a high number of membership is Vietnamese.... Also to be mentioned are hundreds of sisters of various orders, some of which are of Vietnamese origin (such as the Lovers of the Cross).... (2003a: 230–31, 233)

The Vietnamese American Catholic community stands out with its many indigenous religious congregations, including the Congregation of the Mother Co-Redemptrix (CMC, *Dòng Dông Công*), a male religious order based in Carthage, Missouri; the Lovers of the Holy Cross (LHC, *Dòng Mên Thánh Gia*), the oldest and largest of the Vietnamese female religious congregations, both in Vietnam and the United States; the Congregation of Mary, Queen (CMR, *Trinh Vuong*), a female religious order that is an offshoot of the Lovers of the Holy Cross, with its headquarters in Springfield, Missouri; and the Vietnamese Dominican Sisters (headquartered in Houston, Texas).

A Holistic Spirituality

In their pastoral letter *Asian and Pacific Presence*, the U.S. Catholic bishops observe that "Asian and Pacific Catholic Americans and immigrants migrated with the experience and sensibilities of the great religions and spiritual traditions of the world — Buddhism, Confucianism, Hinduism, Islam, Jainism, Judaism, Shintoism, Sikhism, Taoism, and Zoroastrianism — together with Christianity. Their experience of the great religions and spiritual traditions teaches them to live with a profound sense of the sacred, a holistic approach to life and salvation, and a spirituality adapted to their needs and a life-giving vitality" (USCCB 2001: 15). In addition, many Asian American Catholics come from cultures that have been shaped by indigenous spirituality and religiosity, and they invariably find themselves negotiating back and forth between their multiple religious worlds. The comments of Vietnamese American theologian Peter Phan, albeit on Vietnamese American Catholics, are illustrative of the "holistic approach to life and salvation" that arises from the "experience of the great religions and spiritual traditions" that *Asian and Pacific Presence* speaks of:

Asia is the birthplace of almost all world religions (including Christianity!). In Vietnam the three main religious traditions are Confucian, Taoist, and Buddhist. Scratch the surface of every Vietnamese Catholic and you will find a Confucian, a Taoist, and a Buddhist, or more often than not, an indistinguishable mixture of the three. Vietnamese Catholics live within a cultural framework undergirded by Taoist, Confucian, and Buddhist values and moral norms. They are socialized into these values and norms not only through formal teachings but also, and primarily, through thousands of proverbs, folk sayings, songs, and of course, family rituals and cultural festivals. Many Vietnamese Catholics do not find it strange or difficult to inhabit different religious universes. It is this rich and varied religious heritage, latent but pervasive, that Asian American Catholics bring with them to the United States. It will be one of their most significant contributions to the American Church. (2003a: 234)

Martyrdom

Asian and Pacific Presence also celebrates the "long heritage of extraordinary witness of life and martyrdom" in the Asian church: the 120 Chinese martyrs, the 117 Vietnamese martyrs, the 103 Korean martyrs, San Lorenzo Ruiz for Filipino American Catholics, Saint Paul Miki and his companions for Japanese American Catholics, and so on (USCCB 2001: 10–11). For many Asian American Catholics, martyrdom and persecution are not historical footnotes, but contemporary experiences that have caused many to flee their homeland as refugees. The past few decades have witnessed the arrival in the United States of Vietnamese and mainland Chinese Catholics who have been persecuted by communist regimes. Their experiences serve not only to strengthen and enrich their own faith, but also to remind U.S. Christians in general, and U.S. Catholics in particular, who have no experience of martyrdom, not to take their faith for granted.

Conclusion:
The Future of Asian American Churches

The critical studies by scholars of Asian American Christianity call to mind an earlier example, namely, the sociocultural impact of European ethnic churches that sprouted in late-nineteenth and early-twentieth-century America. Scholars have pointed out that Catholic national parishes became territorial enclaves for many European immigrants during this period (see Warner and Srole 1945; Tomasi and Engel 1970; Linkh 1975; Burns 1987). As William Lloyd Warner and Leo Srole pointed out in their study of European immigrant groups in the United States, "The church was the first line of defense behind which these immigrants could organize themselves and with which they could preserve their group, i.e., system, identity" (1945: 160). This point was reiterated by Silvano M. Tomasi when he observed that Italian Catholic parishes "functioned to maintain the ethnic personality by organizing the group around familiar religious and cultural symbols and behavioral mode of the fatherland" (in Tomasi and Engel 1970: 181).

Would contemporary ethnic Asian churches journey on the same path toward assimilation into mainstream white American Christianity that their pre-1965 European counterparts had embarked upon in an earlier age? Perhaps not, for two important reasons. First, as John Lie rightly points out:

> it is no longer assumed that immigrants make a sharp break from their homelands. Rather, pre-immigration networks, cultures and capital remain salient. The sojourn itself is neither unidirectional nor final. Multiple, circular and return migrations, rather than a singular great journey from one sedentary space to another, occur across transnational spaces. People's movements, in other words, follow multifarious trajectories and sustain diverse networks. (1995: 304)

In practical terms, therefore, immigrant Asian American Christians are no longer called upon to break from their pre-immigration past in the manner that their pre-1965 European counterparts did. Rather, with high-speed telecommunication and broadband links, as well as affordable worldwide air travel, they are able to travel at will and keep in touch with relatives in Asia. As a result, they maintain close ties with their familial, ethnic, and cultural roots. Sharon A. Suh puts it well when she says that the "very immediacy of the homeland and ability to exist almost simultaneously in the homeland and the new land has obviated the need for many new immigrants to even worry about full-scale assimilation to American society" (2003: 188). In other words, the border-crossing experience is no longer a unidirectional, once-and-for-all decision. Instead, despite their permanent abode in the United States, Asian American Christians continue to engage in multiple back-and-forth border crossings, negotiating boundaries, relativizing their marginalization, always striving to create a transnational safe space and shape an identity for themselves.

Second, in the decades following the Second World War, European ethnic churches have lost their distinctive identity and character. This is because European immigration to the United States has slowed from a deluge to a mere trickle, and there is no longer any "first generation" to replenish the ranks of those who left and moved away. However, unlike pre-1965 European immigration, Asian immigration to the United States remains open, and thus the "first generation" of Asian immigrants is constantly being replenished. The repeal of earlier restrictions on Asian immigration under the 1965 Hart-Celler Act, together with other factors such as the desire to maintain close familial ties, quest for economic opportunities, as well as ongoing political and religious persecutions in many parts of Asia that show no signs of abating, have resulted in a massive influx of Asian immigrants to the United States.

More significantly, this constant replenishment of the ranks of first-generation Asian immigrants continues to occur as wave after wave of highly educated Asian immigrants arrive, mainly as professionals on employment visas and staying on as permanent residents and naturalized American citizens. In addition, because of the emphasis in many Asian cultures on family ties, many immigrants not only bring in their extended families under the family reunification provisions of U.S. immigration code, but also travel back and forth between the United States and their countries of birth, thereby renewing and strengthening transnational bonds that continue to undergird and maintain their ethnic identities.

Chapter 5

What Are Asian American Theologies?

In this chapter, we define Asian American theologies and outline their ambit, sources, and objectives. Just as there is no single, normative pan–Asian American identity, so too, a universal, monolithic pan–Asian American theology does not exist. As we saw in chapter 1, the term "Asian American" masks a multiplicity and plurality of identities, and more so, within Asian American Christianity in general, and Asian American theologies in particular. Nonetheless, amid such multiplicity and plurality, a review of the varieties of Asian American theologies that have been articulated by various theologians reveals the presence of common building blocks, ideas, and principles that act to unify them under the banner of "Asian American."

Asian American theologies may be defined as critical and pragmatic intercultural theological reflections concerning the significance and implications of the Christian gospel on the distinct life experiences and realities of Asian Americans with firsthand knowledge and experiences of these life realities. Vietnamese American theologian Peter C. Phan puts it well when he describes Asian American theology as "a hybrid theology, neither fully Asian nor fully American, yet authentically American and authentically Asian," which is the "offspring of the marriage of two divergent cultural and religious heritages, a mixture of the two traditions." Phan argues that "[o]n the one hand, with the United States as its home, it faces questions and challenges proper to its social location and has at its disposal theological resources different from those of its countries of origin," and yet "[o]n the other hand, it cannot but dig deeply into its Asian religious and cultural traditions to

find resources to answer these questions and meet these challenges"
(Phan 2003a: xiii–xiv). He goes on to say:

> Paradoxically, while neither fully Asian nor fully American,
> an Asian American theology is *both* Asian and American, em-
> bodying the resources, methodologies, and characteristics of
> both theologies, and in this sense, will be richer than either
> theology by itself. An Asian American theology is by na-
> ture an *intercultural* theology, forged in the cauldron of the
> encounter between two vastly different cultures. (xiv)

Asian American Theologies as Contextual Theologies

Whatever their confessional leanings may be, broadly speaking
Asian American theologies are best understood as *contextual* theologies that seek to juxtapose the life experiences of Asian Americans with the gospel's soteriological, prophetic, ethical, and transformative power. The term "contextualization" was first coined
by the late Taiwanese Presbyterian theologian Ng Chiong Hui
(a.k.a. Shoki Coe) when he was a member of the Theological
Education Fund of the World Council of Churches. In particular,
Ng noted that the worldwide emergence and growth of contextual theologies is the result of a growing concern of the need
for the Christian gospel to be made relevant to the needs and
concerns of actual human living in the contemporary world, in re-
action against the universalist-positivist approaches of traditional
theological methodologies (see Ng 1973, 1980). The necessity for
contextualization has been succinctly expressed by Douglas J. Hall
in the following manner:

> Contextuality in theology means that the form of faith's
> self-understanding is always determined by the historical con-
> figuration in which the community of belief finds itself. It is
> this world which insinuates the questions, the concerns, the
> frustrations and alternatives, the possibilities and impossibil-
> ities by which the content of the faith must be shaped and
> reshaped, and finally confessed. (1994: 84)

Stephen B. Bevans has articulated a working definition of contextual theology that succinctly describes what contextuality in theologizing is all about: a "way of doing theology in which one takes into account: the spirit and message of the gospel; the tradition of the Christian people; the culture in which one is theologizing; and social change in that culture, whether brought about by western technological process or the grass-roots struggle for equality, justice and liberation" (1992: 1). He explains that "theology that is contextual realizes that culture, history, contemporary thought forms, and so forth are to be considered, along with scripture and tradition, as valid sources for theological expression" (Bevans 1992: 2). In contrast to traditional European theologies that are rooted in the *loci theologici* of scripture and tradition, Bevans asserts that contextual theology adds a third theological locus, namely, human experience. In other words, underlying every contextual theology is the triple play of scripture, tradition, and concrete human experiences. Here we see the mutual interaction of the contemporary dimension of daily human experiences with the historical dimensions of scripture and tradition, thereby integrating the present with the past.

In general, the attractiveness of a contextual approach to theologizing is clear for six reasons. First, it recognizes the fact that sociocultural contexts play a very important role in all attempts to live and flesh out the soteriological message of the Christian gospel within new sociocultural contexts. The need for contextualization may be seen in a simple example: historical time periods such as "Late Antiquity," "Middle Ages," "Renaissance," and "Enlightenment" are certainly important and significant time periods in the history of Christianity in Europe, but these periods have no meaning whatsoever for Asian American Christian communities. Their socioreligious contexts have to be determined by events in their time frame and geographical location, history and tradition, culture and language, ethnicity and identity, as well as sociopolitical and economic systems. Second, because it takes a highly nuanced view of sociocultural developments (rather than a simplistic positivistic view), it does not preclude the possibility of the need for the Christian gospel to be countercultural or transcultural in particular sociocultural contexts. Third, it is dynamic because it perceives sociocultural realities not as closed and static systems, but as constantly in a state of flux as a result of increasing globalization and transnationalization. Fourth, it also insists that the Christian gospel cannot be presented as otherworldly, ignoring the suffering, pain, and injustice within particular sociocultural contexts. Fifth, hermeneutical issues within any theological method are necessarily context-dependent and local, inasmuch as the context determines the characterization of the issues, their presuppositions, and the methodological approaches for resolving them. Sixth, the hermeneutics of contextualization seeks to relate and integrate the Christian gospel and the diverse mosaic of Asian American racial-ethnic contexts with each other, because the Christian gospel is not manifested merely in abstract, philosophical, and intellectual ideas and concepts, but rather, in a community's sociocultural thought forms and processes — namely, it is always a contextualized Christian gospel. As the late biblical scholar Jerome Crowe explained succinctly:

> The gospel can only be experienced and communicated in the form of a particular human culture. There is no such thing as a "pure" gospel, untainted by incorporation into a human culture, because the gospel is not a system of divine truths existing somewhere outside this world and untouched by human feeling, language, and customs but God's self-involvement in the concrete circumstances of a people's history and culture. (1997: 153–54)

In this sense, therefore, not just Asian American theologies, but *all* theologies are ultimately contextual in orientation, rooted in the sociocultural milieu of their authors.

Sources and Goals of Asian American Theological Reflections

As contextual theologies, Asian American theologies often eschew abstract or theoretical deductive conjectures in favor of theologizing from the actual happenings in the daily lives of Asian Americans and their theological implications within the framework of the Christian gospel. The contextual foundation of Asian American theologies builds upon the common elements of retrieving, critiquing, reflecting upon, reformulating, and reshaping the varieties of Asian American Christian worldviews, faith identities, and theological endeavors. It seeks to juxtapose the actual life realities and experiences of Asian Americans with the soteriological, prophetic, ethical, and transformative power of the Christian gospel. The deeper implication of this understanding is truly radical. Asian American Christians are not simply sitting on the margin as the passive audience or recipients of the theological insights of others who occupy the center of things. Rather, Asian American Christians move to the center of theologizing, assuming the roles of active participants and collaborators by virtue of their baptismal faith and commitment to the Christian gospel.

Additionally, many Asian American theologies have an inductive dimension; that is, they pay close attention to the real-life experiences of Asian Americans, which in turn shape the locus and task of theologizing. The Asian American lived experiences that form the basis for critical contextual theological reflections encompass a broad spectrum spanning from the diasporic, interstitial, intercultural, and transnational experiences of first-generation Asian immigrants to the United States at one end, and the life experiences of the 1.5 generation and American-born Asian Americans at the other end. These life experiences often center on the construction of their sociocultural identity and are characterized by their contested negotiations of the complex and difficult relationship between their Christian faith and the demands of the gospel, culture, race/ethnicity, and peoplehood within contemporary U.S. society. Indeed, the existential life issues of faith, ethnicity, culture, and identity lie at the very heart of Asian American theologies.

In their theological ruminations, Asian American theologians frequently grapple with, and seek answers to, the following two fundamental questions: (1) What does it mean to be Asian, American, and Christian living in contemporary U.S. society, which is marked by a bewildering diversity and plurality of worldviews, cultures, ethnicities, religions, and philosophies of living? (2) How does one's Asian racial-ethnic identity shape one's Christian faith, theological reflection, and attitude toward others who may not share one's social, cultural, and religious worldviews? The responses to these two questions have been diverse and varied, revealing the fact that Asian American theologizing is neither

monolithic nor uniform. While we shall explore common themes
and approaches here, we should also recognize the diverse ethnic, cultural, philosophical, religious, and personal backgrounds
of Asian American theologians, as well as the influence of their
denomination on their theologizing.

Asian American Systematic Theologies

It would be a mistake to limit the ambit of Asian American theologies to areas that are often assumed to be "relevant" to Asian
Americans — for example, faith and culture, race relations, immigration, evangelism, church planting, as well as young adult and
other pastoral ministries. In reality, an increasing number of Asian
American theologians are seeking to deal with the entire theological tradition that has been handed down, including those aspects
that are commonly regarded as systematic. A common thread that
we find here is the necessity, from the perspectives of both the theologians and their respective audience communities, as well as their
life experiences, to reconsider, reread, and, in the process, re-vision
the received Christian tradition in the interpretation of scripture
and tradition.

In doing so, Asian American theologians are correcting a historical lacuna; many of the traditional or classical models of systematic
theology, biblical hermeneutics, as well as ritual and pastoral practices were developed and systematized without any input by Asian
Americans. By aiming to review and revision the very heart of the
theological task, Asian American theologians are also critiquing the
complacency of mainstream white theologians, challenging them
to rediscover and retrieve elements of the good news of Jesus
Christ that were lost when Christianity was transformed from an
erstwhile religion of the powerless and marginalized that was persecuted by the mighty Roman Empire to the official religion of an
imperial empire.

In this regard, many Asian American theologians have sought
to enrich and reenvision the entire range of the theological enterprise using both Asian and Asian American resources. Examples
of mainstream Asian American constructive systematic theologies

include Jung Young Lee's *A Theology of Change: A Christian Concept of God in Eastern Perspective* (1979) and *The Trinity in Asian Perspective* (1996), Rita Nakashima Brock's *Journeys by Heart: A Christology of Erotic Power* (1988), Grace Ji-Sun Kim's *The Grace of Sophia: A Korean North American Women's Christology* (2002), Andrew Sung Park's *The Wounded Heart of God: The Asian Concept of Han and the Christian Doctrine of Sin* (1993), Peter Phan's "Jesus as the Eldest Son and Ancestor" (2003c), as well as Enoch Wan's endeavors to articulate a transnational Chinese theology of God, Christ, and theological anthropology (1985, 1997, and 1999). In this process, both Asian American Christianity and the wider Christian world as a whole stand to gain from such cross-fertilization of theologies.

Theologizing beyond the Asian American World

There is an increasing recognition by many Asian American theologians that Asian American theologies should not be formulated in isolation from the wider trends that are shaping contemporary U.S. society, both within and outside Asian American racial-ethnic communities. Thus, for Asian American theologies to be truly "American," in addition to being "Asian," Asian American theologians are seeking to contribute to the process of bringing about new understandings and perspectives to U.S. and worldwide Christianity in general, and the shaping of theology and practice in particular. There is a growing recognition that Asian American theologies need to go beyond merely ethnocentric theologies that are narrowly confined to the needs of specific racial-ethnic Asian American communities, to theologies that would also engage with, as well as challenge, the broader Christian world. Vietnamese American Catholic theologian Peter C. Phan explains it well when he writes:

Asian-American theologians have no wish to develop a theology so ethnic and contextual that so-called "main-line" theologians and Church authorities can look upon it at best as an interesting but harmless exercise and at worst as an

entertaining curiosity at a freak show. Rather, their goal is
to produce a theology that is the fruit of a dialogue among
all cultures and systems of thought in which no one can
claim and is granted a superior status, and in which particularity and universality are not related to each other in
mutual contradiction but in dialectical tension, because it is
only by starting from particular points of view that a universal theology can be constructed. The voices of minority
groups and those of the dominant group will make up a new
chorus in which all the distinct and various notes and lyrics
are harmonized together into a new symphony. (Phan 1999c:
xxvii)

As a result, many Asian American theologians are not content
to be limited to theologizing within the comfortable boundaries
of their racial-ethnic communities. Working within the context of
Asian American communities and striving to be interdisciplinary
and ecumenical, an increasing number of Asian American theologians are beginning to respond to the wider sociocultural trends
within the Asian American racial-ethnic communities, as well as
national and transnational trends outside of the Asian American
world. They seek to contribute across racial, ethnic, cultural, and
national boundaries to the universal Christian theological tradition. In doing so, they desire to engage in the task of theological
reflection not in isolation, but in dialogue with white, black, and
Latino/a theologies, as well as other Asian American religious traditions. Ideally, Asian American theologies are not only shaped by,
but also hopefully shaping and cross-fertilizing the wider theological enterprise within white, black, and Latino/a Christianity in the
North American context.

Chapter 6

Who Are the Asian American Theologians?

Asian American theologians are primarily American theologians of Asian descent who carry out their theological reflections in the United States primarily from Asian American perspectives. They are distinct from those Asian theologians in Asia and elsewhere who theologize principally from Asian-centric viewpoints. The practitioners of Asian American theologies hail from a broad cross-section of U.S. Christianity. Historically, Asian American theologians toiled primarily within the various mainline Protestant churches. Since the 1990s, new Asian American theologians are emerging from Catholic, Evangelical, Pentecostal, and non-denominational traditions. While many of these theologians are first-generation immigrants who have settled down in the United States, a small but increasing number are 1.5 and American-born Asians whose worldviews have been shaped by their experiences of growing up and living in the United States.

We begin this chapter by studying the historical backdrop of U.S. society in the 1950s and 1960s and considering how crucial political milestones, significant social and cultural turning points, as well as important theological paradigm shifts that emerged out of the civil rights and Black Power movements during this period had conscientized a nation to the debilitating effects of ethnocentrism, racism, and discrimination. Next, we focus on how these societal changes and shifts provided the impetus for galvanizing many Asian American activists and intellectuals in general, as well as church leaders and theologians in particular, to emulate their African American counterparts in challenging the status quo and fighting for structural changes in church and society.

Finally, we survey the principal Asian American theologians and their theological contributions.

For the purposes of this chapter, we are going to classify Asian American theologians into two categories — the "first generation" and "second generation," identifying the representative thinkers from each generation, as well as analyzing their background and theological contributions. Clearly, it is impossible to provide a detailed study of every single Asian American theologian within the limitations of this chapter. Hence, the choice of names is not meant to be a complete and comprehensive listing of all Asian American theologians, but to highlight the original insights and contributions of those theologians who best represent the variety of trends in both categories.

The Historical Backdrop of the 1950s and 1960s

The seeds for the emergence of Asian American theologies were sown in the mid-1950s, a tumultuous period defined by the civil rights movement that was sweeping the nation. Led by the Reverend Dr. Martin Luther King Jr., African Americans rose up to confront the Jim Crow laws and other institutional and systemic structures that had relegated them to the margins of society. In the process of doing so, they succeeded in redefining their peoplehood and identity, as well as taking charge of their destiny. Who would have known that when Mrs. Rosa Parks boarded a bus on December 1, 1955, in Montgomery, Alabama, and sat on a seat reserved for whites in defiance of the segregation laws of the Deep South, she would set off a maelstrom of civil disobedience ranging from passive defiance to sit-ins, boycotts, riots, and demonstrations, all of which turned U.S. society on its head? The signing of the National Voting Rights Act of 1965 by President Lyndon B. Johnson, the assassination of Malcolm X in 1965, and the birth of the Black Power movement in 1966 signaled the permanent transformation of U.S. society. The myth of white superiority as well as the uncritical assumption of the normative value of white culture, aesthetics, way of life, spirituality, and theologizing were all shattered, making it clear that it was no longer business as usual.

Joining the black civil rights leaders challenging the social, cultural, political, and economic status quo were black theologians and clergy who began to critique what they perceived as biased theological interpretations that subordinated blacks to whites. Their endeavors culminated in the publication of a full-page advertisement in the *New York Times* of July 31, 1966, by the National Committee of Negro Churchmen (NCNC) that presented a manifesto of Black Theology in conjunction with Black Power. As the African American liberation theologian Dwight N. Hopkins explains, the "thesis of the statement was that for too long white people had been exercising power without morality while blacks had been practicing a morality without power" (1999: 7–8).

Hitherto, the black struggle had been carried out mainly in the social, cultural, economic, and political arenas. Now African American pastors and theologians were ready to take the black struggle to the next plane. The next major milestone was the publication in March 1969 of James Cone's classic work, *Black Theology and Black Power*. Hopkins summarizes its major thrusts as follows:

> *Black Theology and Black Power* . . . combined Martin Luther King Jr.'s demand for the church to be a radical institution for individual and social change with Malcolm X's call for African American people to love their beautiful black selves. Basing its arguments on the lessons of Martin and Malcolm, Cone's book concluded that the movement for black folk to exercise their power in white America was not the opposite of the good news of Jesus Christ. In fact, the struggle for liberation was a key example of Jesus' liberation message for all poor people. In other words, carrying out God's call for personal and collective freedom demanded working toward the freedom of the oppressed African American community. And this faithful practice had universal implications for all people who are marginalized and at the bottom of society. (Hopkins 1999: 8)

Emerging Asian American Consciousness

These developments within the African American community, together with the Vietnam War protests, urban riots, and student unrests, inspired and empowered Asian American intellectuals, community and religious leaders, as well as student activists to confront and challenge the pervasive racism and discrimination that were being directed against Asian Americans. For too long, Asian Americans were often derided by many whites as the stereotypical timid, silent, and submissive minorities. Beforehand, Asian Americans tended to be defensive and inward looking. In the face of institutional racism and discrimination in the late 1800s to the early 1900s, they first established mutual aid societies that provided a forum for community support and unity, as well as resources for survival in a society that was often hostile toward them. For example, nineteenth-century Chinese immigrants to the United States formed a network of mutual aid societies called *huiguan,* organized along kinship, dialect, village, region, and occupational lines. Japanese immigrants had a similar network of mutual aid societies termed *kenjinkai,* structured primarily according to regional or prefectural lines. The Koreans established the Friendship Society in San Francisco in 1903, followed by other mutual aid organizations established around nascent Korean Christian churches. Early South Asian immigrants found community and support at the Sikh temple in Stockton, California, which was built in 1912.

Recognizing the limitations of mutual aid societies, Asian immigrants turned to their home governments for assistance, but realized that Asian countries were often either colonized by Western powers (e.g., India, Korea, and the Philippines) or were too weak (e.g., China and Japan) to offer any meaningful assistance to their nationals abroad. This led many first-generation Asian immigrants in the United States in the first half of the twentieth century to conclude that their mistreatment in the United States arose as a result of the powerlessness of their own governments to advocate on their behalf. Hence, they were very enthusiastic in organizing and supporting movements for modernizing the political and social institutions in their homelands, often raising large sums to support reform and independence movements (Wang 1991). As long as Asian immigrants saw their lives in the United States as a temporary sojourn that enabled them to earn enough money to retire back home in their motherland, they were content to focus their efforts on reforming and modernizing their motherlands. This is true not only of early Chinese, Korean, Japanese, and Indian immigrants of the late nineteenth and early twentieth centuries, but also of current first-generation Chinese and Indochinese immigrants who continue to harbor hopes of reforming and transforming the social, economic, and political structures of their ancestral homelands. However, this attitude was not always shared by their American-born children and grandchildren, who have lived all their lives in the United States. These second and subsequent generations of American-born Asians saw their destiny and future in the United States. They did not have strong kinship, social, and economic ties to the countries of their parents and grandparents. Not surprisingly, these Asian Americans are concerned with pursuing their own identities apart from their parents and grandparents, as well as improving their social, economic, and political standing in society. For example, a group of American-born Chinese in California established the Native Sons of the Golden State in 1895, renamed the Chinese American Citizens Alliance (CACA) in 1915, to fight for citizenship rights for Chinese Americans. The second-generation Japanese Americans, known as Nisei, saw themselves as Americans first and established the Japanese American Citizens' League (JACL) in 1930 to campaign for better social, political, and economic rights, as well as overcome all forms of racial discrimination and prejudice.

The 1960s marked a turning point for Asian American consciousness. Influenced and emboldened by the impact of the Black Power movement on the transformation of the U.S. sociopolitical landscape, Asian American student activists worked through student groups such as the Intercollegiate Chinese for Social Action (ICSA), the Philippine American College Endeavor (PACE), and Asian American Political Alliance (AAPA) to initiate civil rights and social action projects that sought to challenge the ingrained racism and discrimination against Asian Americans. They demanded equal rights and opportunities for Asian Americans in the same manner that the blacks fought for and received (Umemoto 1991, Wang 1991, Wei 1993). L. Ling-chi Wang explains that these young Asian Americans challenged the inertia of older mainstream ethnic organizations such as the Chinese Six Companies and the Japanese American Citizens' League. They "fought for community services for the poor and disadvantaged, demanded civil and political rights for all Asian Americans, and pressured major universities to establish Asian American Studies programs" (Wang 1991: 50).

This culminated in the provocative and confrontational "Third World Strike" at the then San Francisco State College (now San Francisco State University) in 1968–69, the longest student-led strike in U.S. history. Organized by the Third World Liberation Front (TWLF), the multiethnic coalition of student groups comprising the ICSA, PACE, AAPA, the Black Students Union (BSU), and the Mexican American Students Confederation (MASC), this strike began on November 6, 1968, and resulted in a shutdown of San Francisco State College that lasted until March 21, 1969. The principal aim of the strike was a complete transformation of the college's education curriculum in general, and the establishment of an Ethnic Studies program in particular. Karen Umemoto explained the rationale for the latter as follows:

> The focus of the strike was a redefinition of education, which in turn was linked to a larger redefinition of American society. These activities were rooted in and also shaped more egalitarian relationships based on mutual respect. While this doctrine was not always fully understood nor always put into practice, it was the beginning of a new set of values and beliefs, a "New World Consciousness." (Umemoto 1991: 4)

At any rate, the success of this strike resulted in the creation of the first School for Ethnic Studies in the United States, which included Asian American studies. More significantly, its success also inspired a string of similar student agitation on college campuses throughout the United States.

The First Generation of Asian American Theologians

The Asian American student activism paved the way for the emergence of the first generation of Asian American theologians in the 1960s and 1970s. They were exclusively Japanese American, Korean American, and Chinese American men who carried out their theologizing from within mainline Protestant traditions. This first generation of Asian American theologians struggled from outside the theological establishment to challenge the entrenched racism and discrimination of both mainstream U.S. society and Christian institutions, focusing primarily on issues of race relations, faith and culture, and social justice that confronted the Japanese American, Korean American, and Chinese American communities at that time. Prominent "first-generation" Asian American theologians include Japanese American theologians Roy I. Sano, Paul M. Nagano, Jitsuo Morikawa, and William Mamoru Shinto; Korean American theologians Jung Young Lee and Sang Hyun Lee; and Chinese American theologians Wesley S. Woo and David Ng.

It should come as no surprise that these Asian American pioneers were working from within mainline Protestant denominations. At this juncture, the explosion in Asian American membership of Evangelical congregations was still some time away, a transformation that would begin in the 1970s and continue unabated until today. Moreover, the Catholic world was still dizzy with excitement from the conclusion of the Second Vatican Council and the significance of the conciliar documents in general; their implications for shaping the relationship between faith, culture, ethnicity, and context had yet to be worked out in a concrete manner.

Inspired by the example of Asian American students, and taking their cue from their African American colleagues, the first generation of Asian American theologians operated outside the mainstream of U.S. mainline Protestant Christianity, fighting for the rights of Asian American Christians to define and shape their own destiny, identity, and theological enterprise. Many of these theological pioneers faced considerable challenges from church, community, and society as they engaged in the task of theological reflection, critiquing all forms of injustice, as well as reinterpreting and re-visioning new theological directions that sought to liberate Asian Americans from their inferior and subordinate status in church and society.

Practically all the first-generation Asian American theologians ran into discrimination or racism within their denominational structures. Indeed, many of them had experienced the negative impact of the ill-advised dismantling of separate, albeit provisional organizational structures for Asian American Christians in mainline U.S. Protestant churches in favor of assimilation and integration into the mainstream of church life. The publication in

1955 of the influential sociological study by Horace R. Cayton and Anne O. Lively, which predicted the eventual demise of Chinese ethnic congregations in the United States, provided the fodder for speeding up the process of assimilation and integration. Within the United Methodist Church, the California Oriental Provisional Conference, which consisted of Chinese, Korean, and Filipino Methodist congregations, was dissolved in 1956, while the Pacific Japanese Provisional Conference was disbanded in 1964. Their member congregations were folded into the regular annual conferences. Ironically, this was accomplished with the full co-operation of Asian American Christian leaders themselves, who accepted the "church's pronouncement of open itinerancy, opportunity for leadership, achievement ladders of salary and position, and higher pension benefits" (Chang 1991: 137).

Nonetheless, the integration did not go as smoothly as envisaged. Jonah Chang, who eventually became the founding executive director of the National Federation of Asian American United Methodists (NFAAUM) admitted that the merger of the Provisional Conferences with regular Conferences was extremely devastating to the morale, church growth, and clergy recruitment of the Asian Americans (Chang 1991: 137). A similar assessment was offered by Japanese American Methodist minister Lester E. Suzuki:

> Although they voted for the mergers, they really didn't belong in spirit to the new Conferences. Their psychology and activities were still ethnically oriented. The Japanese-speaking members could never fit into the new Conference life. The English-speaking ministers and lay people tried valiantly to work together with Japanese in Conference and district affairs, but in reality it was not a success. (1991: 132–33)

Within four years of the merger, the Japanese American Methodist leaders had a change of heart, and looked for ways to reorganize themselves. This would lead to Japanese American Methodist leaders calling for the reestablishment of structures for Japanese American Methodists, and what was being played out among Asian American Methodists would be repeated in Asian American Christian communities within various mainline Protestant denominations.

Within the foregoing backdrop the stage was set for Asian American theologians to emerge and challenge the status quo where church leadership and theologizing were controlled by white Christians. At this juncture, the majority white Christians, who controlled the institutional and theological dimensions of U.S. Christianity, insisted on assimilation and viewed these Asian American lay activists, clergy, and theologians as radical, fringe activists. Paternalism and uncritical racism had relegated Asian American Christians to subordinate positions within Christian institutional structures.

Hence, the first generation of Asian American theologians engaged in debates with their Caucasian counterparts about the ethnocentrism of U.S. Christianity and U.S. theologies. The significance of their struggle lies in the creation of Asian American Christian identity and theologizing. In doing so, these first-generation Asian American theologians grounded their theologies on the issues of social justice and liberation from all forms of institutional and structural racism and discrimination. Let us now take a brief look at three major first-generation Asian American theologians from the Japanese American, Korean American, and Chinese American Christian communities, and study their theological contributions.

Roy Isao Sano

One of the earliest Asian American theologians who emerged in the 1960s is prominent Japanese American Methodist theologian Roy Isao Sano, Emeritus Professor of United Methodist Studies at the Pacific School of Religion, Berkeley, California. Born of immigrant Japanese parents, his childhood experience of being interned together with his family at the Poston Relocation Center during the Second World War shaped his theological worldview and sensitized him to the issues of marginalization and liberation. The writings of major first-generation black liberation theologians such as James Cone, Gayraud S. Wilmore, and J. Deotis Roberts shaped his early theological writings (see, e.g., Sano 1976b: 287, 288; 1976f: 306), leading him to formulate similar theological ideas, approaches, and strategies for Asian American racial-ethnic communities. Sano was Professor of Theology and Pacific and Asian American Ministries at the Pacific School of Religion from 1975 to 1984. In 1984, he became the first Japanese American to be elected as bishop in the United Methodist Church. He served as bishop of Denver (1984–92) and Los Angeles (1992–95). From 1995 to 2000, he was the president of the United Methodist Church's Council of Bishops, before returning to his teaching position at the Pacific School of Religion in 2000 until his retirement.

Sano became an early advocate of Asian American liberation theology, which was patterned after the black liberation theology that Cone and Wilmore had articulated. In the early 1970s, Sano established and directed the Asian American Center for Theology and Strategies (ACTS), later renamed Pacific and Asian American Center for Theology and Strategies (PACTS). PACTS sought to develop Asian American theologies and promote Asian American Christian involvement in liberation movements in church and society. He also edited two seminal collections of Asian American liberation theologies — *Amerasian Theology of Liberation* (1973) and *The Theologies of Asian Americans and Pacific Peoples: A Reader* (1976). Although outdated, both of these Asian American theological collections remain indispensable reading for researchers interested in the early beginnings of Asian American theologies.

Jung Young Lee

Before his untimely death in 1996, Korean American Methodist theologian Jung Young Lee taught at Drew University as professor of systematic theology. Born in North Korea, he fled to South Korea as a refugee, before moving to the United States for graduate theological studies in 1955. His struggle for acceptance within the United Methodist Church led him to develop an Asian American theology of marginality as the fundamental experience of Asian Americans. He was also interested to retrieve what he considered to be important elements from East Asian cultures and traditions that could undergird and inspire an Asian American theology.

In his autobiographical essay (1999), Lee shared his painful realization of the fact that he was "a man without a country." Not only was he not able to belong fully to America, he was also unable to return to live in his native homeland, communist North Korea, which he fled from as a young man (37). To worsen matters, he was denied ordination and appointment to a pastorate on account of his racial origin, despite meeting all the requirements for ordination and full membership in the Ohio Conference of the Methodist Church. The chair of the Board of Ministerial Qualifications went straight to the point: "Unfortunately, no congregation in our conference wants you as their pastor. You know what we mean." Lee knew the painful implications: "I was unappointable because I was of a different race" (35). Thankfully, his bishop intervened, and he was ordained and admitted as a full member of the annual conference.

In his well-known work *Marginality: The Key to Multicultural Theology* (1995), Lee asserted that the loneliness, alienation, and suffering that he experienced came about because of his status as an immigrant. At the same time, he found himself living on the margins of both the Asian and American worlds, living in the "in-between" world (neither Asian nor American) and the "in-both" world (both Asian and American). In response, he believed strongly that the liberation of Asian Americans as a marginal people could only come about if the people at the center are liberated from their exclusivist and discriminatory worldviews. He articulated the case for a new marginality of love and service in a pluralistic society, with no center and therefore no basis for discrimination, to replace the old marginality of power and control, where the center oppresses the margin. For him, this new marginality is grounded in the marginality of Jesus, who lived "in-between" and "in-both" worlds. Besides Lee's theological reflections on marginality, he was also interested to retrieve and embrace traditional Asian cultural and spiritual perspectives in his theological reflections, as may be seen in *A Theology of Change: A Christian Concept of God in Eastern Perspective* (1979) and *The Trinity in Asian Perspective* (1996).

David Ng

When the well-respected Chinese American Presbyterian theologian David Ng passed away in 1997, the Chinese American Christian community lost a talented and versatile theologian and pastor whose writings covered a broad range of topics, including children's ministries (Ng and Thomas 1981), youth ministries (1984a, 1984b), Asian American theology, religious education, and pastoral ministry (1987, 1992, 1996a, and 1996b, and essays in Donald Ng 1988), and one that was close to his heart, Chinese American theological reflection and ministry (1999; Ng and Kim 1996).

Born into a Chinese immigrant family, Ng grew up amid other struggling Chinese immigrant families in the squalid tenements of Chinatown in San Francisco, where opportunities for advancement were scarce. From these humble beginnings, Ng would later serve as pastor (1959–66), Associate for Youth Resource of the United Presbyterian Church's Board of Christian Education (1966–75), Associate Professor of Church Program and Nurture at Austin Theological Seminary (1975–81), Associate General Secretary for Education and Ministry of the National Council of the Churches of Christ in the U.S.A. (1981–86), Associate for Communication and Support in the Educational Division of the Presbyterian Church (USA) (1986–88), and the John K. McLennan Professor of Christian Education at San Francisco Theological Seminary (1988–97).

In much of his writing, Ng is best remembered for his indefatigable commitment to the vision of church as an inclusive and multicultural community of believers that is not only sensitive to cultural diversity and plurality, but also nurtures bonds of solidarity across diverse multicultural faith expressions and ministries of all believers. He was very concerned with issues of religious pluralism and cultural diversity within North American Christianity, as well as the need to build a united and cohesive community that respects and uplifts such diversity and pluralism as definitive aspects of the church. For him, all Christians have unique gifts from their ethnic and cultural contexts that they share with the wider Christian community, thereby transforming and enriching the church as community. As he explained:

> As in the first Christian Pentecost experience, people are realizing they can hear the gospel and understand it in their own tongue. To paraphrase, crudely, the claim in Paul's Letter to the Galatians, even as the Greek Galatians didn't have to practice Jewish rituals to be Christians, Asian North Americans don't have to be 'white' to be Christians. As advocated throughout this book, Asian North Americans have ethnic

and cultural treasures that enrich their Christian life and practice. In such a milieu (perhaps a more appropriate phrase is 'on such a path or such a tao') it is not only all right but it is encouraged of Asian North Americans that their ethnic and cultural identity and heritage be honored, studied, and expressed. (1996b: 287)

More importantly, by asserting cultural diversity and religious pluralism as opportunities to enrich the Christian community, Ng also rejected the notion of the United States as a cultural melting point that would blend diversity "into a large, bland American mush" (1999: 101). In turn, his theological vision of community within much cultural diversity and religious pluralism was shaped by a creative synthesis between his Christian faith, as defined by the New Testament paradigm of *koinonia,* and his own Chinese Confucian cultural heritage, with its profound sense of community. Rejecting the Western preference for individualism, he insisted:

The Confucian sense of community is similar to the New Testament sense of *koinonia.* When Asian North Americans come into the Christian Church they bring with them their sense of community. This sense of community is their contribution to the Church and calls the Church away from an individualistic faith back to a corporate faith. (1999: 101)

Moreover, Ng drew the following profound insight from the Chinese phrase *tuen kai* (in Cantonese) or *tuanqi* (in Mandarin) that is used in the Chinese New Testament to translate the biblical term *koinonia,* which is worth quoting in full:

To capture the richness of the New Testament sense of community the Chinese borrowed terms from Chinese understandings of family and community. These terms carry no sentimental sense of camaraderie and unity of like-minded agreeable folks who choose and create their own "fellowship," as is often the case in North American churches.... *Tuen* means solidarity; *kai* means responsibility. Indeed the Confucian sense of family is that this communal unit is bonded together. But the bond is not by choice — we do not choose our parents or siblings, we are simply family and always will be — family is a "given." Were we to disagree or fail to get along, or even if one of us is a horse thief (or a heretic), we continue to be related to each other and continue to be in solidarity. And as family, we are responsible to each other and for each other. (1999: 102)

Ng was a strong proponent of story or narrative theology (1999: 84), and often utilized an autobiographical style in his theological writings, taking his own life story as an immigrant and a member of a racial-ethnic minority as resources for theologizing. He asserted that theological reflections should begin with the stories of people from their social and cultural contexts, which in turn "become shared resources for everyone on the Way, the *Tao*" (1999: 86). By this, he emphasized that doing theology as Asian Americans meant embarking on a theological journey together:

We Asian North American Christians saw ourselves as companions on the Way — the *Tao* — telling stories to each other and helping each other on the way. *People on the Way* is praxis — a melding of theory and practice. Its theology is a "theology on the Way" rather than a systematic theology. And the theology often is expressed in story form. The reader is left to ponder the story and to draw one's own conclusions or to contribute one's questions to the community's search for answers. (1999: 84)

To understand how Ng came to view solidarity, community building, and journeying on the Way as important components of his theological approach, we have to turn to his early childhood. Ng recalled how he went back and forth between the American public school he attended during the day and the Chinese language school his parents sent him to in the afternoons. His childhood years imprinted in him a remarkable sensitivity not only to the poverty, marginality, and diversity of racial-ethnic minorities, but also to the rich heritage of his Chinese culture as an important source for his theologizing. As he recalled in his autobiographical essay:

I do not recall ever having heard a lecture on Confucian values, certainly not from my father or mother. There were no lectures about inclusive hospitality or generosity. The lofty concepts of family, loyalty, mutuality, reciprocity, filial piety, and such were not taught, at least not in so many words. I simply grew up in the Ng family who lived in Chinatown. Fifty years later while watching Bill Moyers interview Tu Weiming, a Confucian scholar, I knew immediately what Tu meant when he said that Chinese have a "Confucian DNA." I do. (1999: 88)

It was also in this essay that he described his own life as a path of concentric circles centered around community, a theme that resonated with his Confucian background. As he explained:

The Confucian project is a series of concentric circles of relationship in which the individual relates to family, neighborhood, state, and cosmos. Until China and the Chinese came under the influence of Western ideas, every Chinese person's life image or life theme was *community*. In this essay I claim community to be my life theme too. (1999: 85)

The Second Generation of Asian American Theologians

The struggles of the first generation of Asian American theological pioneers paved the way for second-generation Asian American theologians to join the mainstream North American theological circles from the 1980s onwards. Today, second-generation Asian American theologians are slowly but surely gaining the recognition and respect of their white peers. By contrast, it seemed improbable in the 1960s that a uniquely Asian American Christianity and theological way of thinking would emerge. It was not too long ago that white American church leaders and theologians were advocating an assimilation of Asian American Christians into existing structures. Without the struggle of the first generation of Asian American theologians, who fought very hard for years to gain acceptance for Asian American Christians to think theologically and participate in church leadership roles without sacrificing their Asian American identity, second-generation Asian American theologians would not be able to move into the theological mainstream.

Today, many second-generation theologians are able to receive fellowships and research grants for their work in Asian

American Christianity and theology, hold important academic positions in Asian American theology at prestigious universities, and have their writings published in peer-reviewed journals and other mainstream works. Moreover, they have also institutionalized their theological endeavors in academia, including the mainstream American Academy of Religion (AAR), as well as specialized settings such as the Institute for Leadership Development and Study of Pacific and Asian North American Religion (PANA); Pacific, Asian, and North American Asian Women in Theology and Ministry (PANAAWTM); Asian and Pacific Americans and Religion Research Initiative (APARRI); Institute for the Study of Asian American Christianity (ISAAC); Society of Asian North American Christianity Studies (SANACS); and Asian American Women on Leadership (AAWOL).

The second generation of Asian American theologians, who came into prominence in the 1990s and 2000s, hail from a broader and more diverse cross-section of Asian Americans, resulting in very different ways in which they engage with church, community, and society at large. At this juncture, we see the rise of Asian American feminist theologians; biblical scholars; Evangelical, Pentecostal, and Catholic thinkers; theologians from other Asian racial-ethnic communities, e.g., Filipino American, Vietnamese American, Thai American, and Indian American; as well as a new generation of Japanese American, Korean American, and Chinese American theologians. This second generation of Asian American theologians stands out for their creative and innovative interdisciplinary approaches to theologizing on a wide variety of issues. Besides being interested in reconciliation and community transformation, the second-generation theologians are also studying the deeper implications of the relations between (1) faith, ethnicity, and culture, (2) Bible, ethnicity, and culture, and (3) evangelism, ethnicity, and culture. They also strive for the emotional healing, spiritual development, and faith empowerment of all Asian Americans, be they new immigrants or American-born.

On one level, the increase in numbers and the great diversity of the second-generation Asian American theologians from a broader cross-section of society mirror similar trends of Asian American professionals in the wider society. On another level, second-generation Asian American theologies are far more diverse, complex, and nuanced, compared with first-generation theological reflections. Indeed, when we look at the achievements of second-generation Asian American theologians today, we see that they have not only carried forward the endeavors of the first-generation Asian American theologians, but also contributed to the growth and diversity of interests and concerns.

Many second-generation Asian American theologians started out in traditional theological fields before changing gears and embracing Asian American theologizing, returning to their ethnic roots and cultural heritage. Yet at the same time, these second-generation Asian American theologians are far more vocal and critical than their first-generation counterparts about shortcomings in the Asian American sociocultural world. In other words, the second-generation theologians are faced with new challenges. Unlike the first-generation theologians who were marginalized and challenged by the mainstream to fight epic battles to gain acceptance for an entire community and theological way of thinking, the second-generation Asian American theologians and their ways of doing theology are more or less accepted, albeit grudgingly at some institutions.

As a result, while first-generation theologians expended much energy on attacking *external* racism and discrimination, the second-generation theologians are in a position to address, and consequently have taken a far more critical stance on, *internal* challenges and shortcomings. They have shown a greater willingness to reflect on all aspects of Asian American identity, gender, and life experiences, leaving no stone unturned in the process. For example, in his theological reflection on the aftermath of the 1992 Los Angeles riots that pitted blacks against Korean Americans, the Korean American theologian Andrew Sung Park begins by challenging the Korean American Christian community to reexamine their own culpability in their attitudes toward blacks. He goes on to articulate a theology of transmutation — that is, a mutual cooperation, marked by both mutual enrichment and mutual challenge — among the various racial groups in the United States amid much racial diversity. In the process the challenges of racism and discrimination are overcome, interracial relations are strengthened, and past hurts and sufferings (that is, *han*) of victims of racism and discrimination are healed (1996, 2001).

At the same time, we also observe the emergence of more radical Asian American theological reflections on community, racial-ethnic identity, gender, sexual orientation, and ecology/environment being articulated by young Asian American theologians who are willing to challenge the status quo. We explore these developments in the remaining chapters of this book. What is clear now is the fact that a unified and normative pan–Asian American theology is no longer tenable or even desirable amid such differences.

Asian American Feminist Theologians

When we study the diversity of interests and areas of focus of the second-generation Asian American theologians, one of the striking developments is the emergence of Asian American feminist theologians, who were absent among the ranks of the first-generation theologians. Working under the aegis of their professional society, the Pacific, Asian, and North American Asian Women in Theology and Ministry (PANAAWTM), Asian American feminist theologians insist on the need for theologians to include the experiences of Asian American women in the theological enterprise, which have hitherto been ignored or marginalized by church leaders and theologians who are men. Departing from mainstream white feminist theologians, who focus their attention primarily on issues of gender and faith, Asian American feminist theologians are interested in — as well as critique the problems in the interaction between — gender, race, ethnicity, social class, and faith.

More importantly, many Asian American feminist theologians emphasize the double marginality of Asian American women, marginalized by virtue of their gender not only by the patriarchal structures of the church and the wider society, but also by the patriarchy of traditional Asian cultural and religious structures. Moreover, because they are less constrained by traditional theological categories that have been developed by male theologians, Asian American feminist theologians are more open to a creative weaving of theological insights that seek to synthesize what they view as the ideals of traditional Asian cultural and spiritual heritages with the Christian gospel's call to liberation and justice.

Chung Hyun Kyung

Perhaps the best known and most controversial of the Asian American feminist theologians is Chung Hyun Kyung, a Korean American theologian who currently teaches at Union Theological Seminary, author of the seminal work *Struggle to Be the Sun Again: Introducing Asian Women's Theology* (1990), and whose interests range from ecofeminism to Minjung theology. Rooted in the Korean *Minjung* theology, her feminist theology seeks to challenge the patriarchal structures within Korean Confucian culture and worldview that manipulate, abuse, and victimize Korean women. What sets Chung apart is her radical proposal that Korean women embrace those aspects of their Korean cultural-religious traditions, including Shamanism, Buddhism, Confucianism, and modern *Minjung* thought, that would enable them to relativize and transform the existing patriarchal structures in the Korean church and society.

Chung is best remembered for her opening address at the 1991 Assembly of the World Council of Churches (WCC) in Canberra, Australia, where she shocked conservatives with her performance of a dance ritual in which she called upon the Holy Spirit through the spirits of the marginalized and oppressed, including victims of Christian persecutions and women burned as witches, before concluding with an invocation to Guanyin, the female bodhisattva of compassion. While this brazen act shocked and angered the more conservative delegates at the WCC, nonetheless it marks her creativity and passionate commitment to justice and liberation, seeking to transform structures of oppression within Christianity in general, and Asian American Christianity in particular, especially toward women.

Rita Nakashima Brock

Another pioneer of Asian American feminist theology who emerged at the same time as Chung Hyun Kyung is Rita Nakashima Brock, currently co-director of Faith Voices for the Common Good, a progressive think tank for religions that she established together with Brian Sarrazin on November 3, 2004 (Brock 2005: 165). Her previous positions include a variety of teaching positions, as well as director of the Radcliffe Fellowship

Program (formerly the Mary Ingraham Bunting Fellowship Program). Her contributions to Asian American theologies include *Journeys by Heart: A Christology of Erotic Power* (1988), where we find her creative use of the metaphor of "heart" to "turn patriarchy inside out, to reveal its ravaged, faint, fearful, broken heart, and to illuminate the power that heals the heart" (xv). In this book, she also reflects on the ongoing tensions between her Asian and American sensibilities in shaping her bifurcated identity as an Asian American woman:

> My Asian sensibilities lie under the surface of this book like ancient stones overgrown with weeds and new grass.... Those Asian sensibilities, often in conflict with my American ones, tend to see oppositions as false polarities. In looking beyond false polarities and analytic, critical modes of thinking, I seek an intuitive, nonlinear whole. That whole involves a sensitive attunement to my own inner subjective world as the source of the compassionate healing of suffering. Both the Japanese commitment to compassion, inner insight, and generosity and the liberating power of American feminism inform my journey in this book. For I am Asian American. Oppression by both race and gender are facts of my life. (xvi)

Subsequently, Brock went on to write *Casting Stones: Prostitution and Liberation in Asia and the United States* (1996, coauthored with Susan Thistlethwaite), an important study on global prostitution in which she critiques the cultural and religious structures that legitimize prostitution and explores avenues for liberating women from sexual exploitation; and *Proverbs of Ashes: Violence, Redemptive Suffering, and the Search for What Saves Us* (2001, coauthored with Rebecca Ann Parker), in which she rejects the traditional soteriology of redemptive suffering in favor of a soteriology based on love and presence.

Kwok Pui-Lan

A new figure in Asian American feminist theology is Chinese American theologian Kwok Pui-Lan, the William F. Cole Professor of Christian Theology and Spirituality at Episcopal Divinity School in Cambridge, Massachusetts. Kwok is a well-respected biblical scholar and feminist theologian who is interested in combining contemporary biblical hermeneutics and postcolonial thinking with feminist theology and Asian cultural and spiritual resources. Her extensive theological output includes groundbreaking monograph-length works such as *Chinese Women and Christianity, 1860–1927* (1992), *Discovering the Bible in the Non-Biblical World* (1995), *Introducing Asian Feminist Theology* (2000), and *Postcolonial Imagination and Feminist Theology* (2005).

Of these, the most creative and original is her 1995 book, *Discovering the Bible in the Non-Biblical World,* which introduces her trailblazing work in interreligious biblical hermeneutics, and her proposal of a dialogical model of biblical interpretation within the cultural diversity and religious pluralism of Asia, home to the world's major religions with their ancient scriptures. Kwok insists that Asian Christians should read the Bible not as a normative book to the exclusion of other scriptures, but in dialogue with the ancient scriptural works of Asia. She explains her rationale as follows: "Plurality and multiplicity were an integral part of Asian culture, language, and religion long before the rise of postmodernism in the West. We have to avoid superimposing a European framework on the development of Asian hermeneutics, which must remain rooted in its own specific cultural context" (1995: 39).

Asian American Catholic Theologians

Although small in number compared to their mainstream Protestant colleagues, Asian American Catholic theologians have only just begun joining the ranks of second-generation Asian American theologians. Foremost among them is Vietnamese American Catholic theologian Peter C. Phan, the Ignacio Ellacuría Professor of Catholic Social Thought at Georgetown University. A first-generation immigrant from Vietnam who came to the United States in 1975 as a result of the first exodus of Indochinese refugees after the fall of Saigon, Phan describes himself as an "accidental theologian." In his autobiographical essay (1999a), he explains how he did not choose to be a theologian, but that his life as a theologian "betwixt and between" and his approach to theology "between

memory and imagination" have been shaped by his French education in Vietnam; his philosophical studies and theological training
in Hong Kong, Rome, and London; and his life as a first-generation
immigrant to the United States. A recurring theme in his theological writings is that an authentic Asian American theology should be
built upon the three pillars of inculturation, interreligious dialogue,
and liberation from oppression (1999a: 132).

A Korean American Catholic theologian who is a contemporary
of Peter Phan is Anselm Kyungsuk Min, who immigrated to the
United States from Korea. Currently a professor of theology and
philosophy of religion at Claremont Graduate University, Min is
best known for advocating an Asian American theology based on
a "solidarity of others" (1999, 2004). In his 1999 essay, as well
as his more expansive treatment of this topic in his 2004 monograph, Min argues that Asian American theologies in general, and
Korean American theology in particular, should move beyond their
limited racial-ethnic contexts to a more universal, global, and inclusive theology that is defined by the paradigm of "solidarity of
others." Specifically, he describes the Korean American experience
as bounded by four important characteristics: "separation, ambiguity, diversity, and love of the stranger, the other, or xenophilia"
(1999: 149). In turn, these characteristics call for a theology of
"solidarity of others" that is more merely solidarity "with" others
(1999: 157), and that is opposed not simply to "particularism and
tribalism," but also mere "unity of the same" (1999: 155).

Asian American Evangelical Theologians

Asian American Evangelical theologians are relative newcomers to
the Asian American theological landscape. Leading the vanguard
among the emerging Asian American Evangelical theologians is
Timothy Tseng, formerly associate professor of American Religious
History at American Baptist Seminary of the West, Berkeley, California, and currently president of the Board of Directors of the
Institute for the Study of Asian American Christianity (ISAAC), an
organization he helped to establish. While Tseng's primary focus is
in church history, nevertheless he engages in theological reflections
in many of his writings. Generally speaking, Tseng advocates that

an authentic Evangelical theology in general, and Asian American Evangelical theology in particular, should result in concrete transformation of discriminatory and racist social structures (see 2002a, 2002b, 2003a, 2003b).

Korean American theologian Young Lee Hertig exemplifies a new generation of Asian American Evangelical theologians who are seeking to integrate their commitment to the Evangelical theological tradition with the concerns of their contemporary Asian American communities. Formerly the Vera B. Blinn Associate Professor of World Christianity at United Theological Seminary in Dayton, Ohio, Hertig currently teaches in the Global Studies and Sociology Department at Azusa Pacific University. She is also a founding member of the Institute for the Study of Asian American Christianity (ISAAC) and the Asian American Women on Leadership (AAWOL). Her theological writings include *yinism* as an alternative to Western feminism (1998), intergenerational tensions in the Korean American family and church (2001), race reconciliation in the context of the aftermath of the 1992 Los Angeles riots (2003), and cross-cultural mediation (2004). One of her current projects is her research into the possibility of articulating an Asian American Evangelical theology that emerges out of a convergence of *Dao* and Celtic cosmology (2005).

Chinese American Pentecostal theologian Amos Yong, who is Research Professor of Systematic Theology and director of the doctor of philosophy program at Regent University School of Divinity, presents the intriguing case of a theologian whose journey to discover his own beginnings has led him on a convoluted path to Asian American Evangelical theologies. Yong began his theological career by writing extensively on Pentecostalism, pneumatology, gospel and religious pluralism, and interreligious encounter (e.g., 2002, 2003, 2005a, 2008). Recently, he has begun exploring the possibility of articulating a new Asian American Evangelical theology that integrates the dimensions of being Asian, American, and Evangelical in all of their fullness (2007, 2005b). We discuss his thoughts further in chapter 9 of this book.

Chapter 7

Reading the Bible in Asian America

In the preceding chapter, we saw how Asian American theologians are engaged in a quest to discover the manner by which the Christian gospel's message of hope and salvation could be made meaningful and relevant to the contemporary existential concerns of Asian Americans. In turn, this quest for contextuality in the soteriological message of the Christian gospel leads Asian American theologians and biblical scholars to discern, retrieve, critique, reformulate, and reshape the foundational soteriological, prophetic, and ethical aspects of the Christian gospel. They are also inspired to reflect upon how traditional biblical narratives make sense within their personal lives, as well as in the life of their communities. Unfortunately, this is easier said than done.

Just as there is no single and monolithic pan–Asian American identity or theology, so too Asian American biblical scholars realize that a universal and normative Asian American biblical hermeneutics is neither feasible nor desirable. Hence, Asian American biblical scholars are exploring different ways of reading biblical texts through the hybridity, heterogeneity, and multiplicity of Asian American lenses. As Chinese American biblical scholar Tat-siong Benny Liew explains, it is true that one's Asian American identity does play an important role in determining how biblical texts are being read. According to him, "Identity is also formed in the process of reading," such that "there is certain circularity involved in the interaction between identity and interpretation. Identity does not only influence reading, but reading also influences identity" (Liew 2002: 10). In his opinion, if one is looking for "an essentialized reading strategy among Asian Americans," one would be sorely disappointed (Liew 2002: 10).

From its inception in 1995, the Asian and Asian American Biblical Studies Consultation has provided a forum for Asian American biblical scholars to collaborate with each other on articulating the discipline of Asian American biblical hermeneutics. The fruits of their labors include *The Bible in Asian America*, edited by Tatsiong Benny Liew and published as *Semeia* 90/91 (2002), as well as *Ways of Being, Ways of Reading: Asian American Biblical Interpretation*, edited by Mary F. Foskett and Jeffrey Kah-Jin Kuan and published in 2006. In both of these volumes, biblical scholars and theologians from across the Asian American spectrum have contributed groundbreaking essays on the various aspects of Asian American biblical hermeneutics. We explore here the themes and issues that Asian American biblical scholars have raised and discussed in both of these works.

The Dilemma of Asian American Biblical Scholars

One of the earliest issues that Asian American biblical scholars have to grapple with is the primacy that traditional biblical scholarship has given to the historical-critical method. This is because most, if not all Asian American biblical scholars have been trained in the European and North American traditions of biblical scholarship, which emphasize deductive and objective methods of biblical exegesis that focus primarily on exegesis of biblical texts within their historical *Sitz-im-Leben*. As Chinese American biblical scholar Sze-Kar Wan puts it laconically:

> We had no choice but to learn the master's language and narrative before we were allowed a seat at the table. To have insisted on our Asian-American identity, to speak the Asian-American language — before there was any recognizable syntax with which to parse our speech — would have been professional suicide. (2000: 119)

Nevertheless, despite being trained in Europe and North American institutions of higher education and in historical-critical methodologies, many Asian American biblical scholars have come to a realization that they need to challenge the dominant historical-critical hermeneutics of European and North American white biblical scholarship that often ignore important contemporary issues of race, ethnicity, class, culture, as well as questions of power and control in the name of maintaining and promoting critical and objective scholarship. Chinese American biblical scholar Jeffrey Kah-Jin Kuan explains it well when he writes:

> In my own journey to inscribe my own cultural identity, individually and collectively, I began to move in a new direction in my scholarly interests. Trained primarily as a biblical historian in my doctoral studies, I am no longer satisfied with the kind of disinterested inquiry traditional approaches to the interpretation and construction of ancient texts and society prescribe.... My scholarly interest is ... informed by my social location as a diasporic person. It is through this lens that I am trying to make sense of the texts for my primary community of identification — Asian Americans in general and Chinese Americans from Southeast Asia in particular. (2002: 53)

Defining Asian American Biblical Hermeneutics

With the foregoing thoughts in mind, let us consider the possibility of articulating a tentative working definition of Asian American biblical hermeneutics. Chinese American biblical scholar Gale A. Yee has put forward the following definition:

> An Asian American biblical hermeneutics is fashioned by an American of Asian descent who has intentionally adopted a stance of Asian American advocacy. An Asian American biblical hermeneutics "for us" will interpret the biblical text on behalf of Asian American communities, motivating and enlightening them, as well as critiquing and admonishing them. An Asian American biblical hermeneutics "near us" reminds of praxis: as Asian American biblical scholars we need to keep our fingers on the pulse of what is going on in Asian America, religiously and socially. In all of these endeavors, we

must keep in mind that we do not interpret in a vacuum, but must negotiate a white hegemonic guild. Making whiteness visible is one of our challenges in creating our own biblical hermeneutics. (2006: 163)

In particular, Yee further explains that as far as Asian American biblical scholars are concerned, a biblical hermeneutics *"for us* does not 'cater' to Asian American communities, but rather interprets the biblical texts on their behalf" (159). Moreover, she points out that Asian American biblical hermeneutics goes beyond mere validation or affirmation to prophetic critique in oppressive or negative contexts:

The purpose of an Asian American biblical hermeneutics is not to entertain or seek the approval of these communities. Such a hermeneutics may, in fact, critique the ways in which Asian Americans use the Bible to legitimate sexism, racism, or heterosexism in their congregations. Such a hermeneutics may edify, strengthen, and empower Asian American communities. It also may take an oppositional, prophetic role in condemning any biblically based histories of actualities of injustice or oppression within them. (159)

Instead of an objective and detached way of reading the Bible in the abstract, Yee thinks that Asian American biblical scholars "read our own history, experiences, and stories as Asian Americans into the biblical story, as well as liberate ourselves from that story, when it becomes a source of injustice" (159).

At the same time, Yee also warns that Asian American biblical scholars should go beyond merely counteracting "racist biblical interpretations by white society." Her arguments are worth noting:

Highlighting positive images to counter negative ones, however, is methodologically limited, because it is prompted largely by what the white male world thinks, believes, or constructs about Asian Americans. The danger here is allowing the primary focus to be the white male superior.... Biblical interpretation *about* Asian Americans should be guided by the positive *and* negative engagement of these communities with the biblical text and not solely by the negative use of these texts by white society against Americans of Asian descent. (157)

From Historical-Critical Hermeneutics to Contextual Hermeneutics

When Asian American biblical scholars and theologians interpret biblical texts within the context of Asian American life experiences, such that the biblical texts and life experiences interact with each other, new meanings emerge from such encounters that respond to the questions and challenges in the lives of Asian Americans. In turn, these new interpretations go beyond simply affirming the status quo to "provoking the passion for justice and evoking a radical vision for the future" (Eunjoo Mary Kim 2002: 279). What arises from this is a diversity of ways of reading, understanding, and interpreting biblical texts, taking into consideration the concerns and needs of specific Asian American communities, as well as the multicultural and transnational implications arising from the dynamics of their social locations.

This gives rise to a contextual approach to biblical exegesis that seeks to interpret biblical texts within the challenges and issues raised by contemporary Asian American social locations. In this regard, Chinese American biblical scholar Lai-Ling Elizabeth Ngan explains that Asian American biblical interpreters find themselves moving beyond the historical-critical methodologies to seeking

> not only to understand the text in its cultural and historical contexts, but to derive from it its meaning for the present. Since there is no purely objective reading of a text, such readings begin with the presumption that the interpreter's social location and experience will affect the questions and issues that she or he chooses to explore. (Ngan 2006: 71)

In a similar vein, Chinese American biblical scholar Sze-Kar Wan has proposed a *hermeneutics of hyphenation* that would assist Asian American biblical scholars to navigate betwixt and between the two hermeneutical camps of *exegesis* and *eisegesis* in the academic field of biblical studies (2006). He reminds us that because Asian Americans are living in the margins of society, trapped between two cultures and worldviews, they often encounter a "double rejection — rejection by the host culture for being foreign and rejection by the ancestral culture for being impure" (148). Unlike other Asian American scholars and activists who have avoided the use of hyphenation (as in "Asian-Americans"), Wan insists that Asian Americans should embrace the reality of their hyphenation, accepting the doubleness of their lives and constantly seeking a *"conscious integration* of two cultures even as we are keenly aware that we occupy the margins of both cultures" (151). For him, a hermeneutics of hyphenation

> means also *both this and that.* Our tradition is double: we stand with one foot in our ancestral culture and the other in the West. Our text is double: we read the Bible as a sacred text that once lifted our communities from hopeless isolation, but we also read it as it is enfleshed in the experience of the Asian and Asian-American people. Our hermeneutics is double: we earn our entrance into the guild by perfecting our historical-critical task, but we verify its validity continually against the authenticity of our experience in the guild and in society. (151)

On a different note, Japanese American theologian Roy Sano is interested to explore how Asian American Protestant Christian readings of the Bible change with the changing of the context of their lived experiences, especially those involving questions of race relations and sociopolitical identities. He points out that Asian American Protestant Christians adopted two hermeneutical methods to address the issues raised by their contexts: redaction criticism and canonical criticism. The former allows them to address issues of structures and literary styles in biblical passages, thereby enabling new readings of these passages to address their needs and concerns, while the latter enables them to acknowledge the authority of the normative "orthodox canon" that, although part of the biblical tradition, could cause dissonance between the biblical texts and actual lived experiences, while uncovering the "canon within the canon" — that is, the *"operating* canon" that caused such dissonance.

In response, Sano concludes that Asian American Christians "look for comparable situations and the witnesses of [their] ancestors to who God is and what God says and does in those settings," choosing those portions of the Bible as "'*functional canon*' that more appropriately and adequately shapes faith and action in an emerging context" (2002: 117). In other words, the *dynamic* "functional canon" enables Asian American Christians to address the constantly changing environment of their daily lives, while acknowledging the traditional position of the static "orthodox canon." As he explains, this approach "does not suggest that the rest of the orthodox canon is false, but only less appropriate for particular settings" (117). For Sano, because "no individual or community of faith can fully grasp the totality of the Bible" (116), thus the various Asian American racial ethnic communities are able to contextualize biblical passages and reread them to arrive at new insights that address their issues.

Hermeneutics and the Implications of Diasporic and Postcolonial Experiences

A fertile field of study for many Asian American biblical scholars is the intersection of diaspora and postcolonial studies with biblical hermeneutics. A few Asian American biblical scholars have begun examining the diasporic experience as the context for biblical interpretation. Other Asian American biblical scholars are turning to the methodologies and insights from postcolonial studies to read and engage the biblical texts in a new light. The two examples below, one from diasporic studies (Russell Moy) and one from postcolonial studies (Eleazar Fernandez), serve to exemplify how such creative readings and rereadings of biblical texts have given us new and fruitful insights.

Chinese American theologian Russell G. Moy's essay "Resident Aliens of the Diaspora: 1 Peter and Chinese Protestants in San Francisco" (2002) seeks to read 1 Peter in tandem with the nineteenth-century Chinese immigrants of San Francisco. Moy claims that these immigrant Chinese Protestants shared a similar social location and experiences of marginalization and discrimination with the Jews in 1 Peter's community who were resident aliens living in the diasporic world of Asia Minor. Moy makes two claims here.

First, he suggests that the lived experiences of the Chinese Protestants of nineteenth-century San Francisco enable one to understand the sociopolitical context of 1 Peter. Second, and more importantly, he asserts that the Chinese Protestants lived out the vision of 1 Peter through the *Youxue Zhengdaohui,* an independent Chinese immigrant mutual aid society within the white Protestant Christian mission structure. In particular, he claims that the *Youxue Zhengdaohui* enabled these Chinese immigrants to articulate a "both/and" vision of their newly embraced Christian faith, thereby freeing Christianity from its racist and discriminatory nineteenth-century context. In turn, this enabled the Chinese Protestants to define their own destiny by constructing their own identity that preserved the integrity of their faith, culture, and ethnic identity, as well as building bonds of solidarity and fraternity to ensure their survival in the increasingly racist and hostile environment of nineteenth-century California.

In his essay "From Babel to Pentecost: Finding a Home in the Belly of the Empire," Filipino American biblical scholar Eleazar S. Fernandez investigates the politics of exclusion and inclusion in Genesis 11 (the Tower of Babel narrative) and Acts 2 (the Pentecost narrative), juxtapositioning these passages with the Asian American lived experiences of exclusion and inclusion in U.S. society. Working from a postcolonial perspective, Fernandez rereads the Tower of Babel narrative as a subversive countermyth to the dominant Mesopotamian master narrative of *Enuma Elish* that challenges the imperial Babylonian praxis of exclusion and domination. He compares this narrative to the "self-understanding of the white founders of the United States of America" that is "encapsulated in the discourse of 'chosen people' and 'manifest destiny' " to become "the new masters of the world" (2002: 34). Arguing that hegemony and control have no biblical basis, he proposes an alternative vision of the living rooted in the acceptance of diversity and plurality that arises from the grand Pentecost narrative, which conveys "a vision of what it means to live in a pluralistic society" (29).

Hermeneutics and Identity Constructions

Many Asian American biblical scholars are interested in exploring the politics of textual readings and identity constructions, focusing on issues of race, class, and gender. The result is a complex discourse wherein the construction of identity, race/ethnicity, gender, and class either "in" the biblical text or "in the act of reading the text" is in central focus. A careful perusal of the various biblical scholars who have worked in this topic reveals four contrasting approaches. The first category includes scholars like Uriah Yong-Hwan Kim and Eunjoo Mary Kim, who focus on reading biblical texts through the lens of marginality and interstitial living. In the second category, Japanese American biblical scholar Frank Yamada believes that while marginality makes sense for the first-generation Asian Americans, American-born Asian Americans require more nuanced categories that incorporate the realities of plurality, hybridity, and heterogeneity. Exemplifying the third approach, Henry Morisada Rietz challenges conventional approaches to identity construction that focus on similarities while ignoring or erasing differences and particularities. He uses his own identity as a *hapa* (biracial) person to read biblical texts in the context of Asian American bi/multiracial identity constructions. Finally, Mary Foskett considers the implications arising from reading biblical texts through the contexts and perspectives of Asian adoptees of white American families.

Hermeneutics, Marginality, and Identity

Turning to the well-known story of David and Bathsheba (1 Sam. 11) and focusing on the marginalized character of Uriah the Hittite, Korean American biblical scholar Uriah Yong-Hwan Kim argues that this narrative depicts the struggle of a minority group (symbolized by Uriah, a non-Israelite who was a native of Jerusalem and a faithful Yahwist) against the often hypocritical majority group (symbolized by David, the Israelite *par excellence*) (2002). Kim asserts that the story of Uriah is a text of struggle for Israel's identity (75–76). He notes how Uriah's hybrid identity, "betwixt and between" the Israelite and non-Israelite worlds, created an ambiguous situation where he was simultaneously accepted (insofar as he was permitted to serve in the Israelite army as long as he was "wanted" by or "useful" to Israel) and yet rejected when he was no longer needed (he was branded as a "Hittite" and his wife, Bathsheba, was given an unprecedented double identity —

"daughter of Eliam, the wife of Uriah the Hittite") (73, 76–77). While David was "faithful (or made faithful) in observing this cooperation between men in the protection of property (which included women)" (see 1 Sam. 25; 3:14), he apparently saw no problem in breaking from this cooperation to procure Bathsheba for himself. Worse, David covered up his misdeeds by causing Uriah's death. As Uriah was a non-Israelite, David "did not fear the consequences (fear and hostility) that can rise from breaking this cooperation because there was no *goel* (redeemer) for Uriah to avenge his blood" (Hwan Kim 2002: 80). According to Kim, "David did not hesitate in stealing Bathsheba because the cooperation among Israelite men did not extend to the outsiders; moreover, he did not have to fear any retaliation from Uriah's community" (80). In turn, Kim links Uriah's unjust death at the hands of David to the plight of Asian Americans in a U.S. society that welcomes them when they are economically useful and vilifies them when they threaten entrenched interests:

> Uriah's story is familiar to Asian Americans struggling for identity in the U.S. and echoes the tragic story of Vincent Chin. Vincent was a young Chinese American whose mother's great-grandfather was an immigrant railroad laborer in the nineteenth century in the U.S. His father came to the U.S. in 1922 and served in the U.S. army during World War II. But he was killed as a "Jap" because two white auto workers thought that he was a Japanese and blamed him for the loss of their jobs. Incredibly, they did not serve a single day in jail for their crime. It could have easily been Uriah Kim, a Korean American, killed instead of Vincent Chin, a Chinese American, because I would have looked like a Japanese male to the perpetrators as much as Vincent or any other Asian male. After all, we all look alike — Japanese, Chinese, Korean, Vietnamese, Filipino, pick your choice, oh Asian, the "others," non-"Americans." (82)

Similarly, to Korean American theologian Eunjoo Mary Kim, a careful and critical reading of the Bible reveals that "the primary concern of the Bible is our identity formation, that is, *who we are* in the grace of God rather than moralistic exhortation for what we must do" (2002: 278). More importantly, Kim connects the task of interpreting the Bible to the ongoing pain and suffering that Asian Americans encounter in a racist and discriminatory environment. For her, Asian American biblical interpretation should not be passive or inward-looking, but should confront the evil structural power of racism, asking the question: "What kind of future can we imagine for our community in light of the biblical witness?" (280). As she puts it, the necessity for Asian American Christians to "recover the way of reading scriptures in light of identity formation" is based on the fact that the Bible "has the enabling power to transform listeners' lives communally as well as personally." This is all the more important, given that Korean and other Asian American communities are diasporic communities seeking to negotiate an identity in an alien context. One of the tasks of Asian American hermeneutics is to interpret the Bible to illumine and shape a new identity for the community (279).

Hermeneutics, Hybridity, and Identity

Unlike Uriah Kim and Eunjoo Mary Kim, Japanese American biblical scholar Frank Yamada asserts that cultural identity for third and later generations of American-born Asian Americans is messy, complicated, and conflicting. He contends that Asian American biblical interpretation "must move beyond idealized and essentialist notions of culture" and a tendency to utilize the immigrant experience of marginality and liminality as normative of all Asian Americans to "emphasize particularity, contradiction, and complexity in order to counter oversimplified personifications of what constitutes Asian American" (166). In particular, Yamada insists that themes of marginality and liminality are based upon stable, essentialized notions of what it means to be Asian and American (169). As far as he is concerned, Asian American biblical interpretation should "expose conflicts, resist overly simplistic or pure evaluations of cultures or texts, and refuse traditionally held boundaries between texts, interpreters, and the social location of interpreters" (167).

As a result, Yamada proposes "an Asian American biblical interpretation that recognizes *generational difference*, is shaped by *the construction of cultural identity,* and stresses *hybridity* or *hetero-geneity*" (172). He argues that generational differences matter in biblical interpretation because "later generations of Asian Americans will surface different interpretive issues than their first-or second-generation forerunners — themes that reflect their experience of being Asian in America, e.g., hybridity instead of marginality, or tensions of being a citizen within empire rather than longings for homeland" (172). Moreover, a focus on the construction of cultural identity implies that Asian American biblical interpretation is not fixed, but rather dynamic, complex, and nuanced as cultural identity is rearticulated by each generation. By stressing hybridity and heterogeneity over essentialism, Asian American biblical interpretation from a later-generational perspective is able to break down "fixed boundaries and 'pure' notions of culture, both in the culture of the reader and the world of the text" (173).

Hermeneutics and Hapa Identity

In his autobiographical essay "My Father Has No Children: Reflections on a *Hapa* Identity toward a Hermeneutic of Particularity" (2002; see also 2006), Henry Morisada Rietz focuses attention on himself as a biracial *hapa-haole* who claims both German and Japanese ancestries. Rietz acknowledges that his mixed heritage precludes him from claiming one specific identity completely, such that he is the "Other" to both Asian Americans and white Americans. He asserts that his *hapa* identity reveals the limitations of essentialism and homogeneity in Asian American identity constructions that are usually based on boundaries defined by the commonalities of the members, while at the same time accentuating their differences from biracial and multiracial Asian Americans who do not fit neatly into traditional constructions of Asian American identities.

In doing so, Rietz unmasks the painful tension between *inherited* (that is, biological or "blood") reproduction and *constructed* reproduction. He challenges the privileged position of the former by articulating the controversial view that the Asian American identities could be *constructed* without reference to inherited biological ("blood") reproduction. As a solution, he proposes a new model of identity construction that is modeled on *differences* or *particularity* as the basis for community and communication, drawing upon the insights that he has gained from using the hermeneutics of particularity to read the Dead Sea Scrolls. He emphasizes that Asian American identities are not transmitted by inheritance, but shaped by the dynamic process of identity construction politics.

Hermeneutics and Adoptee Identity

In her essay entitled "The Accidents of Being and the Politics of Identity: Biblical Images of Adoption and Asian Adoptees in America" (2002; see also 2006), biblical scholar Mary Foskett, an ethnic Chinese who was adopted by a white American family, explores the vexing question of boundary-setting and biblical hermeneutics within the context of Asian American adoptees of white American families. According to Foskett, Asian American adoptees not only have to contend with the ambiguity and confusion of defining their identity, but also their invisibility and double marginalization to the wider Asian American communities. She rejects the essentialism of the category of "Asian American" that many Asian American theologians and scholars have taken for granted in their theological reflection, confronting headlong the tension between biological reproduction vis-à-vis cultural reproduction in the construction of Asian American communities.

Responding, Foskett turns to the adoption stories in two biblical passages — Exodus 2:1–22 and Romans 8:12–17; 9:1–5 — which she views as complementary paradigms to root her response to this issue. In her rereading of Exodus 2:1–22 (Moses becoming the adopted son of an Egyptian princess), she offers a new vision of Moses' lost identity being replaced by a newly gained identity through his adoption by the Egyptian princess, as well as the ensuring bicultural socialization that resulted in him having to confront painful choices. By interpreting Moses' story as an adoptee's struggle to come to terms with his own identity and purpose in life, Foskett challenges Asian Americans to overcome their indifference toward the plight of Asian American adoptees in the United States, and discover new ways of redefining Asian American identity without essentializing cultural and bloodline identities.

Chapter 8

Race and Race Relations in Asian American Theologies

Asian American theologians, both first and second generations, have reflected critically and deeply on the divisive issues of race, racism, and discrimination against Asian Americans in the United States. This is not unusual, as many Asian American theologians are joining other Asian American community leaders, activists, and intellectuals to campaign actively against all forms of racism and discrimination against Asian Americans. Before discussing the writings of Asian American theologians on this issue, let us first review the historical background about the discourse on race and racism in the United States. In order to understand fully the problem of racism, we have to explore the meaning of the concept of "race," and in conjunction with it, the question of "white privilege" or "whiteness," which defines the normative standard of the "American way of life."

Understanding Race

In popular parlance, "race" is commonly viewed as a biologically inherent trait — that is, determined and inherited from one's family. However, biologists and geneticists strongly disagree with such an essentialist understanding of race. They argue that this viewpoint has no scientific basis because there are no discernible genetic differences in different skin colors. Social theorists would agree, asserting that race is first and foremost an arbitrary social construction that is dependent on the vagaries and contingencies of history, law, politics, and economic domination, defying all attempts to arrive at an objective, normative, and universal definition.

Nevertheless, this viewpoint of "race" as a biologically inherited trait became the basis for the clarion call by nativists throughout American history to preserve a pristine "white" America. It gave rise to antimiscegenation laws, that is, laws that prohibited marriage between a "white" person and a "nonwhite" person. These laws were enacted and enforced in many parts of the United States, until the U.S. Supreme Court unanimously ruled in the celebrated civil rights case of *Loving v. Virginia,* 388 U.S. 1 (1967) that such laws are unconstitutional because they violate the equal protection and due process clauses of the Fourteenth Amendment to the U.S. Constitution (see 388 U.S. 1, 12). In that case, the trial judge who heard the case at first instance made the following infamous statement, ensuring his lasting notoriety in the legal annals of the United States:

> Almighty God created the races white, black, yellow, malay and red, and he placed them on separate continents. And but for the interference with his arrangement there would be no cause for such marriages. The fact that he separated the races shows that he did not intend for the races to mix. (Cited by Justice Warren in 388 U.S. 1, 3)

Chief Justice Earl Warren, who delivered the unanimous judgment of the bench in *Loving v. Virginia,* also noted, that antimiscegenation laws were an endorsement of white supremacy: "The fact that Virginia prohibits only interracial marriages involving white persons demonstrates that the racial classifications must stand on their own justification, as measures designed to maintain White Supremacy" (388 U.S. 1, 11).

More importantly, the category of "race" is not fixed and unchanging. Rather, it is a dynamic concept that is always changing as racial categories are contested, negotiated, redefined, modified, and transformed through social, cultural, political, legal, and economic forces, as Michael Omi and Howard Winant point out throughout their book, *Racial Formation in the United States: From the 1960s to the 1990s* (1994). In truth, the category of race arises when the political elite seeks to categorize people, especially minorities, by *differentiating* them from the dominant majority group. In the U.S. society, this dominant group is commonly labeled as "white."

Historically, "white" was not how the first wave of immigrants from England identified themselves. Instead they saw themselves as "Christian." As historian Winthrop D. Jordan explains: "From the initially most common term *Christian*, . . . there was a marked drift toward *English* and *free*. After about 1680, taking the colonies as a whole, a new term appeared — *white*" (1977: 95). After reviewing the historical evidence, Jordan concludes that the category of "white" was created to delineate the boundary between the English and other colonists on the one hand, who were the dominant class in colonial American society, from the African slaves on the other, the subordinated class who served the dominant class. Matthew Frye Jacobson came to a similar conclusion when he asserts that "whiteness" as a racial identity was first created by the colonial elite for the purpose of defending the nascent American colony from Indian invasions and slave insurrections, and continued by the young republic to ensure that political control remained in the hands of the Anglo-Saxon Protestant elite (Jacobson 1998).

In short, the category of "whiteness" was originally reserved for the descendants of the colonial English elite, the white Anglo-Saxon Protestants, who took over the reins of power after evicting the representatives of the British Crown. This understanding of "white" formed the basis of the provision in the Naturalization Act of 1790 passed by the First Continental Congress, which gave citizenship in the new republic to "free white persons" only. Indeed, all nonwhites, for example, slaves, freed blacks, and Native Americans, were officially excluded from naturalization and the rights and privileges of citizenship. Only with the successful passage of the Fourteenth Amendment to the U.S. Constitution (1868) were blacks granted citizenship rights. The Indian Citizenship Act of 1924 (Snyder Act) stated that Native Americans could become U.S. citizens, and the Immigration and Nationality Act of 1952 (McCarran-Walter Act) legislated that non-European immigrants were eligible for naturalization. In view of the foregoing, it is not surprising that many white Americans uncritically assumed that their culture and way of life were the norms that defined the national fabric of the United States.

It cannot be overemphasized that this category of "whiteness" is not inherently biological, genetic, or even cultural, but rather, a social boundary that is delineated by power and the need for social and political control. Racial and ethnic classification were used by the dominant white Anglo-Saxon Protestants (WASP) class to demarcate, justify, and enforce social, cultural, and economic boundaries between the "white" and "nonwhite" races (Steinberg 2001). This development was not surprising, as the WASPs, who were descendants of the English colonists, held the reins of power in the colonial era and the early formative years of the independent United States. In the process of doing so, the WASPs were able to maintain the power balance and social control in their favor, notwithstanding increasing cultural and ethnic diversity (Allen 1997).

This myth of a homogeneous English-speaking Anglo-Saxon Protestant white race from Europe was shattered with the arrival of other European immigrants — Irish, Jews, Germans — from the mid-nineteenth century onward. What these nineteenth- and early-twentieth-century European immigrants discovered to their chagrin was the reality that the categorization of "white" had nothing to do with skin color. Indeed, fair-skinned Slavic, Irish, Italian, and European Jewish immigrants found themselves categorized as "nonwhite." In other words, "whiteness" is actually an artificial social class category that has everything to do with preserving the perquisites of the dominant WASP class (see Brodkin 1999, Guglielmo and Salerno 2003, Ignatiev 1996, Roediger 1999, 2005). For example, as far as the WASP nativists were concerned, the Irish immigrants were *not* Anglo-Saxon, Protestant, or white (Ignatiev 1996).

More significantly, nineteenth-century immigrants from northern, eastern, and southern Europe, as well as Ireland, found themselves labeled by the WASPs as "undesirables" — they were not quite "white" like the WASPs, although they were certainly a notch above the blacks and Asians. Ethnic European historiographies are full of accounts of Greeks, Italians, Irish, Jews, and other non-WASP Europeans being victimized by white mobs because they did not speak English, they dressed differently, they took jobs away, and so forth. As a result, "whiteness" became an aspirational goal as these European immigrants sought to assimilate into the "whiteness" norm that defined U.S. society. In the process, they had to shed their distinctive native languages, cultural norms, and traditional customs.

From our vantage point today, we see how the category of "whiteness" has undergone shifts in meaning. In the years after the Second World War, this category was expanded to encompass northern, central, and eastern Europeans; the Irish; and European Jews, all of whom were originally classified as "nonwhites" according to nineteenth-century WASP norms. Race theorists identify two principal reasons how these "nonwhite" Europeans were gradually reclassified as "white" in the early twentieth century. First, these "non-white" Europeans were able to assimilate into the mainstream of mid-twentieth-century U.S. society. Second, and more significantly, shifting social, political, ideological, and economic winds in the twentieth century resulted in them becoming reclassified as "whites" over and against black Americans, especially as the civil rights movement garnered strength. There was the perceived necessity to co-opt other Europeans as cohesive voting blocs in the rising tensions between the whites and black Americans that led to the birth of the civil rights movement (see extended discussion in Jacobson 1998, Ignatiev 1996, Brodkin 1999). What this tells us is that "race" is a dynamic sociohistorical category that is concretized in specific historical contexts where the dynamics of power and social relations are contested, negotiated, imposed, and relativized.

Asian Americans and the "Race" Problematic

It was this "white" racial identity norm, which was engrained in all levels of U.S. society, that immigrants from Asia encountered when they arrived in the United States in the nineteenth and twentieth centuries. Although non-Anglo-Saxon Europeans certainly experienced much prejudice and discrimination, nonetheless they were able to experience a fair degree of personal autonomy, and social and economic mobility in the absence of rigidly enforced exclusionary laws, as well as legal, political, and other structural impediments. For example, Italian, German, and Irish unskilled laborers were able to rise through the ranks of the labor force to become foremen, floor and shop supervisors, and union leaders. By contrast, Chinese, Japanese, and Korean unskilled laborers were relegated to working the most dangerous and least desirable jobs in factories, mines, railroads, and other work sites, and denied opportunities for job training and advancement, as well as membership in trade unions.

In particular, although the non-Anglo-Saxon European working-class poor shared the same class and economic discrimination as the Chinese, Japanese, Korean, and Filipino working-class poor in the latter 1800s and early 1900s, the former did not identify themselves in solidarity with the latter. Alexander Saxton summed it up succinctly when he explained that "being white, they benefited by that very exploitation which was compelling the nonwhites to work for low wages or for nothing. Ideologically they were drawn in opposite directions. Racial identification cut at right angles to class consciousness" (1971: 1). Thus, the Chinese laborers were ineligible for union membership and excluded from enjoying the benefits of the labor movement such as better pay, better working conditions, and so forth.

In addition to politicians and labor leaders, even priests and church leaders jumped on this "white" identity platform. For example, Jesuit preacher Father James Bouchard often railed against the Chinese in his popular mission rallies (Burns et al. 2000: 232–33). In one such talk that he gave in 1873 at Saint Francis of Assisi Church in San Francisco as a fundraiser for the Presentation Sisters, Father Bouchard said:

> But suppose that these Chinese that come into our country are all free; could come and sojourn in our country and become citizens if they wished — and Christians too, if they like — still I maintain that they are an inferior race of people and consequently can not be a safe class (that is, if introduced in any considerable number) of people in our country. Their immigration should therefore be opposed — legitimately, of course — I do not countenance violence, or violent and illegal measures; but certainly the immigration of an inferior race must result in great injury to our people and country....
>
> I have said sufficient to show you the inferiority of that race, and the disadvantages to us; as a people, of bringing them among us;... [t]hey are not a people we want; they are far from the laboring class that our country needs, and must have, to develop all its resources — to enrich and ennoble

it — to perpetuate its grand and noble institutions. 'Tis the white race we want. The white man — the head of all his kind in bone and muscle, and pluck and endurance; in intellect a head and shoulder above all other races; a man, even in the natural order, more or less governed by sentiments of honor and the obligations of honesty; and, in addition, more or less under the influence of a conscience trained in accordance with the teachings of Christianity, and controlled by Christian morality in his everyday life; the only race that has ever proved itself capable of self-government, or of really progressive civilization.... (Cited in Burns 2000: 233)

Asian Americans as Unassimilable?

As Asian immigrants found themselves increasingly unwelcome in the latter part of the nineteenth century and early twentieth century, their sociocultural, economic, and political demarcation from other European immigrants was defined and enforced by both the legislative and judicial branches of the U.S. government. This gave rise to legal precedents that defined and maintained racial boundaries and differences between the whites and nonwhites. As a result, the classification of "race" in the United States is more than merely a sociological or political construct. As Ian López explains, it is also a *juridical* construct, namely, legislation and judicial precedents "construct races by setting the standard by which features and ancestry should be read as denoting a White or a non-White person" (1996: 16–17).

In this instance, López is referring to the so-called racial prerequisite cases in which the U.S. courts sought to define the boundaries of what constitute "whiteness" or the white racial identity, thereby determining whether an immigrant is "white" for purposes of qualifying for naturalization. The underlying presumption appears to be that a nonwhite immigrant is *unassimilable* and, hence, *ineligible* for naturalization. We take a closer look below at two important racial perquisite cases that came before the U.S. Supreme Court, namely, *Takao Ozawa v. United States* (1922) and *United States v. Bhagat Singh Thind* (1923). A byproduct of this unfortunate situation is the entrenchment of this legally sanctioned racial inequality as a result of the privileged status being granted by the courts to "whiteness." Ironically, U.S. law ended up creating and maintaining racial inequalities as a result of this artificial reasoning by the highest levels of the judiciary branch of the United States. But more importantly, in the mind-set of all immigrants, Asian Americans included, "white privilege" is so deeply entrenched in U.S. society that it becomes the unassailable social, cultural, political, and even legal norm for judging nonwhites.

Takao Ozawa v. United States

The U.S. Supreme Court's decision in the case of *Takao Ozawa v. United States*, 260 U.S. 178 (1922) reveals that even fair-skinned Asian immigrants were not sufficiently "white" in the eyes of the U.S. courts. When Takao Ozawa's application for naturalization was turned down, he appealed this decision. On March 25, 1916, Judge Charles Clemons of the U.S. District Court for the Territory of Hawaii denied Ozawa's petition for naturalization, holding that although Ozawa was "in every way qualified under the statutes to become an American citizen, except one — he was not white" (quoted in Takaki 1989: 208). Ozawa then appealed to the U.S. Supreme Court, which ruled unanimously against him. Writing the opinion of the bench, Justice George Sutherland acknowledged that had "whiteness" not been a factor, Ozawa would be preeminently qualified for naturalization:

> Including the period of his residence in Hawaii appellant had continuously resided in the United States for 20 years. He was a graduate of the Berkeley, Cal., high school, had been nearly three years a student in the University of California, had educated his children in American schools, his family had attended American churches and he had maintained the use of the English language in his home. That he was well qualified by character and education for citizenship is conceded. (260 U.S. 178, 190)

More significantly, Justice Sutherland held that only Caucasians qualified to be white, even if some Caucasians may not be as fair-skinned as the Japanese. Hence, Ozawa was ineligible for naturalization, notwithstanding his fair skin color. As Justice Sutherland put it in his own words:

> We have been furnished with elaborate briefs in which the meaning of the words "white person" is discussed.... *Manifestly the test afforded by the mere color of the skin of each individual is impracticable, as that differs greatly among persons of the same race, even among Anglo-Saxons, ranging by imperceptible gradations from the fair blond to the swarthy brunette, the latter being darker than many of the lighter hued persons of the brown or yellow races.* Hence to adopt the color test alone would result in a confused overlapping of races and a gradual merging of one into the other, without any practical line of separation. Beginning with the decision of Circuit Judge Sawyer, in Re Ah Yup, 5 Sawy. 155, Fed. Cas. No. 104 (1878), the federal and state courts, in an almost unbroken line, have held that *the words "white person" were meant to indicate only a person of what is popularly known as the Caucasian race....* The effect of the conclusion that the words "white person" means a Caucasian is not to establish a sharp line of demarcation between those who are entitled and those who are not entitled to naturalization, but rather a zone of more or less debatable ground outside of which, upon the one hand, are those clearly eligible, and outside of which, upon the other hand, are those clearly ineligible for citizenship.... The appellant, in the case now under consideration, however, is clearly of a race which is not Caucasian and therefore belongs entirely outside the zone on the negative side. (260 U.S. 178, 197–98, emphasis added)

United States v. Bhagat Singh Thind

Contrary to the popular myth of the essential, unchanging definition of "whiteness," the U.S. courts have vacillated in defining the "whiteness" of specific racial groups. Thus, Armenians were first considered Asiatics before they were considered as white (Takaki 1989: 15). The case of Asian Indians exemplifies the difficulties the U.S. courts faced in deciding whether Asian Indians are "whites" or otherwise. When Asian Indians were considered as "whites," they were eligible for naturalization: see the affirmative decisions of the U.S. Court of Appeals Second Circuit in *United States v. Balsara*, 180 Fed. 694 (1910) and the U.S. Court of Appeals Fifth Circuit in *United States v. Dolla*, 177 Fed. 101 (1910), which held that Asian Indians were "whites."

Inevitably, the question of whether Asian Indians were "white" came before the U.S. Supreme Court in the case of *United States v. Bhagat Singh Thind*, 261 U.S. 204 (1923). Justice George Sutherland, who delivered the judgment of the court six months earlier in the case of *Takao Ozawa v. United States*, struggled to find a way to ensure that Asians remained ineligible for naturalization. Recall that in the case of Takao Ozawa, Justice Sutherland explicitly held that a fair-skinned Japanese was not "white" because the category of "white person" was "meant to indicate only a person of what is popularly known as the Caucasian race" (260 U.S. 178, 197). Faced with a Sikh who asserted that he was eligible for naturalization because he was a Caucasian according to the prevailing scientific consensus, Justice Sutherland now had second thoughts about using "Caucasian" as a yardstick for "white." Indeed, he disavowed the term "Caucasian" as a legal yardstick, backtracking from his earlier decision in the *Takao Ozawa* case:

> The word "Caucasian" is in scarcely better repute. It is at best a conventional term, with an altogether fortuitous origin, which under scientific manipulation, has come to include far more than the unscientific mind suspects.... We venture to think that the average well informed white American would learn with some degree of astonishment that the race to which he belongs is made up of such heterogeneous elements. (26 U.S. 204, 211)

As an alternative, Justice Sutherland turned to the test of popular or commonly held perceptions of whiteness. In this regard, he held that while it "may be true that the blond Scandinavian and the brown Hindu have a common ancestor in the dim reaches of antiquity, but the average man knows perfectly well that there are unmistakable and profound differences between them today" (26 U.S. 204, 209). Despite the inherent subjectivity of such a test, the learned justice nevertheless concluded thus:

What we now hold is that the words "free white persons" are words of common speech, to be interpreted in accordance with the understanding of the common man, synonymous with the word "Caucasian" only as that word is popularly understood. As so understood and used, whatever may be the speculations of the ethnologist, it does not include the body of people to whom the appellee belongs. It is a matter of familiar observation and knowledge that the physical group characteristics of the Hindus render them readily distinguishable from the various groups of persons in this country commonly recognized as white. The children of English, French, German, Italian, Scandinavian, and other European parentage, quickly merge into the mass of our population and lose the distinctive hallmarks of their European origin. *On the other hand, it cannot be doubted that the children born in this country of Hindu parents would retain indefinitely the clear evidence of their ancestry. It is very far from our thought to suggest the slightest question of racial superiority or inferiority. What we suggest is merely racial difference, and it is of such character and extent that the great body of our people instinctively recognize it and reject the thought of assimilation.* (261 U.S. 204, 214–15, emphasis added)

Continuing Prejudice and Stereotyping

While Asians are no longer precluded today from immigrating to and becoming naturalized citizens of the United States, nonetheless they still continue to face ongoing prejudice, racism, and discrimination in their lives in the contemporary United States. In chapter 3, we saw how this is not merely a problem for the first-generation Asian immigrants to the United States, but also for subsequent generations of their American-born progeny who find themselves yet to be fully accepted into the mainstream of society (see Tuan 1998). Notwithstanding the fact that they speak good English, are well educated, and hold good jobs, many Asian American professionals find themselves the target of racial prejudices, stereotyping, or simply sheer ignorance (see discussion in Min and

Kim 1999). It does not help that Asian Americans appear so different physically from the white majority, making them impossible to blend in or assimilate into the white American society. While Asian Americans seek to, and do in reality assimilate culturally, structural assimilation continues to elude them.

In other words, Asian Americans' adoption of the sociocultural norms of white American society does not translate automatically into acceptance by the white American majority as equals. Indeed, cultural assimilation of the dominant values of contemporary U.S. society — for example, individualism, gender and sexual equality, personal freedom, capitalism, and so forth — does not result in entry and full membership in American institutions, as witnessed by the dearth of Asian Americans in the upper echelons of American political, judicial, economic, and corporate institutions. To put it bluntly, Asian Americans struggle with an identity crisis, wondering whether they are forever strangers struggling in the interstices of U.S. society, or honorary whites who are accepted into the mainstream United States to the extent that they do not threaten the privileged position of white Americans.

Asian Americans find themselves always being compared to white Americans, and their success in becoming a part of U.S. society is measured against sociocultural benchmarks set by white Americans, for example, speaking English without an accent. This uncritical image of an assimilation into a melting pot of the American way of life that is often upheld as the American ideal is very misleading because it overlooks the asymmetrical relationship of cultures and power relations. Moreover, it ignores the intractability of the "color line" and ignores the preeminent reality of the dominant power and privilege enjoyed by the dominant white American elite that exerts overarching control over American institutions and determines the criteria and rules for assimilation. Japanese Canadian writer Joy Kagawa puts it bluntly:

> Yet just let us get a little too close — let us stub our toes on the line of privilege — and then watch the reaction from even your most liberal do-gooders. If we don't get our facts exactly right, you whites say, "Look, look, she made a mistake on the third line." You look for errors in our remarks rather than for the truth beyond our errors. And that too is racism. We're all

trapped in it.... Every one of us lives and breathes in structures of racism from the moment we're born. We're caged in standards controlled by people of privilege — standards of truth and goodness, standards of excellence, standards of beauty which are standards of privilege through and through, and those are the bars that deny our specific realities and lock us out of even your most anti-racist institutions. (Cited in Liew 2002: 5)

Asian American Theological Responses to Racism

As a result of the radical racialization of Asian American lives, Asian American theologians have engaged in critical theological reflections on the questions of racism, discrimination, and prejudice. Japanese American theologian Fumitaka Matsuoka defines racism as follows:

Racism is socially defined as a structural and systemic deprivation of the human rights and dignity of people of color by those who are in positions of dominance. Racism is more than that, however. It is the negation of relation and the absence of direction for a collective human life due to the devaluation of life generated within societal institutions functioning as powers and principalities in our communal life. In this sense, racism is an obstacle to the formation of a common peoplehood. The negation of relation and the absence of direction are evil not because of some conceptional notion of evil but because of a total attitude expressed in both life and thought. (Matsuoka 1997: 58)

In reflecting upon these painful experiences, Asian American theologians are not content with accepting the status quo. Rather, they endeavor to challenge the social setup, exploring how Asian Americans see themselves vis-à-vis a racist status quo, envisioning a new world where Asian Americans are able to claim their place in the social fabric, and constructing theological resources to enable Asian Americans to achieve these goals. Reflecting upon the place, identity, and minority experiences of their communities in the racist atmosphere of U.S. society, they decry the ethnocentrism and condescending attitudes of many white American church leaders and theologians, who assume blithely a universal and normative (read: Anglo-Saxon) way and experience of Christian theologizing and living that Asian American Christians were expected to assimilate into, as opposed to culturally diverse ways and experiences of Christian theologizing and living.

Theologies of Marginality

In view of the foregoing, it is not surprising that many Asian American theologians view Asian American life experiences through the lens of marginality. We explore here a few representative examples of this theological approach.

Jung Young Lee: Marginality as the Center of Life-giving Creativity

The late Korean American theologian Jung Young Lee reflected on the loneliness, alienation, and suffering that he encountered in the United States. As a first-generation Korean American, he was almost denied ordination and appointment of pastorship on account of his racial origin, despite meeting all the requirements for ordination and full membership in the Ohio Conference of the Methodist Church. He recalled how wherever he went, people asked him when was he going home. He realized that while he did not belong to America, he could not return to his country, North Korea, either. He spoke of the United States as a land of exile, where the color of his skin, the shape of his face, and the peculiar character of his culture alienated him. As a result of these painful life experiences, Lee articulated a theology of marginality for Korean Americans as perpetual immigrant, living "in-between" and "in-both." Specifically, Lee's theology of marginality redefines the margin as the center of life-giving creativity (Jung Young Lee 1995, 1999).

Paul Nagano: Affirming Marginality

In his theological autobiography, "A Japanese-American Pilgrimage: Theological Reflections" (1999), Japanese American Baptist theologian Paul Nagano reflected on his dehumanizing wartime experiences of being stripped of his rights and interned as an "enemy alien" in a concentration camp despite his American citizenship. For him, this internment experience led him to reflect seriously on how his marginality *humanized* him as he defined his being and identity. He defines marginalization as never being at the center, never being fully accepted or being treated on the same level as the dominant majority, and concludes:

> My journey at the margin of the American society and my search for identity as a Japanese American have led me to conclude that my marginality is a permanent predicament, no matter what changes may take place in the attitude of the majority whites toward non-whites. Human nature tends to seek power over and control of others; and people at the center do not willingly give up their dominant position in favor of those who are on the margin. (1999: 78–79)

To the younger Japanese who try to assimilate as much as possible into American society, Nagano offers them a threefold advice: affirm their Japanese American identity while frankly acknowledging their marginality, develop strategies of solidarity and common action with other marginalized ethnic groups, and work for the coming of the reign of God on the global level (79).

Peter C. Phan: Marginality, Memory, and Imagination

Building upon the insights of the first-generation Korean American theologians, Vietnamese American Catholic theologian Peter C. Phan has articulated a new theology of marginality that is centered around the twin poles of "memory" and "imagination" in his essay "Betwixt and Between: Doing Theology with Memory and Imagination" (1999a, cf. 1999b). Focusing on the life experiences of the Vietnamese American community, Phan asserts that Vietnamese Americans "share one common trait and fundamental predicament: immigrants they all are. And being immigrant means being at the margin, or being in-between or being betwixt and between" (1999b: 162–63). Even those who are born in the United States and like to think of themselves as assimilated are, in reality, often perceived as "immigrants" and members of a minority group by mainstream U.S. society.

According to Phan, whether they accept it or otherwise, Vietnamese Americans live "betwixt and between" two worlds: the native homeland from which their families left, and the adopted countries which graciously offered them sanctuary and an opportunity to begin life anew. Living in-between two worlds, their quest for self-identity is defined by a marginality that is "often marked with excessive impressionableness, rootlessness, and an inordinate desire for longing" (1999a: 113). In particular, Phan captures succinctly the sense of fragility, rootlessness, and transitoriness that arises from living in exile and in a state of betwixt and between in the visual metaphor of the mobile home, "a ubiquitous and distinctive feature of the American landscape and yet a cultural oxymoron for Asians, for whom home means a permanent place, rooted in the earth, where one is born and dies" (126–27).

On the one hand, as immigrants in alien lands who have to interact with other peoples and cultures, Vietnamese Americans discover that total and unequivocal assimilation into the ubiquitous mainstream white American way of life is often not possible. Instead, they will always stand out as different because of the color of their hair, eyes, or skin, or even the way they speak, eat, and walk. On the other hand, Vietnamese Americans also realize that they can never go back in time because the culture, history, and way of life of the old Vietnam no longer exist today. At the same time, Phan sees living "betwixt and between" two worlds, Vietnamese and American, is not totally disadvantageous. Paradoxically, this marginality enables Vietnamese Americans to belong simultaneously to both worlds, as well as to shape their self-identity and destiny as people who stand not only in-between these two worlds, but also as people who journey confidently toward a new world that empowers them to transcend the limitations of their marginality, thereby fully realizing their human potentiality.

Reflecting on this state of affairs, Phan goes on to articulate a theology of marginality, a "theology betwixt and between" or "theology done with both memory and imagination," that is, "contemplating the past and creating the future at the same time." He argues that while memory "anchors the theologian in the ocean of history and tradition," imagination "thrusts the theologian into a new world or at least a different way of being in the world," empowering the theologian "to break out of the limits of the past and bring human potentialities to full flourishing" (114). Here, it is important to note that "memory" is not about nostalgic reminiscences about the past. As Phan explains:

> Remembering is not producing reality exactly as it happened (Leopold van Ranke's *"wie es eigentlich gewesen"*) but *re-creating* it imaginatively; it is re-*membering* disparate fragments of the past together and forming them into a new pattern under the pressure of present experiences, with a view to shaping a possible future. (114)

Indeed, Phan views the mutual interaction of memory and imagination as the epistemological equivalents of *yin* and *yang*, such that "without memory, theology would be empty; without imagination, it would be blind" (115). At the same time, he cautions that doing theology merely with memory and imagination could lead to solipsism, "if it is not accompanied by an explicit attention to the sociopolitical and economic dimensions of human existence and to what Gustavo Gutiérrez calls 'the underside of history' " (130). Hence, he insists that in addition to the hermeneutics of retrieval (memory) and reconstruction (imagination), "there must be a hermeneutics of suspicion, to be practiced with fairness and humility, to unmask forms of repression and oppression embedded in the text and in the social and ecclesial structures" (130).

According to Phan, humans who live in time "do not experience the past as something irretrievably lost and gone but as truly present, effectively shaping our identity and our destiny" (128). In his words, "The past is gathered up and preserved in our *memory*, and the future is anticipated and made real in our *imagination*" (129). Living in contemporary U.S. society, Vietnamese Americans bring their memories, expectations, beliefs, and hopes to bear on their daily lives. However, it does not stop there: in turn, they are inspired by their imagination to enter into as well as to experience and be transformed by new possibilities communicated by the challenges and opportunities posed by contemporary U.S. society. Thus, through this memory-imagination epistemological matrix, Vietnamese Americans transcend their marginality to discover who they really are (*memory*) and open up a window to new and exciting vistas (*imagination*).

Theologies of Reconciliation and Healing

Young Lee Hertig: Yinism in Race Reconciliation

Taking the 1992 Los Angeles riots and the California Civil Rights Initiative (CCRI), better known as Proposition 209, which sought to dismantle affirmative action programs within the state of California, as starting points, Korean American theologian Young Lee Hertig challenges Korean Americans to take seriously their civic responsibilities and participate in the ongoing debates on race relations and racism in the U.S. public square (Hertig 2003). She argues that the painful aftermath of the 1992 Los Angeles riots, where Korean mom-and-pop storeowners were caught in the black-white crossfire that followed the Rodney King beating, ought to jolt the complacent Korean immigrant Christians who were comfortably ensconced in their Koreantown enclaves, challenging them to redefine their identity within the contested terrain of their relation to their black neighbors.

According to Hertig, many Korean Americans saw the burning of their businesses as the loss of their hopes and aspirations of achieving the American Dream. Seeking to address the theological and ecclesiological narratives that hinder the Korean immigrant church from public engagement, Hertig points to an enclave mentality with a dualistic theological understanding that is centered around "otherworldly theology and programs on the one hand, and this-worldly materialism on the other," where "the dominant theme of the sermons preached on Sunday mornings focuses on 'If you obey and serve the church by giving all sorts of offerings and tithes, you and your children will be blessed'" (139). In her words:

> The reason the Korean immigrant church lacks a public voice primarily lies on the theological bias. The doubly reinforced dualistic theology from Confucian and Puritan

theology, which promotes otherworldly faith, promotes public disengagement. Fused with Puritan fundamentalism and Confucian fundamentalism, Korean immigrant churches still uphold the separation of proclamation and social action. (139)

Paradoxically, the sense of victimhood, alienation, and powerlessness in confronting the naked public square causes immigrant first-generation Korean Christians to withdraw inward into the protective cocoon of the Korean church. Hertig observes that this propensity to look inward is true not only of the first-generation Korean immigrants, but also of the 1.5 generation and American-born Koreans, who also find comfort among themselves. She concludes:

> The Korean immigrant church is like an island of *usness* within the sea of the mainstream *otherness*. The very existence of the immigrant church is rooted in ethnicity, which forms its own static tribal value against the unfamiliar mainstream culture. The very need for the common heritage disconnects it from the public arena. (140)

In response, Hertig asserts that Korean American Christians are called to balance their desire for a racially homogeneous Korean community on the one hand, and the richness of heterogeneous unity on the other, with their racial-ethnic neighbors in an inclusive and holistic fashion. For her, the weakness of the Korean immigrant church in its "public expression of faith derives from its theological and cultural fundamentalism on the one hand and lack of internalization of faith on the other" (141). She argues that only when the Korean immigrant church balances its inward and outward journey can it transcend the theological and cultural dualism that holds it back from engaging in public witnessing to the transforming power of the gospel. To facilitate this transformation, she adapts the Daoist yin-yang cosmology to construct an alternative theological and epistemological paradigm of *yinism* as a model for holistic social activism for the Korean and Asian North American church. For her, the inclusiveness of *yinism* reconciles the pitfall of the dualistic and dichotomous paradigm that divides rather than connects the diverse parts, bridging both *usness* and *otherness* to become whole.

Deborah Lee: Talk Story and the Practice of Family or Kinship

Chinese American theologian Deborah Lee takes a different approach to the problem of racism and the distrust, violence, and wounds that are generated (2003). She suggests that one has to address not only the painful wounds of racism that Asian Americans experience, but also the pains and scars that they bring with them. For her, the twin challenge of reconciliation and healing goes beyond the white–Asian American struggle to encompass reconciliation and healing of the pains and scars within Asian American communities themselves, as evidenced from her example of conflict within the Vietnamese American community of Westminster in Southern California.

Specifically, Lee proposes two "concrete human acts" to promote racial healing and reconciliation. The first is "talk story" or "talking story" — that is, creating a liminal, holy, and grace-filled space for storytellers and listeners to share their lives, pains, struggles, and hopes at a deep, personal level. The second is a renewed understanding of the practice of family or kinship that draws attention to the relational ties that engender "unconditional love and the ability to embrace differences and yet still love," and the sharing of "rituals to maintain and reinforce the kinship, such as the sharing of food, history, time, and resources" (154). In this regard, Lee draws a parallel between reconciliation and healing within a typical multigenerational Asian American family and multigenerational Asian American communities:

> There is often little choice regarding into what family you are born and who becomes part of your extended family. Fate, or this random sorting process, has brought us together. What if we took these fateful ties seriously and used our relationality, inherent in kinship, as a starting point to break down barriers and promote deeper understanding? What would it mean to go deep and really embrace and reconcile with the differences and tensions in our own families? (154–55)

Timothy Tseng: Overcoming Racism and Orientalism

Timothy Tseng has gone one step further to ask deeper questions about why Asian Americans continue to be targets of racism, prejudice, and stereotyping. In his essay "Beyond Orientalism and Assimilation: The Asian American as Historical Subject" (2003a), Tseng argues that as long as Asian Americans and their life experiences are perceived through Orientalist or assimilationist lenses, they would be seen as "innately foreign" or "completely assimilated," or to use Mia Tuan's (1998) phrases, "forever foreigner" or "honorary white":

> To assert that American religious historiography has viewed Asian Americans through Orientalist lenses is to suggest that Asian Americans have been perceived as innately foreign or completely assimilated. This is no less true for American historiography in general and popular perceptions as well. Historian Gary Okihiro contends that the images of the "yellow peril" and the "model minority" are "flip sides of the same coin" of the American racial construction of Asian Americans. In other words, whatever it is that makes Asians different from what is considered American is construed as something that is permanent or something to be erased. The few contemporary American religious historians who give attention to Asian Americans gravitate toward either an assimilationist reading of the Asian American Christianity or a sentimentalized and disembodied Orientalist reading of non-Christian Asian religious communities. Asian cultural difference is either erased beneath the canopy of white Christianity or constructed as the "other." ... (Tseng 2003a: 58)

Moreover, Tseng points out that "both the traditional study of Christian history and the comparative religious studies approach to American religious history have been color-blind to the racialized aspects of the Asian American experience. In part, this 'color-blindness' has been created by and continues to perpetuate Orientalism in American religious historiography" (58). He questions the conventional assumptions of the sociological theories articulated by Robert E. Park and others that Asian immigrants would be able to assimilate into the American society as easily as European immigrants. While acknowledging that "the recognition of racial differences has led to racism and social strife," Tseng nevertheless argues that the "nonrecognition or erasure of racial difference" has not resulted in a reduction of racism and discrimination against Asian Americans. He concludes that the racial tensions "develop in contexts of both enforced assimilation and segregation." This suggests social dynamics that are much more complex than the mere presence of racial difference. For him, one has to consider the underlying "power dynamics, patterns of privilege, and the ideology of race" in one's theological reflection on racism (62).

More importantly, Tseng argues that these perceptions also legitimize stereotypes and prejudices in society as well as in Christian churches, whereby Asian Americans are objectified as the inscrutable "other." He proposes a new framework where Asian Americans become the masters of their own destiny, as *subjects* of their own history and destiny, freeing themselves from the Orientalist/assimilationist paradigms. He insists that this new framework cannot ignore the history of Asian American suffering and oppression. Indeed, he views that the accurate historiographic description of Asian Americans that explores all dimensions of the Asian American life experience, including suffering and oppression, would pave the way for all to see how U.S. society marginalizes and discriminates against minorities, and how these behaviors can be changed.

Chapter 9

Asian American Evangelical Theologies

Emerging Trends and Challenges

Since the 1990s, Evangelical Christianity has witnessed a resurgence in the United States. With their emptying pews and graying hairs, many traditional mainline Protestant churches in the United States have largely been supplanted by Evangelical churches as one of the fastest-growing segments of U.S. Christianity. Generally speaking, Evangelical Christians emphasize the necessity of accepting Jesus Christ as one's personal Lord and Savior, repenting of one's sins and allowing oneself to be born again, as well as sharing the good news of salvation with those who have yet to accept Jesus Christ as their personal Lord and Savior. Evangelicals ground their faith around four core foundational beliefs: (1) belief in the inerrancy of the Bible, (2) belief in the sinful nature of the human race as a result of Adam's fall, (3) belief in the necessity of Jesus Christ for salvation, and (4) belief in the fulfillment of the Great Commission (Matt. 28:16–20) to proclaim the gospel to non-Christians. In particular, Evangelicals perceive personal conversion and spiritual rebirth, evangelism, and church growth as going hand in hand, inspiring them to seek out souls for Jesus Christ after they themselves have committed their lives to the gospel.

Powering the rapid growth of Evangelical Christianity in contemporary U.S. society is the rise of the seeker-friendly megachurch movement that is inspired and led by well-known and hugely successful megachurches such as Lakewood Church (Houston), Willow Creek Community Church (South Barrington, Illinois), and Rick Warren's Saddleback Church (Lake Forest, California). In particular, the seeker-friendly megachurch movement reaches out to

143

many unchurched Americans by tapping into their yearning for self-purpose and self-empowerment. The immense popularity of Rick Warren's *The Purpose-Driven Life: What on Earth Am I Here For?* (2002) is testimony to this explosive growth in Evangelical Christianity. Indeed, even the secular media such as *Business Week* (see Symonds 2005) and the *Economist* (2005) are sitting up and taking notice of this phenomenal growth.

More importantly, many Gen-Yers and Millennials flock to these megachurches, attracted by their informal yet inspirational worship services, uplifted by contemporary praise and worship music, as well as finding their personal, psychological, and emotional needs being nourished by the many therapeutic and support ministries. On the one hand, the successes of these megachurches have put pressure on many mainline Protestant churches to adapt and graft many of the megachurches' ideas and approaches onto a more traditional and formal ecclesial framework. On the other hand, critics have expressed their disquiet about the uncritical use of entrepreneurial, business, and various aspects of contemporary popular culture by megachurches in their quest for new members.

Rapid Growth of Asian American Evangelical Christianity

The remarkable growth in American Evangelicalism is also mirrored in Asian American Christianity. Not only are Asian Americans mainly Christian, popular stereotypes to the contrary notwithstanding (see Goldman 1991), a significant majority of these Asian American Christians are Evangelical. Indeed, Asian American Evangelical Christianity is flourishing especially among the cohort of Gen-Yers and Millennials in the Korean American (see Ecklund 2006, Rebecca Y. Kim 2006) and Chinese American (see Yang 1999; Tseng 2002b, 2003b) communities. This growth is fueled in large part by the evangelistic witnessing of parachurch organizations such as Campus Crusade for Christ and the InterVarsity Christian Fellowship, both of which have significant Asian American membership. Rebecca Kim summarizes the important role played by these parachurch organizations in Asian American outreach:

Today, there are more than fifty Evangelical Christian groups at the University of California (UC) at Berkeley and the University of California at Los Angeles (UCLA), and 80 percent of their members are Asian American (Busto 1996; Chang 2000). On the East Coast, one out of four Evangelical college students at New York City colleges and universities are Asian American (Carnes and Yang 2004). At Harvard, Asian Americans constitute 70 percent of the Harvard Radcliffe Christian Fellowship ... (Chang 2000: 1). At Yale, the Campus Crusade for Christ is now 90 percent Asian, which is astonishing considering that twenty years ago it was 100 percent white. Like Yale, Stanford's InterVarsity Christian Fellowship (IVCF) has become almost entirely Asian .... (Rebecca Y. Kim 2006: 1)

Scholars are fascinated by the fact that many more unchurched Asian Americans are attracted to Evangelical Christianity rather than to mainline Protestant or Catholic Christianity. Rudy Busto attempts to explain this phenomenon by pointing out that, broadly speaking, Asian American Gen-Yers and Millennials are attracted by the "universalist message of evangelical Christianity" that "bolsters a type of 'built in' dis-identification from non-evangelicals in general ('the world') prompting an alternative identity based not on race/ethnicity, but on faith," and therefore "[t]aking the theological call for Christians to be apart from the world (as in 1 John 2:15) — or more generally, 'chosen' one step further, it may be helpful to think about Asian American evangelicals as part of a larger Christian people or 'incipient ethnicity' " (Busto 1996: 140–41). In other words, for these Asian American Christians, the Evangelical subculture of U.S. Christianity has become the defining point for their identity construction.

Korean American Evangelicalism

Busto's general observations about the growth of Asian American Evangelicalism as a result of the interaction between Evangelicalism's certitude of faith and Asian Americans' struggle to construct their identity are supported by further insights from fellow Asian American sociologist Antony Alumkal (1999, 2002, 2003). From his ethnographical studies of second-generation Korean American Evangelical Christians, Alumkal observes that many Korean Americans are attracted to Evangelicalism's clear and unambiguous stance on the necessity of grounding one's true identity on one's faith in Jesus Christ rather than in one's ethnicity or race. In particular, Alumkal's respondents express their dilemma of having to cope with the paradox of living up to a highly racialized "model minority" image of successful Korean Americans, while at the same time being marginalized for being the model minority. He also observes that Korean American Evangelical churches offer their members "a place where they could de-emphasize their racial minority status by proclaiming (in language characteristic of contemporary Evangelicalism) that while they were proud of being Korean Americans, their 'true' identities were as (evangelical) Christians" (1999: 139). In a subsequent essay, Alumkal explains further:

> Much of the discourse I heard during participant observation and interviews emphasized the certainty that an evangelical-style Christian faith provided. Individuals who struggled with reconciling their Chinese or Korean identities with their American identities took comfort in the fact that their *true* identities were as Christians. (2002: 248)

Moreover, Alumkal goes on to say that "the culturally and racially 'liminal' space that second-generation Asian Americans inhabit can heighten their need for certainty and encourage their acceptance of contemporary American evangelical theology" (2002: 248).

Chinese American Evangelicalism

Chinese American Christianity is predominantly Evangelical in orientation, and even historic mainline Protestant Chinese American congregations are increasingly turning Evangelical (Tseng 2003b: 244; 2005). Chinese American sociologist Fenggang Yang observes that most Chinese immigrants who embrace Christianity upon their arrival in the United States choose Evangelical Christianity over mainline Protestant or Catholic Christianity, and in the process are fueling the explosive growth of conservative Evangelical

Chinese American churches which are independent of any denominational ties. A convert to Evangelical Christianity himself who has conducted extensive research and ethnographical studies on the growth of Chinese American Evangelical Christians, Yang suggests that for Chinese immigrants in the United States who embrace Christianity in general, and Evangelical Christianity in particular, "three important identities undergo construction and reconstruction. As converts, they achieve a Christian identity; as immigrants, they achieve an American identity; and as Chinese, their identity is challenged by their emigration away from China and their diverse diasporic experiences" (Yang 1999: 9).

Echoing the perception held by Busto and Alumkal, Fenggang Yang thinks that many Chinese immigrant families are attracted to Evangelical Christianity because "for new Chinese immigrants, both premigration traumas and postmigration uncertainties in modern American society fortify their desire for absoluteness and certainty" that Evangelical Christianity is able to provide (94). Additionally, Yang notes that "the attraction of evangelical Christianity to Chinese immigrants also comes from its perceived compatibility with Confucian moral values," and therefore, "absolute evangelical beliefs provide a foundation upon which Chinese church members can justify the strict moral and behavioral values that they impose on themselves and their children" (94).

Responding to Yang's findings, Chinese American church historian Timothy Tseng points out that while Yang is right "to posit the changing Chinese context and changing Chinese Diasporic identity as external factors that have shaped and are continuing to shape a distinctive Chinese evangelical identity," he fails to "explore the internal history of the Chinese Protestants themselves or the historical contexts" that are crucial for understanding the paradigm shift from mainline Protestantism to Evangelicalism (Tseng 2003b: 245–46). In addition, Tseng notes that Yang's research "remains 'America-centered' and does not give enough attention to the Diasporic contexts" that these Chinese American Christians have emerged from before immigrating to the United States (246). As far as Tseng is concerned, although Chinese American Christianity may have had its roots in mainline Protestantism, the Chinese communist victory in 1949 together with the significant immigration to the United States of Chinese Christians from China,

Taiwan, and the Chinese Diaspora who are imbued with a "separatist" Evangelical outlook "have so completely reconstructed the community over the past thirty years that evangelicalism is now clearly the predominant form of Chinese Christianity" (246–47, 261–63; see also Tseng 2005). In particular, Tseng identifies the roots of contemporary Chinese American Evangelicalism as an "indigenous form of Chinese Christianity" shaped and propagated by fundamentalist Chinese evangelists — for example, Watchman Nee, John Sung, Andrew Gih, Torrey Shih, Thomas Wang, Moses Chow, and Christiana Tsai — and emerging from "the millennial yearnings and popular religiosity of ordinary Chinese people" (Tseng 2003b: 257).

Asian American Evangelical Identity Construction

In his ethnographical study of Asian American pan-ethnic congregations in the San Francisco Bay area, sociologist Russell Jeung discovered that mainline Protestant and Evangelical Asian American congregations approach the issue of Asian American identity construction in diametrically opposite ways (2002a; see also 2005). According to Jeung, mainline Protestant pan–Asian American Christians tend to consider themselves as belonging to "a racial minority group with a common history of cultural oppression and racism," while Evangelical Asian American Christians tend to view Asian Americans as "a spiritual consumer target group made up of personal networks and lifestyle affinities" (2002a: 212). In other words, while mainline Protestant Asian American Christians emphasize the importance of communal Asian American identity construction and the Asian American struggle against racism and discrimination, Evangelical Asian American Christians ground their emphasis on personal spiritual formation and church growth, focusing on individuals with common family patterns, psychological issues, and social needs.

Going one step further, Jeung observes that many Asian American Evangelicals tend to view their racial-ethnic identity as separate from their spiritual identity: "Being Asian American is a cultural background that is associated with family patterns, a lifestyle, and a social set of relationships. Being Christian is an interior and spiritual state of being that should influence how one relates and behaves in this world" (230). Hence, one's Asian American identity and one's Christian identity are parallel identities, with one's Christian identity being "more real and authentic" (230). As Jeung puts it:

> As therapeutic language and values have seeped into American evangelical discourse, so they have entered the evangelical Asian American churches. GFC [Grace Faith Church] teaches its Asian American members that their identities should be spiritual in nature. At times, Asian American Christians may have to renounce Asian cultural practices that are unhealthy or dysfunctional. They can then affirm their "true" identities and gain freedom as the children of God. This spiritual identity also includes a calling to evangelize others. Given this mission, Asian American Christians are to reach out to their friends and families. (232)

In particular, Jeung attributes the rapid growth of Asian American Evangelical Christianity to the interaction of two important forces. First, Asian Americans are attracted to Evangelical churches because of those churches' focus on family dynamics and psychological issues involving self-worth and identity constructions that are challenged by the pressure to succeed, overbearing parental control, high family expectations, and other dysfunctional family structures (224). Second, the use of the church-growth seeker strategy of "friendship evangelism" — that is, Asian American Evangelicals inviting their friends, who are also mainly Asian Americans to begin with, to small group gatherings and activities — has served to introduce Christianity over time "to their non-Christian friends in a 'nonthreatening, nondogmatic' manner" (227).

"The 'Scandal' of the 'Model Minority' Mind?"

In an essay entitled "The Scandal of the 'Model Minority' Mind? The Bible and Second-Generation Asian American Evangelicals" (2002), Antony Alumkal challenges what he perceives to be the theological complacency of Asian American Evangelicals. Alumkal takes his cue from Mark Noll's *The Scandal of the Evangelical Mind* (1994) in which Noll claimed that the American Evangelical subculture generally suffers from a lack of intellectual rigor, especially in its approach to biblical hermeneutics and the sciences. Alumkal also draws upon his ethnographical study of Chinese American and Korean American Evangelical congregations, asserting that second-generation Asian American Evangelicals, many of whom are highly educated and successful middle- and upper-middle-class Americans, have assimilated uncritically the same worldview of their white counterparts by accepting "mainstream American evangelical theology as synonymous with 'Christianity'" (2002: 239; see also 2003).

As far as Alumkal is concerned, in uncritically essentializing the U.S. Evangelical Christian subculture, many Asian American Evangelicals are unaware of its Anglo-American roots. He also notes the paradoxical result that their university-level training in the sciences has reinforced biblical literalism by treating the Bible as a scientific text. Moreover, Alumkal laments the fact that "many second-generation Asian American Christians do not appear to be interested in developing their own contributions to Christian theology," preferring to utilize theologies articulated by white American Evangelicals (2002: 249). Responding, Alumkal threw down the gauntlet at Asian American Evangelicals:

> Creating a distinctly Asian American evangelical theology would require Asian Americans to step out of the comfortable certainty that the contemporary evangelical subculture promotes. They would need to recognize that much of evangelical theology, including biblical theology, far from representing "old-time religion" or "orthodoxy," is of relatively recent vintage and has been shaped by particular cultural influences. Only then would Asian American evangelicals be able to escape the scandal of the evangelical mind. (249)

As someone of ethnic Indian and Filipino descent who identifies with mainline Christianity, Alumkal's critical assessment of Asian American Evangelical Christianity and its lack of theological curiosity is understandable. Nonetheless, Alumkal's critical views are also shared by the Chinese American church historian Timothy Tseng, who is an ordained pastor and committed

Evangelical Christian himself. In a thought-provoking essay entitled "Second-Generation Chinese Evangelical Use of the Bible in Identity Discourse in North America" (2002a), Tseng provides a much-needed discussion on the rapid growth of Evangelicalism among second-generation Chinese American Christians, commonly known as American-born Chinese (ABCs), as well as their biblical hermeneutics. Specifically, he argues that ABC Evangelical biblical hermeneutics are oriented according to the twin poles of (1) the European immigrant experience of assimilation into U.S. society as the model for their Asian American identity discourse, and (2) a white American "evangelical universalism" that subordinates racial identities.

Like Alumkal, Tseng challenges ABCs to break out of uncritical assimilationist and Orientalist ways of reading the Bible that they have adopted from white American Evangelicals. In his essay, Tseng cites the writings of English-speaking ABCs who correlated the Hebrew-speaking Christians to the Chinese-born Chinese Americans who insisted on retaining their Chinese language and culture in worship, and the Greek-speaking Christians to the English-speaking American-born Chinese Americans who insisted on using English and American cultural resources in their worship. Rightly or wrongly, the ABCs identify their own marginality with the marginality of the Hellenistic Christians at the hands of the Hebrew Christians. Tseng challenges this uncritical reading of Acts 6:1–7, proposing an alternative reading of these characters as Anglo-American Christians, thereby breaking open new understandings in Asian American Evangelicalism with respect to the wider discussion on race, ethnicity, culture, and identity formation. He explains at some length:

> What is missing in Chinese American evangelical appropriation of Acts 6 is a critique of how structural racism operates in white American evangelical circles. Without tools for structural analysis, ABC evangelicals may be in danger of making "whiteness" their norm and perhaps open themselves up to criticism that they are "investing in whiteness." Without an interrogation of white evangelical norms, analysis of their ministries is circumscribed by an understanding of "assimilation" that assumes European immigrant experience as the

basis for their identity discourse. Furthermore, by uncritically embracing a mainstream American evangelical theological universalism, their own experiences as racialized people in church and society are dismissed. This strategy of "investing in whiteness" allows anti-Asian consciousness in the fabric of American history and contemporary society to seep into the way American-born Chinese perceive Chinese immigrants. (2002a: 263)

In another essay, "Asian Pacific American Christianity in a Post-Ethnic Future" (2002b), which was originally presented at the Japanese Baptist Church's Seattle Centennial Celebration in 1999, Tseng discusses three reasons that many 1.5 generation and American-born Asian Evangelical Christians are ambivalent about their Asian American identities and the issue of racism. First, he recognizes the fact that many Asian American Christians view questions of race, racial identity, and racial discrimination not in structural or institutional terms, but as personal and attitudinal issues. He attributes this development to the fact that many Asian American Christians grew up in the suburbs among Caucasians, raised in an environment where racial identity is subsumed under a broader universal Evangelical faith identity that has been defined by white Evangelicals. Indeed, Tseng acknowledges the increasing reality of many of these Asian Americans viewing their race and ethnicity as merely a question of personal preference. This shift results in an increasingly held viewpoint that solutions to the problems of racism ought to be shifted away from the political process toward individualistic racial reconciliation projects.

Second, Tseng points to the growing influence of neoconservative thinking against affirmative action policies in favor of so-called color-blind policies — that is, policies emphasizing racial non-recognition. Third, he identifies the growing chasm between an earlier generation of Asian American theologians and the emerging younger Evangelical Asian American Christian leadership. At the same time, he also recognizes the reality of a "popular" Evangelical viewpoint that universalizes Christian identity while erasing particular racial-ethnic identities. In his opinion, this popular thinking is rooted in a gnostic dualism between spirit and flesh, and which emphasizes that one can become simply a "Christian" while being indifferent to the particularities of denominational life or racial-ethnic identities and politics.

As a result, many Asian American Evangelical pastors and church leaders are unwilling or unable to confront the issue of racial discrimination or wrestle with the historical and contemporary reality of racism against Asian Americans. Tseng identifies and challenges the two underlying sociological assumptions that undergird their thinking. First, they assume that the discrimination that Asian Americans experience is closer to the kind experienced by European immigrants rather than that experienced by blacks, such that discrimination will eventually disappear as Asian Americans assimilate into American society. Second, they assume that Asian Americans would assimilate just as easily as European immigrants assimilate, and therefore ethnic churches are only a temporary phenomenon that will disappear once all Asian Americans join the mainstream.

In response, Tseng cites Mia Tuan's trailblazing work, *Forever Foreigners or Honorary Whites? The Asian Ethnic Experience Today* (1998), for his contention that Asian American immigrants are not treated like European immigrants. In her study, Tuan uncovers the harsh reality that notwithstanding the model minority label that has been bestowed upon them, third- through fifth-generation Chinese and Japanese in California who have achieved high educational and professional status find themselves unable to integrate easily into white mainstream America. Like African Americans, the physical features of Asian Americans remain obstacles for full integration. Unlike African Americans, Asian Americans continue to be labeled as "foreign." On this basis, while young Asian Americans may have the freedom to choose their ethnic identities in private, they are denied this freedom in public. On this basis, Tseng concludes that Asian American Evangelical Christians are wrong to deny that "white privilege" continues to create a climate of anti-Asian racism.

Drawing upon the theological thought of Miroslav Volf (1996), Tseng insists that while ethnic and racial identities may not be rigid and fixed, nonetheless they are still part of who we are as humans, created by God, such that ethnic and racial identities have intrinsic value to God. Hence, he argues that racial separation, privileging, and racial injustice are all clearly offensive to God. He asserts that the postethnic perspective which assumes that all Americans can choose their ethnic identities freely is a "white privilege" that Asian Americans do not enjoy. Hence, he calls upon Asian American Evangelical Christians to acknowledge the historical and contemporary all-pervasive reality of racism and white racial privileging, as well as challenging this sinful reality through prophetic witnessing, however uncomfortable this may be. For him, talking about "race reconciliation" is dodging the issue, because in the minds of most American Christians, the races that appear in need of reconciliation are blacks and whites, rather than Asians and whites or Asians and blacks. In reality, the truth remains that Asians and whites, as well as Asians and blacks are also greatly in need of reconciliation.

Emergence of Asian American Evangelical Theologies

Unlike their mainline colleagues, Asian American Evangelical theologians have only begun reflecting theologically through Asian American and Evangelical lenses. To begin with, many Asian American Evangelicals are generally uncomfortable with the theological perspectives and language of mainline Protestant Asian American theologians, as church historian Timothy Tseng rightly notes (Tseng 2002b). Theologian Jeffrey Jue exemplifies one such Asian American Evangelical theologian who acknowledges that he is unable to accept the liberal and nonfoundationalist framework of mainline Protestant Asian American theologies (Jue 2006: 103–9). Other Asian American Evangelical theologians struggle with their ambiguity toward their mainline Protestant colleagues. For example, Paul Chang-Ha Lim acknowledges that while he finds himself "distancing from some of the constructive *theological* construal of the likes of C. S. Song, the late Jung Young Lee, Andrew Sung Park, etc." on the basis that their theologies are "relatively unsuitable for my own individual theological perspective(s) and institutionally less than expedient," nonetheless he has found "their *personal* narratives poignant, powerfully evocative, and profoundly gripping." Indeed, he wonders: "Can I *like, ad-mire, respect* their theological pilgrimage while remaining less than thoroughly convinced in the final analysis?" (Lim 2006: 45).

Not surprisingly, many young Asian American Evangelical scholars have emerged from the shadow, paving new theological paths and carrying out in-depth, critical theological reflections. Their work has been encouraged and nurtured by Asian American Evangelical organizations such as the L² Foundation and the Institute for the Study of Asian American Christianity (ISAAC). Both of these organizations have taken a number of significant steps to nurture and mentor young theologians, scholars, and church leaders to serve Asian American Evangelical churches.

L² Foundation

The L² Foundation was launched by the Chou Family Foundation in 2001 to develop the leadership and legacy of Asian Americans by providing support, mentoring, and resources. The Foundation has produced a youth ministry resource, *Asian American Youth Ministry* (Chuang 2006), which discusses the issues and approaches on Asian American youth ministry from an Evangelical perspective. In November 2002, the L² Foundation organized a theology forum of twelve Asian American theologians and scholars to engage in critical theological reflection. The papers from this forum were collected and published in a monograph entitled *Conversations: Asian American Evangelical Theologies in Formation* (Chuang and Tseng 2006).

At this forum, Jeffrey Jue outlined succinctly the broad goals and objectives of articulating a distinctive Asian American Evangelical theology and biblical hermeneutics. In his opinion, Asian American Evangelical theology ought to be

a theology that is both biblically consistent and culturally sensitive...As Scripture is the revelation of God, meaning therefore must be found in the text and not the experience of the Asian American reader. Redemptive history, given in the Bible, regulates the meaning and message, which is ultimately the redemptive plan of God from the beginning to the consummation. Asian American theology must seek to maintain the unity and integrity of that plan as it has been recorded in Scripture. However, the communication of this message, along with the response which calls the hearer/reader to identify and participate in that plan, must be sensitive to a variety of individual issues, including ethnicity. Asian Americans respond to the redemptive historical message from an Asian American context. Subsequently, Asian American biblical interpreters should take into account their Asian American context, but they must be careful to distinguish their context from the biblical history of redemption. Biblical interpretations should not be based upon an individual's experiences; instead, experiences shape each individual's response to the biblical message. Experience is not the foundation, but response is born out of experience. The task of Asian American biblical interpretation, and more broadly theology, is to communicate the supernatural revelation of God, as it has been revealed in redemptive history and recorded in the Bible, to a specific Asian American context with the goal of calling the reader/hearer to respond. (2006: 113–14)

Institute for the Study of Asian American Christianity (ISAAC)

In 2006, a group of six Asian American Evangelical theologians and pastors led by Chinese American church historian Timothy Tseng established the Institute for the Study of Asian American Christianity (ISAAC) to develop educational, theological, organizational, and outreach resources for Asian American Christianity. Primarily Evangelical in orientation, ISAAC's objectives include providing strategic opportunities for Asian American Christians to participate fully in the church, academy, and public life in North America and the world through a three-pronged approach. First, ISAAC seeks to equip culturally competent and biblically grounded professional and lay leaders for the Asian American churches and communities. Second, it hopes to educate the seminary, the university, the church, and the public about Asian American Christian history, presence, perspectives, and prospects. Finally, ISAAC endeavors to encourage research that brings breadth and depth to contemporary understandings of Asian American Christianity. Although it is deeply committed to its Evangelical roots, ISAAC has sought to reach out to other Asian American Christian theologians through the Society of Asian North American Christianity Studies (SANACS), which functions as an ecumenical meeting place for dialogue and collaboration among Asian American Evangelical, mainline Protestant, Pentecostal, and Catholic theologians.

Constructing Asian American Evangelical Theologies

The development of Asian American Evangelical theologies received a major boost when the American Academy of Religion's Asian North American Religion, Culture, and Society Group (ANARCS) and the Evangelical Theology Group organized a panel discussion entitled "Constructing Asian American Evangelical Theologies" at the 2005 Annual Meeting of the AAR. This panel represented an important milestone for Asian American Evangelical theologies. For the first time, Asian American Evangelical theologians and other interested scholars, both Evangelical and non-Evangelical, were able to gather together to engage in a public discussion and dialogue on the goals, methods, and contents of Asian American Evangelical theologies. By all accounts, there was standing room only at this panel, which was very well received by the panelists, respondents, and participants. The next sections of this chapter discuss two major papers presented at this panel: Young Lee Hertig's "Why Asian American Evangelical Theologies?" and Amos Yong's "What Asian, Which American? Whose *Evangelion*? Whither Asian American Evangelical Theology?"

"Why Asian American Evangelical Theologies?"

In a paper entitled "Why Asian American Evangelical Theologies?" (Hertig 2005), Young Lee Hertig began by laying out the case for Asian American Evangelical theologies:

First of all Asian American Evangelical Theologies have not been represented in theological discourses which are significant sources of inquiry. Secondly, Asian American Evangelical Seminarians who go through training in American Seminaries today tend to find themselves ill-prepared when they start their ministry in Asian American churches. Thirdly, color- and culture-blind theological education in general denies innate Asian collective subconsciousness.... Fourthly, with the lack of theological, cultural, and personal identities that integrate particular Asian American experiences, current pastoral leadership crisis poses a serious problem for the future of the Asian American Evangelical church. Despite the vitality of the Pan Asian American congregational trend, an effort toward Asian American theological construction will define who we are as *Asian, American,* and *Evangelical.*

In particular, Hertig acknowledges that her approach is shaped by her multiple hybrid identities as Korean, American, female, wife, mother, instructor, and itinerant pastor, who is both Evangelical and ecumenical. Her tentative contribution is a *Yinist* theology that is a holistic Asian American Evangelical theology which integrates both Celtic and Daoist worldviews in a creative synthesis. "Yinist" refers to the female energy in Daoism. This female energy is comprehensive because it encompasses gender, ecology, nature, health, and God. This yin is holistic, dynamic, synthesizing, and complementary with yang, the male energy. Yinist feminism, therefore, diffuses false sets of dichotomy deriving from the dualistic paradigm: male against female, human being against nature, god apart from human being, this world apart from the other world (1998). In this respect, Hertig finds a remarkable convergence between the Daoist and Celtic worldviews: "both traditions share holistic worldviews that could balance the yang dominant value, an extreme value that harms all sectors of living organisms" (2005). Moreover, she thinks that both worldviews provide the opportunity to overcome dualistic "either-or" perspectives that are divisive and oppressive. What excites Hertig is the potential of the *Yinist* theological paradigm to fill a spiritual hunger for existential meaning among many second-generation Asian American Evangelicals arising from ecclesial and community structures that emphasize proper performance of social conventions and reward external success. In her assessment, the *Yinist* theology is able to retrieve marginalized voices, thereby nurturing and empowering Asian American Evangelicals to articulate and nourish authentic community-building in their faith communities.

More significantly, Hertig argues that Yinist theology portrays Jesus not as a powerful and almighty ruler and judge who demands obedience, but as someone "vulnerable, humble, merciful, loving, sacrificial, and steadfast" who "reverses the cultural concept of power through his withdrawal, vulnerability, sacrifice, acceptance, and love." She rereads the story of Jesus' encounter with a Samaritan woman at the well (John 4:4–42) as exemplifying "a Yinist praxis that brings wholeness to a broken woman." Moreover, Hertig claims that "the current emerging generation's pursuit of God is not *yangish* (masculine energy) omnipotent, almighty, *the bigger the better,* but rather *yinish* (feminine energy), a nurturing God" who exemplifies the reciprocal relationship and mutual respect that Jesus showed the Samaritan woman at the well. Specifically, she views Yinist theology as offering an alternative theological paradigm for 1.5 and later generations of Korean American Christians who want to go beyond the first-generation Korean Americans' emphasis on results, performance, power, and hierarchy to construct their *own* identity as an egalitarian community of believers. In doing so, Yinist theology seeks to transform and empower the lives of these younger Korean American Christians, who often find themselves marginalized in the hierarchy of many Korean American churches, just as a Yinist Jesus empowered the Samaritan woman at the well by redefining her life and identity (2005).

"What Asian, Which American? Whose Evangelion?"

In a paper entitled "What Asian, Which American? Whose *Evangelion?* Whither Asian American Evangelical Theology?" (Yong 2005b; see also 2005c, 2007), Asian American Pentecostal theologian Amos Yong acknowledges a dearth of theological reflections on the part of Asian American Evangelicals. This is not surprising, because the quest to define and articulate an Asian American Evangelical theology is fraught with pitfalls, as there are many diverse Asian American Evangelical communities with different histories, cultures, languages, and experiences. As a result, many Asian American Evangelicals tend to sidestep such diversity and plurality by thinking about their Evangelical theology in normative and universalist terms.

Not surprisingly, Yong thinks that this state of affairs is not satisfactory. He argues that a viable Asian American Evangelical theology must take into account the various sociohistorical contexts of Asian Americans, as well as the issues of globalization, transnationalization, intergenerational dynamics, and cultural assimilation. His tentative proposal for an Asian American Evangelical theology is undergirded by three foundational pillars. First, he insists that Asian American Evangelical theology cannot be any less than Asian. As he explains, "contemporary Asian American Evangelical theology must responsibly engage that which is distinctively Asian, prophetically judging what needs to be judged according to the gospel on the one hand, even while being reconciled to all things good as made possible by the redemptive power of the gospel on the other" (Yong 2005b).

Second, Yong argues that an Asian American Evangelical theology must also engage the American context intentionally. He explains that while Asian American Evangelicals have much to be grateful for in America, they also have to wrestle critically with the continuing injustice, greed, racism, and discrimination, as well as the other social, cultural, political, and economic ills that continue to affect the contemporary United States. As a committed Pentecostal himself, he proposes that "Azusa Street, Los Angeles, symbolizes and encapsulates the promise and challenge of American life: the promise of reconciliation across ethnic, racial, class, and gender lines; the challenge of how to live out this reconciliation in a world that remains fallen and in need of full redemption." As far as he is concerned, an Asian American Evangelical theology must serve as a prophetic catalyst for the Asian American Evangelical Church to become "a community of reconciling transformation, speaking prophetically against injustice on the one hand, and yet bringing healing to the 'nations' within this land on the other."

Third, Yong concludes that an authentic Asian American Evangelical theology must also be "resolutely and vigorously evangelical."

Eschewing uncritical universalist notions of Evangelicalism that "whitewash" cultures and ethnicities, Yong goes on:

> there is no ahistorical *evangelion* disconnected from Asia or America. Rather, the *evangelion* in Asian American Evangelical theology is precisely the good news as encountered concretely by Asian Americans in history. Thus, evangelical theology must be trinitarian, by which I take to mean both incarnational and Pentecostal in terms of taking historicity, embodiment, and pneumatic empowerment seriously, and in terms of prophetically critiquing the accommodations of previous formulations of evangelical theology to any kind of ideological captivity. Further, evangelical theology must emphasize not only orthodoxy but also orthopraxis and orthopathy, by which I mean both embracing rightly oriented belief and confession and rightly oriented action and affection, and resisting any bifurcation of heart and mind, mind and soul, spirit and body. Finally, evangelical theology must be the whole gospel for the whole person for the whole world, by which I mean not only proclaiming and living out a holistic soteriology in terms of being explicit about the personal, confessional, embodied, social, environmental, spiritual, and eschatological dimensions of the saving work of Christ by the Spirit, but also rejecting any attempt to reduce the redemptive work of the trinitarian God to any one of these aspects.

While Yong's threefold proposal does not lay out the concrete specifics of the *contents* of Asian American Evangelical theology, nevertheless his proposal represents an important methodological step for other Asian American Evangelical theologians to build upon. To his credit, Yong has articulated a balanced Asian American Evangelical theological method that takes all three adjectives — Asian, American, and Evangelical — seriously. In addition, his call to Asian American Evangelical theologians to take orthodoxy, orthopraxis, and orthopathy seriously testifies to his vision of a balanced and holistic approach to theological reflection that goes beyond merely being mind-centric to body-centric and spirit-centric.

Chapter 10

The Future of
Asian American Theologies

Asian American theologies have come a long way since the early 1960s. If one were to look back in history to see how far Asian American theologies have evolved in that time, one could not help but be impressed by the great strides that two generations of Asian American theologians have made through five decades of struggle as advocates for renewal, change, and transformation in their communities, their churches, and the broader U.S. society. Although Asian American theologians are but a minority in the wider U.S. theological community, they have contributed significantly to the vitality of the theological endeavors and achievements of the entire community of U.S. theologians. Let us review the accomplishments of these theologians, taking stock of their successes and setbacks, as well as looking to future developments and challenges ahead.

If we could say one thing about Asian American theologians, it would be that they often go beyond merely translating the norms and approaches of European and North American white theologies for use in their faith communities. Indeed, Asian American theologians generally eschew the uncritical transplanting of a priori and universal norms of European and North American white theologies in various Asian American contexts. Asian American theologians reject the naive presumption that white theologies are normative, perennial, ahistorical, acultural, and therefore universally relevant and applicable without regard to the specific life experiences and continuing needs of Asian American faith communities. In turning to the contextualization of the Christian gospel's soteriological message in the midst of the contemporary vibrant life experiences of Asian American Christians, Asian American theologians have signaled their commitment to engage in an ongoing quest to articulate ways of theologizing, using the rich and diverse resources of their own racial-ethnic communities.

Without a doubt, Asian Americans face significant challenges in their quest to construct and shape a meaningful identity, peoplehood, worldview, and moral order as a minority community in the sociocultural environment of a contemporary United States that may not always be sympathetic to their concerns. The many sociological studies that have been carried out on Asian Americans and their religious life experiences reveal that Asian Americans, whether immigrant or American-born, whether mainline Protestant, Evangelical, Pentecostal, or Catholic, have established deep roots and are constantly being renewed with ongoing, new immigration of "first-generation" members under "family reunification" and other immigration opportunities in the post-1965 period. Immigration is no longer a one-way street that entails an absolute, conclusive break from the old country, uprooting Asians and transplanting them in the United States.

This paradigm shift from the absolute and unidirectional migration patterns of the past to the dynamic and multidirectional transnational movements of the present marks a momentous Copernican turn for Asian Americans, leading to a multiplicity of heterogenized, hybridized, and conflicting constructions of identity and relations in relation to the dominant white American mainstream. For many, if not the majority of Asian American Christians, their religious identity becomes a defining aspect of who they are. What is clear from the various sociological studies discussed in this book is the fact that Asian American religious practices are more than merely the nostalgic longings of immigrant Asian Americans for their distant past. Rather, these religious practices are, in reality, the central means whereby various Asian American communities define and shape their own transnational and hybridized identity in the United States. In other words, religion is a potent force in shaping and reproducing sociocultural identity in Asian American communities, as well as a powerful symbolic framework through which such identity and self-awareness may be constructed. These developments are the signs of the times that challenge Asian American theologians as they reflect theologically on what it means to be Asian, American, and Christian in contemporary U.S. society.

Toward a Common Asian American Theological Method

In chapter 6, we saw how in contrast to the first-generation Asian American theologians — all of whom were either Japanese, Chinese, or Korean American male theologians working within mainline Protestant Christianity — the second-generation Asian American theologians are diverse and pluralistic. These contemporary Asian American theologians are men and women, progressive and conservative, mainline Protestant, Evangelical, Pentecostal, and Catholic working within a variety of Asian American racial-ethnic communities with their own histories, traditions, and identity constructions. Would it be possible to construct a common Asian American theological method amid such plurality and diversity?

To be sure, a single, uniform, and normative Asian American theology is neither feasible nor desirable in the context of multiple heterogeneous, hybridized, and contested identities. For example, Asian American Catholic theologians might be interested in constructing a contemporary Asian American Catholic theology that is intercultural and transnational, while remaining Catholic. In contrast, Asian American Pentecostal theologians might be interested in exploring the pneumatological implications of their theologizing. Asian American Evangelical theologians might hold different perspectives on ecclesiology from Asian American Catholic theologians. As such, instead of thinking about a common theology, it would be more feasible and realistic to consider the possibility of a broad-based common theological method that would unite disparate Asian American theologies from multiple confessional settings together in a spirit of *koinonia*, collaboration, and dialogue that arises from a shared sense of being Asian, American, and Christian, thereby transcending past denominational and ideological battles that first emerged in sixteenth-century Europe.

Clearly, Asian American theologians, both first and second generations, have written a great deal on the inspiration behind, thematic orientations of, and impact of their theologizing, reflecting deeply on a variety of issues and concerns. However, one looks in vain for any detailed proposal or discussion about a common Asian American theological method, other than brief or indirect allusions and references. Indeed, a striking observation of the theological endeavors of the first- and second-generation theologians that we reviewed in the preceding chapters of this book is the lack of any explicit systematic presentation of an Asian American theological method. Instead, we see that the interests of Asian American theologians are fundamentally pastoral and pragmatic; they wish to ascertain how Jesus Christ and his message of hope and salvation are relevant and meaningful to contemporary Asian Americans who are struggling to cope with contemporary existential life issues, how Asian Americans could encounter the saving reality of Jesus Christ in their daily lives, and how the gospel could transform their lives, respond to their concerns, and fulfill their longings and aspirations, thereby bringing them joy and hope amid life's challenges.

In view of the foregoing, it should not surprise us that thinking about a common theological method is not high on the agenda of many Asian American theologians. This is not to say that Asian American theologians lack a coherent method for doing theology, because in the first place, one's theological method is usually not something that is systematically articulated a priori — that is, at the very beginning before one embarks on any theological endeavor. On the one hand, various classical European theological-philosophical perspectives have traditionally insisted that method ought to precede content. On the other hand, from a practical and pragmatic perspective, one cannot but acknowledge the fact that theological endeavors are often carried out primarily based on particular issues, or in response to particular needs. Consequently, as is the case in the articulation of Asian American theologies, theological method is something that is presumed or even improvised along the way in an evolutionary manner as the theological content is being developed.

Perhaps the time is ripe now for Asian American theologians to stand back and reflect critically about the possibility of constructing a common Asian American theological method, and in doing so address the legitimacy and future viability of Asian American theologies. With the foregoing concerns in mind, I would like to propose a common theological method for constructing Asian

American theologies that would unite Asian American theologians across confessional, denominational, and theological divides around the following four propositions.

Proposition 1:
Empathy, Commitment, Service, and Advocacy

Asian American theologies are united by and built upon a spirit of deep empathy for Asian Americans. In turn, this spirit of empathy leads Asian American theologies to commitment, service, and advocacy to Asian Americans.

United by their *empathy* with the life experiences of their fellow Asian Americans, Asian American theologians engage in a common theological quest that commits them to serve and advocate for Asian Americans. By going beyond merely sympathizing with Asian Americans to empathizing with them, Asian American theologians seek to transcend all paternalistic and manipulative theological approaches that appropriate and instrumentalize the life experiences of Asian Americans as *ancillae theologiae*. Such instrumentalization of Asian American life experiences as theological fodder is not only reductionistic and manipulative, it also fails to respect the integrity of these life experiences as meaningful experiences. Moreover, Asian American theologies cannot be reduced to the objective and abstract theological discussions in the intellectual arena of the university or academy that have no real connection with Asian American life realities. Indeed, one problem about classical academic theologies as conceived in the Christian West is that they are often either articulated apart from, or in priority over community life, practice, and spirituality.

In contrast, Asian American theologies broaden the ambit of what theologizing is all about. Asian American theologians reject all attempts at doing theology *in* Asian American communities, doing theology *for* the benefit of Asian American communities, or even doing theology *about* their Asian American communities, viewing all these approaches as condescending and patronizing. Instead, Asian American theologians seek to do Asian American theology *together* with their communities and in solidarity with their daily life experiences as Asians, Americans, and Christians, exploring the intersections of faith, ethnicity, culture, and identity. In this regard, Asian American theologians are deeply committed to and immersed in the daily lives of Asian Americans, not as detached and objective outsiders who study Asian Americans from afar while remaining safely and comfortably ensconced in the ivory towers of academia, but as insiders and active participants who are bound in solidarity with them, listening to their hopes and aspirations, and seeking to understand the gospel within their lives.

To put it differently, Asian American theologians' theological reflections are deeply rooted in, and thus cannot be separated from, the rich and profound life experiences of Asian American Christians. These experiences are more than mere starting points for theologizing. They also complement the Christian gospel as referents for doing contextual theology. As a result of this empathy, commitment, and service to life, Asian American theologies are intimately linked to real human persons with their histories, cultures, traditions, struggles, dreams, and aspirations in a particular place and time. In this way, the real-life experiences of Asian Americans are brought into the very core of Asian American theologies.

Seen in this light, Asian American theologies envision a holistic integration of the gospel and faith on the one hand, and culture, identity, and contemporary life experiences on the other hand. They reject bifurcated and dualistic visions that pit one side against the other, where the "flesh" (culture, identity, and life experiences) is perceived as somewhat inferior to "spirit" (gospel and faith). Instead, Asian American theologies take seriously the pain, suffering, victimization, oppression, and alienation experienced by all Asian Americans in their daily lives, seeking to lift up, transform, and redeem these life realities. Hence, the human relational dimension is embedded as an integral part of theological endeavors. In turn, Asian American theologies empower Asian Americans to live their lives to the full as Asian, American, and Christian.

In view of our foregoing discussion, we see that all Asian American theologies share a common twofold foundational framework. First, Asian American theologies are shaped by an *epistemological* perspective that enables one to truly know, understand, empathize, commit to, and advocate for the hopes and needs of Asian Americans. Second, and more importantly, Asian American theologies are rooted in a foundational *theological* perspective that recognizes the divine presence and workings in the daily life experiences of Asian Americans. This underlying theological perspective is rooted in the mystery of the Incarnation that exemplifies God's solidarity with human beings in the particularities of their life experiences: "And the Word became flesh and lived among us" (John 1:14).

Proposition 2: Reading the Signs of the Times

Asian American theologies seek to read the signs of the times.

In their theological reflections, Asian American theologians endeavor to read the signs of the times, seeking to understand and challenge the political, sociocultural, economic, and racial status quo. This process may take the forms of uncovering, challenging, and transforming sociocultural, communal, and ecclesial structures that cause racism and discrimination (e.g., Jung Young Lee, Sang Hyun Lee, and Fumitaka Matsuoka), patriarchal and gender discrimination (e.g., Chung Hyun Kyung, Rita Nakashima Brock, and Kwok Pui-Lan), uncritical assimilation into the dominant sociocultural ethos (e.g., Antony Alumkal and Timothy Tseng), or racial and ethnic essentialism (e.g., Mary Foskett and Henry Morisada Rietz).

Such prophetic challenges recall Jesus' own prophetic challenge to the political, sociocultural, economic, and racial status quo of his day. Just as Jesus' preaching and deeds transformed people and enabled them to see the world around them in a new light, so too, Asian American theologians aim to overcome the destructive forces in the life experiences of their fellow Asian Americans, helping them to break free from structures that trap them in bondage and captivity, promoting structures that foster human dignity in their daily living, as well as creating a genuine and deep-seated spirit of *koinonia* among generations of Asian Americans, as well as between Asian Americans and other Americans within and outside Christianity. In doing so, Asian American theologians are able to remind all Asian Americans that their Christian faith is neither individualistic nor inward looking in orientation, but rather, it has wider social and public consequences.

Proposition 3: Traditioning

Contemporary Asian American theologies respond to the challenges of multiplicity, hybridity, and changing contexts by engaging in traditioning — that is, strategic and situational ways of constructing theologies that empower Asian Americans in their effective engagement with the world around them.

The label "Asian American" is a double-edged sword. On the one hand, it is a useful label to define a pan-ethnic identity that serves to unite disparate ethnic Asian American communities under a common umbrella in contemporary sociopolitical discourse, giving them a united and collective voice vis-à-vis the dominant white mainstream. On the other hand, it is also problematic insofar as its categories break down when confronted with adoptees and bi/multiracial Asian Americans who are the products of interracial marriages. Indeed, the presence of adoptees and bi/multiracial Asian Americans challenges the uncritical presumption of a normative, monolithic, and static notion of "Asianness." The incongruity arising from their presence serves as a reminder that identity is negotiated and constructed, neither given nor born, and neither static nor fixed. Are adoptees and bi/multiracial Asian Americans authentically Asian Americans? Would they be able to do authentic Asian American theological reflections? Are they legitimate subjects of Asian American theologizing?

The foregoing dilemma did not arise in the minds of first-generation Asian American theologians. Instead, as a result of the historical wider race debates of the 1950s through the 1970s, first-generation Asian American theologians focused almost single-mindedly on the issues of marginality and liminality that arose as a result of the racism and discrimination within U.S. society in general, and the U.S. church in particular. Idealized and essentialized biological and cultural notions of what constituted "Asian" and "American" identities undergirded their theological reflections. They naively assumed that their essentialized definitions of "Asian" and "American" were stable and normative. In this regard, they had unknowingly and uncritically adopted the mind-set of their assimilationist white counterparts who, likewise, also assumed that definitions of identity and culture were stable, normative, and unchanging. Clearly, both groups viewed whites and Asian Americans as stable and homogeneous groups, glossing over differences and particularities in general, as well as the reality that identity constructs are dynamic and affected by external and internal forces in particular.

While it is easy to challenge these uncritical bipolar constructs today, nonetheless we must realize that these constructs made perfect sense for first-generation Asian American theologians who were dealing with issues of assimilation, dislocation, and discrimination. In their minds, they were fighting for Asian Americans to get their rightful positions and entitlements in church and society. With the benefit of hindsight, we now see that this uncritical assimilationist perspective presumed not only a stable and normative view of identity construct, but also the naive presumption that rights and privileges of white Americans were the ideals of the American Dream that they should aspire to, without challenging their inequities and other exploitative or questionable aspects.

In addition, an increasing number of second-generation Asian American theologians are challenging the uncritical privileging of certain biological traits that purport to define Asian American identity. Instead of using essentialized notions in their theological reflections, they are beginning to pay attention to the particularities of identity constructions that are shaped by forces of hybridity and heterogeneity. In the case of many 1.5 generation and subsequent generations of American-born Asian Americans, traditional Asian racial-ethnic identities and sociocultural norms are often voluntarily chosen, challenged, rejected, or relativized. Moreover, the increasing hybridity and heterogeneity in Asian America is exemplified not only by the increasing presence of Asian adoptees of white American families (as Mary Foskett points out), but also by Asian Americans who outmarry and end up with bi/multiracial identities (as discussed by Henry Morisada Rietz). Both Foskett and Rietz do not fit neatly into essentialized and clearly demarcated biologically defined racial-ethnic categories of Asian Americans. Indeed, Rietz's writings reveal that he considers himself both Asian and white American. Would that make him any less Asian or white American?

As a result, Asian American theologians are moving beyond idealized and essentialized notions of identity and culture to reflect critically on conflict, particularity, and hybridity, and how these notions affect and shape their theological endeavors. They realize that bipolar dichotomies such as insider-outsider, homeland–host country, center-margin, and so forth are no longer tenable. All Asian American theologians are constantly reformulating their theological reflections in a context that is marked by multiplicity, hybridity, and conflicts, and not just those Asian American theologians who belong to the 1.5 and subsequent generations. This is because Asian Americans of all generations and categories, theologians and nontheologians alike, are constantly negotiating and renegotiating their identities, rendering their identities fluid, hybridized, and contested in their globalized and transnationalized world.

In view of the foregoing developments, contemporary Asian American theologians across the denominational and theological divide are beginning to move away from *tradition-maintenance* — that is, clinging on to ethnic-bound traditions, customs, and theological positions from the "Old World" at all costs — in favor of what I would call *traditioning,* which I define as the largely unconscious and ongoing process of shaping, constructing, and negotiating new traditions, practices, and theological positions that seek to address the issues and questions confronting all Asian Americans, be they immigrant, American-born, adoptee, or bi/multiracial. The theological process of "traditioning" is not something new or peculiar to Asian American theologies. Other theologians such as Dale Irvin (1998), Simon Chan (2000), and Amos Yong (2002) have reflected about various aspects of traditioning in other contexts in their theological writings. For example, Asian theologian Simon Chan observes that traditioning ensures that the Pentecostal faith tradition is handed down to a new generation "in a way that *takes account of the new context of a new generation of faithful"* (Chan 2000: 20, emphasis added).

However, the most succinct yet deeply profound articulation of traditioning is found in the remarks that the late Jaroslav Pelikan made in an interview with Joseph Carey that appeared in the June 26, 1989, issue of *U.S. News & World Report:*

Tradition is not fixed for all time.... It is the perpetuation of *a changing, developing identity.* Tradition is the living faith

of the dead; traditionalism is the dead faith of the living. Tradition lives *in conversation with the past,* while *remembering
where we are* and *when we are* and that *it is we who have
to decide.* Traditionalism supposes that nothing should ever
be done for the first time, so all that is needed to solve any
problem is to arrive at the supposedly unanimous testimony
of this homogenized tradition. (Carey 1989, emphasis added)

Pelikan's insights have far-reaching consequences for theological
reflections. Although he did not use the specific phrase "traditioning," it is clear from the extended quotation that the verb
"traditioning" best describes what Pelikan had in mind when he
spoke about a tradition that "lives *in conversation with the past,*
while *remembering where we are* and *when we are* and that *it
is we who have to decide.*" In other words, Pelikan unequivo-
cally eschewed the static traditionalism that clings tenaciously to
past theological precedents without any regard for the contemporary context and its specific needs, in favor of an active and
dynamic traditioning in theological reflections that pays attention
to contemporary social locations, needs, and challenges.

Moreover, Pelikan's statement highlights the fact that traditioning questions simplistic and uncritical reproductions of past
theological reflections, rejecting all attempts at fossilizing or ar-
chaizing the present in a state of theological stasis, as well as
challenging any notion that theologizing is ahistorical, atemporal,
and independent of sociocultural changes. Instead, traditioning entails critical theological reflections about a community's present
and future. By going beyond mere replication of historical theological precedents, traditioning seeks to retell, reinterpret, and
nuance one's theological reflections with new layers of meaningfulness that address the concerns of the present context. Traditioning
also pursues strategic, dynamic, creative, and contextualized interpretations of the Christian gospel, mediating between historical
theological precedents and current concerns, thereby endeavor-
ing to create a coherent theology that unites the rich legacy of
historical theological precedents with contemporary needs and
challenges.

In other words, traditioning is dynamic and flexible. It is open
to life realities, as well as healthy theological renewal and change

that are integral to a community's social location and context, while remaining in conversation with the past. Rather than looking for a single normative and essentialistic meaning in theologizing, traditioning seeks hybridized and multiple meaningfulness, embodying and integrating both differences and consensus, past and present, precedent and innovation, authority and creativity, thereby facilitating the articulation of new meanings for the present and future. As a result, the theological tradition is constantly being renegotiated, renewed, and nuanced.

As a constitutive element of a common Asian American theological method, traditioning provides the impetus for Asian American theological reflections to be dynamic, situational, and strategic, differentiating between elements, as well as privileging the faith development of "a new generation of faithful." Through the process of traditioning, all Asian American theologians are able to engage in, nuance, and redefine theologies in a creative, strategic, flexible, and innovative manner to empower Asian Americans in their effective engagement with the world around them. Traditioning enables contemporary Asian American theologians to transcend the biological and cultural essentialism of the first generation of Asian American theologians to address the concerns and aspirations of American-born Asian Americans, Asian American adoptees, bi/multiracial Asian Americans, or even transnational first-generation Asian Americans who are becoming increasingly adept at balancing the multiple worlds that they move back and forth between.

By going beyond the simplistic cultural essentialism and sociopolitical nationalism of the first-generation Asian American theologians who had emphasized the acquisition of rights and entitlements, traditioning enables second-generation Asian American theologians to grapple with the ambiguities that emerge when the blurring of the boundaries between Asians and Asian Americans is giving rise to an increasingly multivalent and complex intertwining of social, cultural, and religious identities. Through traditioning, the Asian American past can be integrated with diverse and pluralistic contexts of contemporary Asian America, giving all Asian Americans a coherent sense of communal consensus, belonging, identity, and direction.

Proposition 4: Authenticity and Credibility

The authenticity and credibility of Asian American theologies are rooted in the creative tension between the vertical dimension of the Christian gospel and its soteriological message on the one hand, and the horizontal dimension of life experiences of Asian Americans on the other hand.

Finally, we have to deal with the question of evaluating the authenticity and credibility of Asian American theologies; these theologies are authentically and credibly Christian, Asian, and American. In this regard, many Asian American theologians are often tempted to use the praxis of a community's own experiences and actions as the principal criterion for authenticating their theologies. Nevertheless, the praxis of a community, however liberative it may appear to be, cannot be the principal criterion for authenticating one's theologies; there is an absence of any external theological criteria for critically unearthing any potential failures, biases, or shortcomings in a theological method that is structured primarily upon a community's praxis and which in turn relies upon this very same praxis as the principal criterion for authenticity and credibility. In particular, without such external criteria for critical evaluation, Asian American theologies run the risk of being reduced to mere ideology. Hence, where a community's praxis is a constitutive element of a theology, there is a necessity for using external criteria that are outside of a community's praxis to judge the authenticity and credibility of such praxis.

The credibility and authenticity of an Asian American theology is best judged within the matrix of a creative tension between the vertical and horizontal dimensions of theologizing, whereby the Christian gospel and human experience encounter each other in a mutual dialogical relationship. The vertical dimension of theologizing refers to Asian American theologies' internal coherence with the gospel and its soteriological message, while the horizontal dimension of theologizing refers to these theologies' external coherence with the Asian American communities' life experiences. To the extent that Asian American theologies are authentic and credible, they should be able to transcend all forms of bipolar and oppositional dichotomies to define, articulate, and uphold in a holistic manner the reality that Asian American theologies are, first and foremost, authentically Christian, while at the same time truly Asian and American.

On the one hand, the internal coherence of any Asian American theology to the gospel is necessary for it to be specifically Christian and not one of many syncretistic fads that come and go in a postmodern world. On the other hand, the vertical dimension cannot be the only dimension of authenticity and credibility, because it does not necessarily follow that theologies which worked successfully in the past or other contexts (e.g., North American and European white theologies) would ipso facto work effectively in a variety of contemporary Asian American contexts. More importantly, making the vertical dimension of theologizing the sole criterion for the authenticity and credibility of Asian American theologies results in a failure to recognize that theologizing is not an abstract or intellectual endeavor, but rather, it is something done concretely within a community, by a community, and for this community as it seeks to understand and develop its multiple, heterogenized, and hybridized identit(ies) as Christian, Asian, and American.

To the extent that an Asian American theology is faithful to both the vertical and horizontal dimensions of theologizing, it is truly authentic Christian theologizing when it responds credibly to the signs of the times: the social, cultural, political, economic, identity, and religious aspects that define and shape the daily lives of Asian Americans. Such credibility also demands that it respond to the challenges posed by social, cultural, economic, and political anomie. In doing so, it also seeks to portray a vision of the gospel that is at the same time universal (it is faithful to its founding stories and narratives) and local (that these founding stories and narratives are being appropriated, contextualized, juxtaposed, and applied in local Asian American contexts).

In the final analysis, unless Asian American theologies emerge from and are nourished by the gospel, they cannot be truly liberative, prophetic, and transformative. Instead, such theologies run the risk of a distortive emphasis on the materialist aspects of salvation. On the other hand, fidelity to the gospel goes beyond the mere proclamation of the universality of the unique redemptive role of Jesus Christ, to a fidelity to make present Jesus' radical vision of bringing about God's reign within the wider picture of the drama of Asian American daily living here and now. In other words, by paying careful attention to both tradition and praxis, as well as historicity and temporality, an Asian American theology is able to communicate the salvific reality of the Christian gospel in the facticity and events in the Asian American milieu.

References

Legislation and Treaties Cited

Burlingame Treaty of 1868

California Civil Rights Initiative of 1995 (Proposition 209)

California Criminal Proceedings Act of 1850

Chinese Exclusion Act of 1882

Chinese Exclusion Act of 1902

Chinese Exclusion Repeal Act of 1943 (Magnuson Act)

Civil Liberties Act of 1988

Displaced Persons Act of 1948

Displaced Persons Act of 1950

Fourteenth Amendment to the United States Constitution (1868)

Geary Act of 1892

Gentlemen's Agreement of 1907

Immigration Act of 1917 (Asiatic Barred Zone Act)

Immigration Act of 1924 (Johnson-Reed Act, Japanese Exclusion Act, or Asian Exclusion Act)

Immigration and Nationality Act of 1952 (McCarran-Walter Act)

Immigration and Nationality Act of 1965 (Hart-Celler Act)

Indian Citizenship Act of 1924 (Snyder Act)

Luce-Celler Act of 1946

National Voting Rights Act of 1965

Naturalization Act of 1790

Philippines Independence Act of 1934 (Tydings-McDuffie Act)

Proposition 209 (see California Civil Rights Initiative of 1995)

Refugee Relief Act of 1953

War Brides Act of 1945

Case Law Cited

Loving v. Virginia, 388 U.S. 1 (1967)

People v. Hall, 4 Cal. 399 (1854)

Takao Ozawa v. United States, 260 U.S. 178 (1922)

United States v. Balsara, 180 Fed. 694 (1910)

United States v. Bhagat Singh Thind, 261 U.S. 204 (1923)

United States v. Dolla, 177 Fed. 101 (1910)

Books and Articles Cited

Allen, Theodore W.
　1997　*The Invention of the White Race. Volume 2: The Origins of Racial Oppression in Anglo-America.* New York: Verso.
Alumkal, Antony W.
　1999　"Preserving Patriarchy: Assimilation, Gender Norms, and Second-Generation Korean American Evangelicals." *Qualitative Sociology* 22, no. 2: 127–40.
　2002　"The Scandal of the 'Model Minority' Mind? The Bible and Second-Generation Asian American Evangelicals." *Semeia* 90/91: 237–50.
　2003　*Asian American Evangelical Churches: Race, Ethnicity, and Assimilation in the Second Generation.* New York: LFB Scholarly Publishing.
Bankston, Carl L.
　2000　"Vietnamese-American Catholicism: Transplanted and Flourishing." *U.S. Catholic Historian* 18, no. 1: 36–53.
Basch, Linda, Nina Glick Schiller, and Cristina Szanton-Blanc, eds.
　1994　*Nations Unbound: Transnational Projects, Postcolonial Predicaments, and Deterritorialized Nation States.* Langhorne, PA: Gordon and Breach.

Bevans, Stephen B.
1992   *Models of Contextual Theology.* Maryknoll, NY: Orbis Books.
Blalock, Hubert M., Jr.
1975   *Toward a Theory of Minority-Group Relations.* New York: Wiley.
Borah, Eloisa Gomez
1995/96   "Filipinos in Unamuno's California Expedition of 1587." *Amerasia Journal* 21: 175–83.
Brock, Rita Nakashima
1988   *Journeys by Heart: A Christology of Erotic Power.* New York: Crossroad.
1992   "Dusting the Bible on the Floor: The Loss of Innocence and the Power of Wisdom in Asian American Women's Writing." *In God's Image* 11, no. 3: 3–9.
1996a   "Critical Reflections on Asian American Religious Identity: Response — Clearing the Tangled Vines." *Amerasia Journal* 22, no. 1: 181–86.
1996b   "Private, Public, and Somewhere in Between: Lessons from the History of Asian-Pacific American Women." *Journal of Feminist Studies in Religion* 12, no. 1: 127–32.
1998   "Interstitial Integrity: Reflections toward an Asian American Woman's Theology." In *Introduction to Christian Theology: Contemporary North American Perspectives,* ed. Roger A. Badham, 183–96. Louisville, KY: Westminster John Knox Press.
2005   "Fantastic Coherence." *Journal of Feminist Studies in Religion* 21, no. 1: 155–73.
Brock, Rita Nakashima, and Naomi Southard
1987   "The Other Half of the Basket: Asian American Women and the Search for a Theological Home." *Journal of Feminist Studies in Religion* 3, no. 2: 135–50.
Brock, Rita Nakashima, and Rebecca Ann Parker
2001   *Proverbs of Ashes: Violence, Redemptive Suffering, and the Search for What Saves Us.* Boston: Beacon Press.
Brock, Rita Nakashima, and Susan Brooks Thistlethwaite
1996   *Casting Stones: Prostitution and Liberation in Asia and the United States.* Minneapolis: Augsburg Fortress.
Brodkin, Karen
1999   *How Jews Became White Folks and What That Says about Race in America.* New Brunswick, NJ: Rutgers University Press.

Bundang, Rachel A. R.
1998   " 'May You Storm Heaven with Your Prayers': Devotions to
         Mary and Jesus in Filipino American Catholic Life." Paper
         presented at the Asian North American Religion, Culture,
         and Society (ANARCS) Group of the American Academy of
         Religion Annual Meeting.
2002   "Home As Memory, Metaphor, and Promise in Asian/Pacific
         American Religious Experience." *Semeia* 90/91: 87–104.
Burns, Jeffrey M.
1987   *The Catholic American Parish: A History from the 1850s to
         the Present.* New York: Paulist Press.
Burns, Jeffrey M., Ellen Skerrett, and Joseph M. White, eds.
2000   *Keeping Faith: European and Asian Catholic Immigrants.*
         Maryknoll, NY: Orbis Books.
Busto, Rudy
1996   "The Gospel According to the Model Minority? Hazarding
         an Interpretation of Asian American Evangelical College
         Students." *Amerasia Journal* 22: 133–47.
Carey, Joseph
1989   "Christianity as an Enfolding Circle." *U.S. News & World
         Report* 106, no. 25: 57.
Carnes, Tony, and Fenggang Yang, eds.
2004   *Asian American Religions: The Making and Remaking of
         Borders and Boundaries.* New York: New York University
         Press.
Cayton, Horace R., and Anne O. Lively
1955   *The Chinese in the United States and the Chinese Christian
         Church.* New York: Bureau of Research and Survey, National
         Council of Churches of Christ in the United States.
Chan, Simon
2000   *Pentecostal Theology and the Christian Spiritual Tradition.*
         London: Sheffield Academic Press.
Chan, Sucheng
1991   *Asian Americans: An Interpretive History.* Boston: Twayne.
Chang, Carrie
2000   "Amen. Pass the Kimchee: Why Are Asian Americans on
         Colleges Converting to Christianity in Droves?" *Monolid: An
         Asian American Magazine for Those Who Aren't Blinking* 1,
         no. 1: 1–9.
Chang, Jonah
1991   "Movement of Self-Empowerment: History of the National
         Federation of Asian American United Methodists." In *Churches*

Aflame: Asian Americans and United Methodism, ed. Artemio
Guillermo, 135–53. Nashville: Abingdon Press.

Cheng, Lucie, and Philip Q. Yang
2000   "The 'Model Minority' Deconstructed." In *Contemporary
Asian America: A Multidisciplinary Reader,* ed. Min Zhou and
James V. Gatewood, 459–82. New York: New York University
Press.

Chuang, D.J.
2006   *Asian American Youth Ministry.* Washington, DC: L^2
Foundation.

Chuang, D.J., and Timothy Tseng
2006   *Conversations: Asian American Evangelical Theologies in
Formation.* Washington, DC: L^2 Foundation.

Chung Hyun Kyung
1990   *Struggle to Be the Sun Again: Introducing Asian Women's
Theology.* Maryknoll, NY: Orbis Books.

Crowe, Jerome
1997   *From Jerusalem to Antioch: The Gospel across Cultures.*
Collegeville, MN: Liturgical Press.

Ebaugh, Helen Rose
2005   *Handbook of Religion and Social Institutions.* New York:
Springer.

Ebaugh, Helen Rose, and Janet Saltzman Chafetz, eds.
2000   *Religion and the New Immigrants: Continuities and Adap-
tations in Immigrant Congregations.* Walnut Creek, CA:
AltaMira Press.

2002   *Religions across Borders: Transnational Immigrant Networks.*
Walnut Creek, CA: AltaMira Press.

Eck, Diana L.
2001   *A New Religious America: How a "Christian Country" Has
Become the World's Most Religiously Diverse Nation.* San
Francisco: HarperSanFrancisco.

Ecklund, Elaine Howard
2006   *Korean American Evangelicals: New Models for Civic Life.*
New York: Oxford University Press.

Economist
2005   "Jesus, CEO: Churches as Businesses." *Economist*
(December 24, 2005): 41–44.

Espina, Marina E.
1988   *Filipinos in Louisiana.* New Orleans: A. F. Laborde & Sons.

Fernandez, Eleazar S.
    2001   "Exodus toward Egypt: Filipino-Americans' Struggle to Realize
            the Promised Land in America." In *A Dream Unfinished:
            Theological Reflections on America from the Margins,* ed.
            Eleazar S. Fernandez and Fernando F. Segovia, 167–81.
            Maryknoll, NY: Orbis Books.
    2002   "From Babel to Pentecost: Finding a Home in the Belly of the
            Empire." *Semeia* 90/91: 29–50.
    2003a   "Postcolonial Exorcism and Reconstruction: Filipino Ameri-
            cans' Search for Postcolonial Subjecthood." In *Realizing the
            America of Our Hearts: Theological Voices of Asian Ameri-
            cans,* ed. Fumitaka Matsuoka and Eleazar S. Fernandez, 75–98.
            St. Louis: Chalice Press.
    2003b   "America from the Hearts of a Diasporized People: A Di-
            asporized Heart." In *Realizing the America of Our Hearts:
            Theological Voices of Asian Americans,* ed. Fumitaka Mat-
            suoka and Eleazar S. Fernandez, 253–73. St. Louis: Chalice
            Press.
Foskett, Mary F.
    2002   "The Accidents of Being and the Politics of Identity: Biblical
            Images of Adoption and Asian Adoptees in America." *Semeia*
            90/91: 135–44.
    2006   "Obscured Beginnings: Lessons from the Study of Christian
            Origins." In *Ways of Being, Ways of Reading: Asian American
            Biblical Interpretation,* ed. Mary F. Foskett and Jeffrey Kah-Jin
            Kuan, 178–91. St. Louis: Chalice Press.
Foskett, Mary F., and Jeffrey Kah-Jin Kuan, eds.
    2006   *Ways of Being, Ways of Reading: Asian American Biblical
            Interpretation.* St. Louis: Chalice Press.
Gerona-Adkins, Rita M.
    2001   "Asian Pacific Americans Display Support for Arab, Sikh
            Americans." *Asian Fortune* 9, no. 10 (October): 23.
Goldman, Ari L.
    1991   "Portrait of Religion in U.S. Holds Dozens of Surprises." *New
            York Times* (April 10, 1991): A1.
Guest, Kenneth J.
    2003   *God in Chinatown: Religion and Survival in New York's
            Evolving Immigrant Community.* New York: New York
            University Press.
    2005   "Religion and Transnational Migration in the New China-
            town." In *Immigrant Faiths: Transforming Religious Life
            in America,* ed. Karen I. Leonard, Alex Stepick, Manuel A.

Vasquez, and Jennifer Holdaway, 145–63. Lanham, MD: AltaMira Press.

Guglielmo, Jennifer, and Salvatore Salerno, eds.
2003   *Are Italians White? How Race Is Made in America.* New York: Routledge.

Gyory, Andrew
1998   *Closing the Gate: Race, Politics, and the Chinese Exclusion Act.* Chapel Hill: University of North Carolina Press.

Ha, Thao
2002   "The Evolution of Remittances from Family to Faith: The Vietnamese Case." In *Religions across Borders: Transnational Immigrant Networks,* ed. Helen Rose Ebaugh and Janet Saltzman Chafetz, 111–28. Walnut Creek, CA: AltaMira Press.

Hall, Douglas
1994   *Thinking the Faith: Christian Theology in a North American Context.* Minneapolis: Augsburg.

Hearn, Lafcadio
1883   "Saint Malo: A Lacustrine Village in Louisiana." *Harper's Weekly.* March 31, 1883.

Hertig, Young Lee
1998   "The Asian-American Alternative to Feminism: A Yinist Paradigm." *Missiology* 26, no. 1: 15–22.
2001   *Cultural Tug of War: Korean Immigrant Family and Church in Transition.* Nashville: Abingdon Press.
2003   "The Korean Immigrant Church and Naked Public Square." In *Realizing the America of Our Hearts: Theological Voices of Asian Americans,* ed. Fumitaka Matsuoka and Eleazar S. Fernandez, 131–46. St. Louis: Chalice Press.
2004   "Cross-cultural Mediation: From Exclusion to Inclusion." In *Mission in Acts: Ancient Narratives for a Postmodern Context,* ed. Robert Gallagher and Paul Hertig, 59–72. Maryknoll, NY: Orbis Books.
2005   "Why Asian American Evangelical Theologies?" Paper presented at the American Academy of Religion, Philadelphia, November 20.

Hing, Bill Ong
1993   *Making and Remaking Asian America through Immigration Policy, 1850–1990.* Stanford, CA: Stanford University Press.

Hollinger, David A.
1995   *Postethnic America: Beyond Multiculturalism.* New York: Basic Books.

Hopkins, Dwight N.
1999   *Introducing Black Theology of Liberation*. Maryknoll, NY:
        Orbis Books.
Hsu, Francis L. K.
1971   *The Challenge of the American Dream: The Chinese in the
        United States*. Belmont, CA: Wadsworth.
Hunter, James
1987   *Evangelicalism: The Coming Generation*. Chicago: University
        of Chicago Press.
Hurh, Won Moo
1977   "Comparative Study of Korean Immigrants in the United
        States: A Typology." In *Koreans in America*, ed. Byong-Suh
        Kin et al., 73–95. Memphis: Association of Korean Christian
        Scholars in North America.
Hurh, Won Moo, and Kwang Chung Kim
1984   *Korean Immigrants in America: A Structural Analysis of Ethnic
        Confinement and Adhesive Assimilation*. Rutherford, NJ:
        Fairleigh Dickinson University Press.
1989   "The 'Success Image' of Asian Americans: Its Validity, and
        Its Practical and Theoretical Implications." *Ethnic and Racial
        Studies* 12, no. 4: 512–38.
1990   "Religious Participation of Korean Immigrants in the United
        States." *Journal of the Scientific Study of Religion* 29, no. 1:
        19–34.
Ignatiev, Noel
1996   *How the Irish Became White*. New edition. New York:
        Routledge.
Irvin, Dale T.
1998   *Christian Histories, Christian Traditioning: Rendering
        Accounts*. Maryknoll, NY: Orbis Books.
Iwamura, Jane Naomi, and Paul Spickard, eds.
2003   *Revealing the Sacred in Asian and Pacific America*. New York:
        Routledge.
Jacobson, Matthew Frye
1998   *Whiteness of a Different Color: European Immigrants and the
        Alchemy of Race*. Cambridge, MA: Harvard University Press.
Jensen, Richard J., and Cara J. Abeyta
1987   "The Minority in the Middle: Asian-American Dissent in the
        1960s and 1970s." *Western Journal of Speech Communication*
        51: 404–16.
Jeung, Russell
2002a   "Evangelical and Mainline Teachings on Asian American
        Identity." *Semeia* 90/91: 211–36.

2002b "Asian American Pan-Ethnic Formation and Congregational Culture." In *Religions in Asian America: Building Faith Communities,* ed. Pyong Gap Min and Jung Ha Kim, 215–43. Walnut Creek, CA: AltaMira Press.

2003 "New Asian American Churches and Symbolic Racial Identity." In *Revealing the Sacred in Asian and Pacific America,* ed. Jane Naomi Iwamura and Paul Spickard, 225–40. New York: Routledge.

2005 *Faithful Generations: Race and New American Churches.* New Brunswick, NJ: Rutgers University Press.

Jordan, Winthrop D.
1977 *White over Black: American Attitudes toward the Negro, 1550–1812.* New York: Norton.

Jue, Jeffrey K.
2006 "Asian American Theology: A Modern and Postmodern Dilemma." In *Conversations: Asian American Evangelical Theologies in Formation,* ed. D.J. Chuang and Timothy Tseng, 99–119. Washington, DC: L² Foundation.

Kim, Eunjoo Mary
1999 *Preaching the Presence of God: A Homiletic from an Asian American Perspective.* Valley Forge, PA: Judson Press.

2002 "Hermeneutics and Asian American Preaching." *Semeia* 90/91: 269–90.

Kim, Grace Ji-Sun
2002 *The Grace of Sophia: A Korean North American Women's Christology.* Cleveland: Pilgrim Press.

Kim, Jung Ha
1999 "The Labor of Compassion: Voices of Churched Korean American Women." In *New Spiritual Homes: Religion and Asian Americans,* ed. David K. Yoo, 202–17. Honolulu: University of Hawaii Press.

Kim, Rebecca Y.
2006 *God's New Whiz Kids: Korean American Evangelicals on Campus.* New York: New York University Press.

Kim, Uriah Yong-Hwan
2002 "Uriah the Hittite: A (Con)text of Struggle for Identity." *Semeia* 90/91: 69–85.

2006 "The *Realpolitik* of Liminality in Josiah's Kingdom and Asian America." In *Ways of Being, Ways of Reading: Asian American Biblical Interpretation,* ed. Mary F. Foskett and Jeffrey Kah-Jin Kuan, 84–98. St. Louis: Chalice Press.

Kogawa, Joy
1992 *Itsuka.* New York: Anchor.

Kuan, Jeffrey Kah-Jin
2000   "Diasporic Reading of a Diasporic Text: Identity Politics
        and Race Relations and the Book of Esther." In *Interpreting
        Beyond Borders,* ed. Fernando F. Segovia, 161–73. Sheffield:
        Sheffield Academic Press.
2002   "My Journey into Diasporic Hermeneutics." *Union Seminary
        Quarterly Review* 56: 50–54.
Kwok Pui-Lan
1992   *Chinese Women and Christianity, 1860–1927.* Atlanta:
        Scholars Press.
1995   *Discovering the Bible in the Non-Biblical World.* Maryknoll,
        NY: Orbis Books.
1996   "Diversity within Us: The Challenge of Community among
        Asian and Asian-American Women." *In God's Image* 15, no. 1:
        51–53.
2000   *Introducing Asian Feminist Theology.* Cleveland: Pilgrim Press.
2004   "Finding a Home for Ruth: Gender, Sexuality, and the Politics
        of Otherness." In *New Paradigms for Bible Study: The Bible in
        the Third Millennium,* ed. Robert M. Fowler, Edith Blumhofer,
        and Fernando F. Segovia, 135–54. New York: Trinity Press
        International.
2005   *Postcolonial Imagination and Feminist Theology.* Louisville,
        KY: Westminster John Knox Press.
Kwok Pui-Lan, ed.
1997   "Asian and Asian American Women's Voices." *Journal of Asian
        and Asian American Theology* 2, no. 1.
Lee, Deborah
2003   "Faith Practices for Racial Healing and Reconciliation." In
        *Realizing the America of Our Hearts: Theological Voices
        of Asian Americans,* ed. Fumitaka Matsuoka and Eleazar S.
        Fernandez, 147–57. St. Louis: Chalice Press.
Lee, Jung Young
1979   *A Theology of Change: A Christian Concept of God in Eastern
        Perspective.* Maryknoll, NY: Orbis Books.
1993   "Marginality: A Multi-Ethnic Approach to Theology from
        an Asian-American Perspective." *Asia Journal of Theology* 7,
        no. 2: 244–53.
1995   *Marginality: The Key to Multicultural Theology.* Minneapolis:
        Fortress Press.
1996   *The Trinity in Asian Perspective.* Nashville: Abingdon Press.
1999   "A Life In-Between: A Korean-American Journey." In *Journeys
        at the Margin: Toward an Autobiographical Theology in*

American-Asian Perspective, ed. Peter C. Phan and Jung Young Lee, 23–39. Collegeville, MN: Liturgical Press.

Lee, Robert G.
1999 *Orientals: Asian Americans in Popular Culture.* Philadelphia: Temple University Press.

Lee, Sang Hyun
1980 "Called to Be Pilgrims: Toward a Theology within the Korean American Context." In *The Korean Immigrant in America,* ed. Byong-suh Kim and Sang Hyun Lee, 37–74. Montclair, NJ: Association of Korean Christian Scholars in North America.

1987 "Called to Be Pilgrims: Toward an Asian-American Theology from the Korean Immigrant Perspective." In *Korean American Ministry: A Resource Book,* ed. Sang Hyun Lee, 90–120. Princeton: Princeton Theological Seminary.

1991 "Korean American Presbyterians: A Need for Ethnic Particularity and the Challenge of Christian Pilgrimage." In *The Diversity of Discipleship: Presbyterians and Twentieth Century Christian Witness,* ed. Milton J. Coalter, John M. Mulder, and Louis B. Weeks, 312–30. Louisville, KY: Westminster/John Knox Press.

1996a "How Shall We Sing the Lord's Song in a Strange Land?" *Journal of Asian and Asian American Theology* 1, no. 1: 77–81.

1996b "Pilgrimage and Home in the Wilderness of Marginality: Symbols and Context in Asian American Theology." In *Korean Americans and Their Religions: Pilgrims and Missionaries from a Different Shore,* ed. Ho-Youn Kwon, Kwang Chung-Kim, and R. Stephen Warner, 55–69. University Park: Pennsylvania State University Press.

2003 "Marginality as Coerced Liminality: Toward an Understanding of the Context of Asian American Theology." In *Realizing the America of Our Hearts: Theological Voices of Asian Americans,* ed. Fumitaka Matsuoka and Eleazar S. Fernandez, 11–28. St. Louis: Chalice Press.

Leonard, Karen I., Alex Stepick, Manuel A. Vasquez, and Jennifer Holdaway, eds.
2005 *Immigrant Faiths: Transforming Religious Life in America.* Lanham, MD: AltaMira Press.

Levitt, Peggy
2001 *The Transnational Villagers.* Berkeley: University of California Press.

2005 "Immigration." In *Handbook of Religious and Social Institutions*, ed. Helen Rose Ebaugh, 391–410. New York: Springer.

Lie, John
1995 "From International Migration to Transnational Diaspora." *Contemporary Sociology* 24, no. 4: 303–6.

Liew, Tat-siong Benny
2001 "Reading with Yin Yang Eyes: Negotiating the Ideological Dilemma of a Chinese American Biblical Hermeneutics." *Biblical Interpretation* 9, no. 3: 309–35.
2002 "Introduction: Whose Bible? Which (Asian) America?" *Semeia* 90/91: 1–26.

Lim, Paul Chang-Ha
2006 "Beyond Han: A Korean American Evangelical Theologian's Reflections." In *Conversations: Asian American Evangelical Theologies in Formation*, ed. D.J. Chuang and Timothy Tseng, 43–53. Washington, DC: L² Foundation.

Linkh, Richard M.
1975 *American Catholicism and European Immigrants: 1900–1924*. Staten Island, NY: Center for Migration Studies.

Liu, Eric
1988 *The Accidental Asian: Notes of a Native Speaker*. New York: Random House.

López, Ian F.
1996 *White by Law: The Legal Construction of Race*. New York: New York University Press.

Lowe, Lisa
1991 "Heterogeneity, Hybridity, Multiplicity: Marking Asian American Differences." *Diaspora* 1: 24–44.

Matsuoka, Fumitaka
1995 *Out of Silence: Emerging Themes in Asian American Churches*. Cleveland: Pilgrim Press.
1997 *The Color of Faith: Building Community in a Multiracial Society*. Cleveland: United Church Press.
2003 "Creating Community Amidst the Memories of Historic Injuries." In *Realizing the America of Our Hearts: Theological Voices of Asian Americans*, ed. Fumitaka Matsuoka and Eleazar S. Fernandez, 29–40. St. Louis: Chalice Press.

Matsuoka, Fumitaka, and Eleazar S. Fernandez, eds.
2003 *Realizing the America of Our Hearts: Theological Voices of Asian Americans*. St. Louis: Chalice Press.

McClain, Charles J.
1994 *In Search of Equality: The Chinese Struggle against Discrimination in Nineteenth-Century America.* Berkeley: University of California Press.
McLaren, Peter
1997 *Revolutionary Multiculturalism: Pedagogies of Dissent for the New Millennium.* Boulder, CO: Westview Press.
Miller, Stuart Creighton
1969 *The Unwelcome Immigrant: The American Image of the Chinese, 1785–1882.* Berkeley: University of California Press.
Min, Anselm Kyongsuk
1989 *Dialectic of Salvation: Issues in Theology of Liberation.* Albany: State University of New York Press.
1999 "From Autobiography to Fellowship of Others: Reflections on Doing Ethnic Theology Today." In *Journeys at the Margin: Toward an Autobiographical Theology in American-Asian Perspective,* ed. Peter C. Phan and Jung Young Lee, 135–59. Collegeville, MN: Liturgical Press.
2004 *The Solidarity of Others in a Divided World: A Postmodern Theology after Postmodernism.* London: T&T Clark International.
Min, Pyong Gap
2003 "Immigrants' Religion and Ethnicity: A Comparison of Korean Christian and Indian Hindu Immigrants." In *Revealing the Sacred in Asian and Pacific America,* ed. Jane Naomi Iwamura and Paul Spickard, 125–41. New York: Routledge.
Min, Pyong Gap, and Jung Ha Kim, eds.
2002 *Religions in Asian America: Building Faith Communities.* Walnut Creek, CA: AltaMira Press.
Min, Pyong Gap, and Rose Kim, eds.
1999 *Struggle for Ethnic Identity: Narratives by Asian American Professionals.* Walnut Creek, CA: AltaMira.
Moy, Russell G.
1993 "Biculturalism, Race, and the Bible." *Religious Education* 88, no. 3: 415–33.
2000 "American Racism: The Null Curriculum in Religious Education." *Religious Education* 95, no. 2: 120–33.
2002 "Resident Aliens of the Diaspora: 1 Peter and Chinese Protestants in San Francisco." *Semeia* 90/91: 51–67.
Nagano, Paul M.
1976a "The Japanese Americans' Search for Identity, Ethnic Pluralism, and a Christian Basis of Permanent Identity." In *The Theologies of Asian Americans and Pacific Peoples: A Reader,* comp.

Roy I. Sano, 225–53. Berkeley, CA: Asian American Center for Theology and Strategies, Pacific School of Religion.

1976b   "Biblical and Theological Statement for the Asian American Baptist Caucus." In *The Theologies of Asian Americans and Pacific Peoples: A Reader,* comp. Roy I. Sano, 450–56. Berkeley, CA: Asian American Center for Theology and Strategies, Pacific School of Religion.

1996   "My Theological and Identity Odyssey." *Journal of Asian and Asian American Theology* 1, no. 1: 4–9.

1999   "A Japanese-American Pilgrimage: Theological Reflections." In *Journeys at the Margin: Toward an Autobiographical Theology in American-Asian Perspective,* ed. Peter C. Phan and Jung Young Lee, 63–79. Collegeville, MN: Liturgical Press.

Nakanishi, Don T.

2000   "A Quota on Excellence? The Asian American Admissions Debate." In *Contemporary Asian America: A Multidisciplinary Reader,* ed. Min Zhou and James V. Gatewood, 483–98. New York: New York University Press.

Ng, Chiong Hui (Shoki Coe)

1973   "In Search of Renewal in Theological Education." *Theological Education* 9: 233–43.

1980   "Contextualization as the Way toward Reform." In *Asian Christian Theology: Emerging Themes,* ed. Douglas J. Elwood, 48–55. Philadelphia: Westminster Press.

Ng, David

1976   "The Chinaman's Chances Are Improving." In *The Theologies of Asian Americans and Pacific Peoples: A Reader,* comp. Roy I. Sano, 153–55. Berkeley, CA: Asian Center for Theology and Strategies, Pacific School of Religion.

1984a   *Developing Leaders for Youth Ministry.* Valley Forge, PA: Judson Press.

1984b   *Youth in the Community of Disciples.* Valley Forge, PA: Judson Press.

1987   "Sojourners Bearing Gifts: Pacific Asian American Christian Education." In *Ethnicity in the Education of the Church,* ed. Charles R. Foster, 7–23. Nashville: Scarritt Press.

1992   Working with Pacific Asian American families. In *Faith and Families: A Parish Program for Parenting In Faith Growth,* ed. Thomas Bright and John Roberto, chap. 5. New Rochelle, NY: Catholic Family Series.

1996a   "Introduction." In *People on the Way: Asian North Americans Discovering Christ, Culture and Community,* ed. David Ng, xv–xxix. Valley Forge, PA: Judson Press.

1996b "Varieties of Congregations or Varieties of People." In *People on the Way: Asian North Americans Discovering Christ, Culture and Community,* ed. David Ng, 281–300. Valley Forge, PA: Judson Press.

1999 "A Path of Concentric Circles: Toward an Autobiographical Theology of Community." In *Journeys at the Margin: Toward an Autobiographical Theology in American-Asian Perspective,* ed. Peter C. Phan and Jung Young Lee, 81–102. Collegeville, MN: Liturgical Press.

Ng, David, ed.
1996c *People on the Way: Asian North Americans Discovering Christ, Culture and Community.* Valley Forge, PA: Judson Press.

Ng, David, and Heup Young Kim
1996 "The Central Issue of Community: An Example of Asian North American Theology on the Way." In *People on the Way: Asian North Americans Discovering Christ, Culture and Community,* ed. David Ng, 25–41. Valley Forge, PA: Judson Press.

Ng, David, and Virginia Thomas
1981 *Children in the Worshiping Community.* Atlanta: John Knox Press.

Ng, Donald, ed.
1988 *Asian Pacific American Youth Ministry.* Valley Forge, PA: Judson Press.

Ngan, Lai Ling Elizabeth
2006 "Neither Here nor There: Boundary and Identity in the Hagar Story." In *Ways of Being, Ways of Reading: Asian American Biblical Interpretation,* ed. Mary F. Foskett and Jeffrey Kah-Jin Kuan, 70–83. St. Louis: Chalice Press.

Noll, Mark A.
1994 *The Scandal of the Evangelical Mind.* Grand Rapids: Eerdmans.

Omi, Michael, and Howard Winant
1994 *Racial Formation in the United States: From the 1960s to the 1990s.* New York: Routledge.

Ong, Aihwa
1999 *Flexible Citizenship: The Cultural Location of Transnationality.* Durham, NC: Duke University Press.

Ong, Aihwa, and Donald Nonini, eds.
1997 *Ungrounded Empires: The Cultural Politics of Modern Chinese Transnationalism.* New York: Routledge.

Osajima, Keith
2000 "Asian Americans as the Model Minority: An Analysis of the Popular Press Image in the 1960s and 1980s." In *Contemporary Asian America: A Multidisciplinary Reader,* ed.

Min Zhou and James V. Gatewood, 459–82. New York: New York University Press.

Park, Andrew Sung

1993   *The Wounded Heart of God: The Asian Concept of Han and the Christian Doctrine of Sin.* Nashville: Abingdon Press.

1996   *Racial Conflict and Healing: An Asian-American Theological Perspective.* Maryknoll, NY: Orbis Books.

1999   "Church and Theology: My Theological Journey." In *Journeys at the Margin: Toward an Autobiographical Theology in American-Asian Perspective,* ed. Peter C. Phan and Jung Young Lee, 161–72. Collegeville, MN: Liturgical Press.

2001   "A Theology of Transmutation." In *A Dream Unfinished: Theological Reflections on America from the Margins,* ed. Eleazar S. Fernandez and Fernando F. Segovia, 152–66. Maryknoll, NY: Orbis Books.

2003   "A Theology of Tao (Way): Han, *Sin, and Evil.*" In *Realizing the America of Our Hearts: Theological Voices of Asian Americans,* ed. Fumitaka Matsuoka and Eleazar S. Fernandez, 41–54. St. Louis: Chalice Press.

2004   *From Hurt to Healing: A Theology of the Wounded.* Nashville: Abingdon Press.

Phan, Peter C.

1999a   "Betwixt and Between: Doing Theology with Memory and Imagination." In *Journeys at the Margin: Toward an Autobiographical Theology in American-Asian Perspective,* ed. Peter C. Phan and Jung Young Lee, 113–33. Collegeville, MN: Liturgical Press.

1999b   "Asian Catholics in the United States: Challenges and Opportunities for the Church." *Mission Studies* 16, no. 2: 151–74.

1999c   "An Asian-American Theology: Believing and Thinking at the Boundaries." In *Journeys at the Margin: Toward an Autobiographical Theology in American-Asian Perspective,* ed. Peter C. Phan and Jung Young Lee, xi–xxvii. Collegeville, MN: Liturgical Press.

2001   "The Dragon and the Eagle: Toward a Vietnamese-American Theology." *Theology Digest* 49, no. 3: 203–18.

2002   "Mary in Vietnamese Piety and Theology: A Contemporary Perspective." *Ephemerides Mariologicae* 51: 457–71.

2003a   *Christianity with an Asian Face: Asian American Theology in the Making.* Maryknoll, NY: Orbis Books.

2003b "The Experience of Migration as Source of Intercultural Theology in the United States." In Peter C. Phan, *Christianity with an Asian Face: Asian American Theology in the Making*, 3–25. Maryknoll, NY: Orbis Books.

2003c "Jesus as the Eldest Son and Ancestor." In Peter C. Phan, *Christianity with an Asian Face: Asian American Theology in the Making*, 125–45. Maryknoll, NY: Orbis Books.

2003d "The Experience of Migration as Source of Intercultural Theology in the United States." In Peter C. Phan, *Christianity with an Asian Face: Asian American Theology in the Making*, 3–25. Maryknoll, NY: Orbis Books.

Phan, Peter C., and Jung Young Lee, eds.

1999 *Journeys at the Margin: Toward an Autobiographical Theology in American-Asian Perspective*. Collegeville, MN: Liturgical Press.

Porterfield, Amanda

2001 *The Transformation of American Religion: The Story of a Late-Twentieth-Century Awakening*. New York: Oxford University Press.

Rietz, Henry W. Morisada

2002 "My Father Has No Children: Reflections on a *Hapa* Identity toward a Hermeneutic of Particularity." *Semeia* 90/91: 145–57.

2006 "Living Past: A *Hapa* Identifying with the Exodus, the Exile, and the Internment." In *Ways of Being, Ways of Reading: Asian American Biblical Interpretation*, ed. Mary F. Foskett and Jeffrey Kah-Jin Kuan, 192–203. St. Louis: Chalice Press.

Roediger, David R.

1999 *The Wages of Whiteness: Race and the Making of the American Working Class*. Revised edition. New York: Verso.

2005 *Working toward Whiteness: How America's Immigrants Become White. The Strange Journey from Ellis Island to the Suburbs*. New York: Basic Books.

Rutledge, Paul James

1985 *The Role of Religion in Ethnic Self-Identity: A Vietnamese Community*. Lanham, MD: University Press of America.

1992 *The Vietnamese Experience in America*. Bloomington: University of Indiana Press.

Sahagun, Louis

2007 "Creating a Better Life for Children of Saigu." *Los Angeles Times*, June 10.

Salyer, Lucy E.
1995   *Laws Harsh as Tigers: Chinese Immigrants and the Shaping of Modern Immigration Law.* Chapel Hill: University of North Carolina Press.
2004   "Baptism by Fire: Race, Military Service and U.S. Citizenship Policy, 1918–1935." *Journal of American History* 91: 847–76.

Sano, Roy I.
1973   *Amerasian Theology of Liberation: A Reader.* Monograph available at the Pacific and Asian American Center for Theology and Strategies Collection. Graduate Theological Union Archives, Berkeley CA.
1976a   "Cultural Genocide and Cultural Liberation through Amerasian Protestantism." In *The Theologies of Asian Americans and Pacific Peoples: A Reader,* comp. Roy I. Sano, 28–50. Berkeley, CA: Asian Center for Theology and Strategies, Pacific School of Religion.
1976b   "Ministry for a Liberating Ethnicity." In *The Theologies of Asian Americans and Pacific Peoples: A Reader,* comp. Roy I. Sano, 281–95. Berkeley, CA: Asian American Center for Theology and Strategies, Pacific School of Religion.
1976c   "Yes, We'll Have No More Bananas in Church." In *The Theologies of Asian Americans and Pacific Peoples: A Reader,* comp. Roy I. Sano, 51–54. Berkeley, CA: Asian American Center for Theology and Strategies, Pacific School of Religion.
1976d   "This Matter of Integration." In *The Theologies of Asian Americans and Pacific Peoples: A Reader,* comp. Roy I. Sano, 262–63. Berkeley, CA: Asian American Center for Theology and Strategies, Pacific School of Religion.
1976e   "The Church: One Holy Catholic and Apostolic." In *The Theologies of Asian Americans and Pacific Peoples: A Reader,* comp. Roy I. Sano, 264–80. Berkeley, CA: Asian American Center for Theology and Strategies, Pacific School of Religion.
1976f   "The Bible and Pacific Basin Peoples." In *The Theologies of Asian Americans and Pacific Peoples: A Reader,* comp. Roy I. Sano, 296–309. Berkeley, CA: Asian American Center for Theology and Strategies, Pacific School of Religion.
1982   *From Every Nation without Number: Racial and Ethnic Diversity in United Methodism.* Nashville: Abingdon Press.
2002   "Shifts in Reading the Bible: Hermeneutical Moves among Asian Americans." *Semeia* 90/91: 105–18.

Saxton, Alexander
1971   *The Indispensable Enemy: Labor and the Anti-Chinese Movement in California*. Berkeley: University of California Press.
Shin, Eui Hang, and Hyung Park
1988   "An Analysis of the Causes of Schisms in Ethnic Churches: The Case of Korean-American Churches." *Sociological Analysis* 49:234–48.
Steinberg, Stephen
2001   *The Ethnic Myth: Race, Ethnicity, and Class in America*. 3rd ed. Boston: Beacon Press.
Suh, Sharon A.
2003   " 'To Be Buddhist Is to Be Korean': The Rhetorical Use of Authenticity and the Homeland in the Construction of Post-Immigration Identities." In *Revealing the Sacred in Asian and Pacific America*, ed. Jane Naomi Iwamura and Paul Spickard, 177–91. New York: Routledge.
Suzuki, Lester E.
1991   "Persecution, Alienation, Recognition: History of Japanese Methodist Churches." In *Churches Aflame: Asian Americans and United Methodism*, ed. Artemio Guillermo, 113–34. Nashville: Abingdon Press.
Symonds, William C.
2005   "Earthly Empires: How Evangelical Churches Are Borrowing from the Business Playbook." *BusinessWeek* (May 23), 78–88.
Takagi, Dana
1992   *The Retreat from Race: Asian-American Admissions and Racial Politics*. New Brunswick, NJ: Rutgers University Press.
Takaki, Ronald
1989   *Strangers from a Different Shore: A History of Asian Americans*. Boston: Little, Brown.
Thomas, William Isaac, and Florian Znaniecki
1918   *The Polish Peasant in Europe and America*. Chicago: University of Chicago Press.
Tomasi, Silvano M., and Madeline H. Engel, eds.
1970   *The Italian Experience in the United States*. Staten Island, NY: Center for Migration Studies.
Toteja, Greeta
2001   "Indian-Americans Become Targets of Retaliatory Attacks." *Asian Fortune* 9, no. 10 (October): 32.
Tseng, Timothy
2002a   "Second-Generation Chinese Evangelical Use of the Bible in Identity Discourse in North America." *Semeia* 90/91: 251–67.

2002b   "Asian Pacific American Christianity in a Post-Ethnic Future." *American Baptist Quarterly* 21, no. 3: 277–92.

2003a   "Beyond Orientalism and Assimilation: The Asian American as Historical Subject." In *Realizing the America of Our Hearts: Theological Voices of Asian Americans*, ed. Fumitaka Matsuoka and Eleazar S. Fernandez, 55–72. St. Louis: Chalice Press.

2003b   "Trans-Pacific Transpositions: Continuities and Discontinuities in Chinese North American Protestantism Since 1965." In *Revealing the Sacred in Asian and Pacific America*, ed. Jane Naomi Iwamura and Paul Spickard, 241–71. New York: Routledge.

2005   "The Evangelical Reconstruction of Chinese American Protestantism." Paper presented at the Institute for the Study of American Evangelicalism's Symposium on the Changing Face of American Evangelicalism. October 13–14.

Tuan, Mia
1998   *Forever Foreigners or Honorary Whites? The Asian Ethnic Experience Today.* New Brunswick, NJ: Rutgers University Press.

Turner, Jonathan H. and Edna Bonacich
1980   "Toward a Composite Theory of Middleman Minorities." *Ethnicity* 7: 144–58.

Umemoto, Karen
1991   "On Strike! San Francisco State College Strike, 1968–1969, The Role of Asian American Students." *Amerasia Journal* 15, no. 1: 3–41.

U.S. Census Bureau
2002a   *A Profile of the Nation's Foreign-Born Population from Asia (2000 Update).* Census Brief: Current Population Survey, CENBR/01–3. Washington, DC: U.S. Census Bureau.

2002b   *Population Profile of the United States: 2000.* Washington, DC: U.S. Census Bureau.

2002c   *The Asian Population: 2000.* Census 2000 Brief, C2KBR/01–16. Washington, DC: U.S. Census Bureau.

2003   *The Asian and Pacific Islander Population in the United States: March 2002.* Current Population Reports, P20–540. Washington, DC: U.S. Census Bureau.

2004a   *Asian Pacific American Heritage Month: May 2004.* Facts for Features, CB04–FF.06. Washington, DC: U.S. Census Bureau.

2004b   *U.S. Interim Projections by Age, Sex, Race, and Hispanic Origin.* Washington, DC: U.S. Census Bureau.

United States Conference of Catholic Bishops (USCCB)
    2001   *Asian and Pacific Presence: Harmony in Faith.* Washington, DC: USCCB.
United States Conference of Catholic Bishops, Office for the Pastoral Care of Migrants and Refugees (USCCB-PCMR)
    1992   *The Pastoral Care of Immigrants from the Philippines.*
Volf, Miroslav
    1996   *Exclusion and Embrace: A Theological Exploration of Identity, Otherness, and Reconciliation.* Nashville: Abingdon Press.
Wan, Enoch
    1985   "Tao—The Chinese Theology of God-Man." *His Dominion* 2, no. 3: 24–27.
    1997   *Debunking the Old and Formulating the New: An Exploration to Formulating Sino-Theology* [in Chinese]. Toronto, Canada: Chinese Christian Communication.
    1999   *Sino-Theology: A Survey Study* [in Chinese]. Toronto: Chinese Christian Communication.
Wan, Sze-Kar
    2000   "Does Diaspora Identity Imply Some Sort of Universality? An Asian-American Reading of Ablations." In *Interpreting beyond Borders,* ed. Fernando F. Segovia, 107–31. Sheffield: Sheffield Academic Press.
    2006   "Betwixt and Between: Toward a Hermeneutics of Hyphenation." In *Ways of Being, Ways of Reading: Asian American Biblical Interpretation,* ed. Mary F. Foskett and Jeffrey Kah-Jin Kuan, 137–51. St. Louis: Chalice Press.
Wang, L. Ling-chi
    1991   "The Politics of Ethnic Identity and Empowerment: The Asian American Community since the 1960s." *Asian American Policy Review* 2: 43–56.
Warner, William Lloyd, and Leo Srole
    1945   *The Social Systems of American Ethnic Groups.* New Haven: Yale University Press.
Warren, Rick
    2002   *The Purpose-Driven Life: What on Earth Am I Here For?* Grand Rapids: Zondervan.
Wei, William
    1993   *The Asian American Movement.* Philadelphia: Temple University Press.
Williams, Raymond Brady
    1996   *Christian Pluralism in the United States: The Indian Immigrant Experience.* Cambridge: Cambridge University Press.

Winant, Howard
1994   *Racial Conditions: Politics, Theory, Comparisons.* Minneapolis:
        University of Minnesota Press.
Wu, Cheng-Tsu, ed.
1971   *Chink: A Documentary History of Anti-Chinese Prejudice in
        America.* New York: Meridian.
Yamada, Frank M.
2006   "Constructing Hybridity and Heterogeneity: Asian American
        Biblical Interpretation from a Third-Generation Perspective."
        In *Ways of Being, Ways of Reading: Asian American Biblical
        Interpretation,* ed. Mary F. Foskett and Jeffrey Kah-Jin Kuan,
        164–77. St. Louis: Chalice Press.
Yang, Fenggang
1999   *Chinese Christians in America: Conversion, Assimilation,
        and Adhesive Identities.* University Park: Pennsylvania State
        University Press.
2002a   "Chinese Christian Transnationalism: Diverse Networks of a
        Houston Church." In *Religions across Borders: Transnational
        Immigrant Networks,* ed. Helen Rose Ebaugh and Jane
        Saltzman Chafetz, 129–48. Walnut Creek, CA: AltaMira Press.
2002b   "Religious Diversity among the Chinese in America." In
        Religions in Asian America: Building Faith Communities, ed.
        Pyong Gap Min and Jung Ha Kim, 71–98. Walnut Creek, CA:
        AltaMira Press.
Yee, Gale A.
2006   "Yin/Yang Is Not Me: An Exploration into an Asian American
        Biblical Hermeneutics." In *Ways of Being, Ways of Reading:
        Asian American Biblical Interpretation,* ed. Mary F. Foskett
        and Jeffrey Kah-Jin Kuan, 152–63. St. Louis: Chalice Press.
Yong, Amos
2002   *Spirit-Word-Community: Theological Hermeneutics in
        Trinitarian Perspective.* Burlington, VT: Ashgate.
2003   *Beyond the Impasse: Toward a Pneumatological Theology of
        Religions.* Grand Rapids: Baker.
2005a   *The Spirit Poured Out on All Flesh: Pentecostalism and the
        Possibility of Global Theology.* Grand Rapids: Baker.
2005b   "What Asian, Which American? Whose *Evangelion?* Whither
        Asian American Evangelical Theology?" Paper presented at the
        American Academy of Religion, Philadelphia, November 20.
        Forthcoming in the *Evangelical Review of Theology.*
2005c   "The Future of Evangelical Theology: Asian and Asian
        American Interrogations." Lecture presented at Harvard
        Divinity School, December 19.

2007   "The Future of Asian Pentecostal Theology: An Asian American Assessment." *Asian Journal of Pentecostal Studies* 10, no. 1: 22–41.

2008   *Hospitality and the Other: Pentecost, Christian Practices, and the Neighbor.* Faith Meets Faith. Maryknoll, NY: Orbis Books.

Yoo, David K., ed.

1999   *New Spiritual Homes: Religion and Asian Americans.* Honolulu: University of Hawaii Press.

Zhou, Min, and Carl Bankston III, eds.

1998   *Growing Up American: How Vietnamese Children Adapt to Life in the United States.* New York: Russell Sage Foundation.

Zhou, Min, and James V. Gatewood, eds.

2000   *Contemporary Asian America: A Multidisciplinary Reader.* New York: New York University Press.

Index

Underlined references indicate tables.

accent-losing programs, 42
*Accidental Asian: Notes of a Native
Speaker* (Liu), 49–50
acculturation, 41–42
additive assimilation, 44
adhesive assimilation, 44
adhesive integration, 63
adoptees, 116, 120, 169, 170
Alumkal, Antony, 145–46, 149–50,
168
Amerasian Theology of Liberation
(Sano), 94
American Academy of Religion (AAR),
100, 157
anti-Asian hysteria, in the twentieth
century, 29–32
antimiscegenation laws, 29, 122
Arab Americans, abuse against, 48
Asia, diversity of cultures from, 2–3
Asian adoptees, of white American
families, 116, 120, 169, 170
Asian American, label of, as double-
edged sword, 169
Asian American Catholicism, 64–74
Asian American Center for Theology
and Strategies, 94
Asian American Christianity. *See also*
Asian American Christians, Asian
American theologies
churches, future of, 74–76
effect on, of transnationalism, 56
emergence of, 58–59
moving to the center of theologizing,
81
Asian American Christians. *See also*
Asian American Christianity,
Asian American theologies
facing paternalism and uncritical
racism, 93

growth and vitality of churches for,
59–61
most diverse group of U.S. Christians,
xi
Asian American Political Alliance
(AAPA), 89, 90
Asian Americans
biblical scholars, dilemma of, 109–10
demographical overview, 3–19
consciousness of, emerging, 87–90
discrimination against, 38, 60
education of, 4, <u>10</u>, <u>15</u>
Evangelical identity construction
among, 148–49
Evangelical theologies emerging
among, 154–57
family income of, 4, <u>11</u>, <u>15</u>
fastest-growing segment of U.S.
population, 4–5
as forever foreigners, 41, 44–45,
50–51, 141
geographical distribution of, 5–6,
<u>16–19</u>
heterogeneity of, 2–3
hidden majority of, 37
holistic approach of, to life and
salvation, 73
as honorary whites, 44
identity, shaping of, in 21st-century
United States, 49–56
identity crisis of, 132
identity in flux, 2
liberation of, as a marginal people,
95
maintaining close ties with Asian
roots, 75
as masters of their own destiny, 142
as middle minority, 39–40
mistaken assumptions about religion
of, 57–58

Asian Americans (*continued*)
　most diverse U.S. racial group, 3–4
　occupations of, 4, 11, 15
　outmarrying among, 3–4
　perceived as model minority, 37–39
　population of, 8
　population profiles, 10–11
　predominantly Christian, xii
　"race" problematic and, 125–27
　racism against, 44–48
　rapid growth among, of Evangelical
　　Christianity, 144–45, 149, 151
　self-definition of, 1
　stereotypes of, 88
　story of, compared to Uriah's,
　　116–17
　straight-line assimilation not
　　available to, 42–43
　theological complacency of
　　Evangelicals, 149–54, 159–60
　top twelve groups of, 9
　transnationalism of, 52–56
　treated differently from European
　　immigrants, 125–27
　U.S. Census Bureau definition of,
　　1, 2
　universities' discrimination against,
　　38
　viewed in romanticized terms, xi
Asian American theologians, 85–86
　accomplishments of, 162–63
　Catholic, 105–6
　Evangelical, 106–7
　feminist, 102–5
　first generation, 90–99, 101
　first- and second-generation,
　　differences between, 169–70
　racism and discrimination toward,
　　91–92
　second generation, 99–102
　seeking answers to fundamental
　　questions, 81–82
Asian American theologies. *See also*
　Asian American Christianity,
　Asian American Christians,
　Evangelical Christianity
　biblical hermeneutics of, 108
　contextual foundation of, 80–81
　as contextual theologies, 78–80

creating common method for,
　164–76
　defined, 77
　Evangelical, 143–61
　future of, 162–76
　historical backdrop for (1950s and
　　1960s), 86–87
　inductive dimension of, 81
　liberation theology, 94
　of marginality, 134–38
　moving beyond ethnocentric
　　theologies, 83–84
　of reconciliation and healing, 138–42
　responses of, to racism, 133–34
　shaped by epistemological and foun-
　　dational theological perspectives,
　　167–68
　systematic, 82–83
Asian American Women on Leadership
　(AAWOL), 100, 107
Asian American Youth Ministry, 155
Asian and Asian American Biblical
　Studies Consultation, 109
Asian-born U.S. population
　profile of, 15
　top five countries of origin, 14
Asian countries, leading in immigrant-
　sending, 5
Asian Exclusion Act, 30
Asian Indians, court decisions regarding
　"whiteness" of, 129–31
Asian North American Religion,
　Culture, and Society Group
　(ANARCS), 157
Asian and Pacific Americans and
　Religion Research Initiative
　(APARRI), 100
*Asian and Pacific Presence: Harmony in
　Faith* (USCCB), 64–66, 73, 74
Asians, immigration of, 20–35. *See
　also categories for individual
　immigrant groups*
Asiatic Barred Zone Act, 30
Asiatic Exclusion League, 29
assimilationist argument, 51
authenticity, as element of common
　Asian American theology, 174–76
Basch, Linda, 52
Bevans, Stephen B., 79

Bible
  approaches to, in Asian America, 108–20
  functional and orthodox canons of, 113–14
  interpretation of, for Asian Americans, 156
  Bible in Asian America (Liew, ed.), 109
biblical hermeneutics
  Asian American, defining, 110–12
  moving from historical-critical to contextual, 112–14
biblical scholars, dilemma of, 109–10
bi/multiracial identity, 116, 169, 170
Black Power movement, 86–87, 89
Black Students Union (BSU), 90
black theology, 86
Black Theology and Black Power (Cone), 87
Blade Runner, 46–47
Bouchard, James, 126–27
Brock, Rita Nakashima, 83, 103–4, 168
Buddhists, Vietnamese, 56
Bui, Francis, 70
Bundang, Rachel A. R., 68
Burlingame, Anson, 22
Burlingame Treaty, 22, 26
Busto, Rudy, 145

California Civil Rights Initiative (CCRI), 138
California Gold Rush, 20–22
California Oriental Provisional Conference, 92
Campus Crusade for Christ, 144–45
canonical criticism, 113
Carey, Joseph, 171–72
Casting Stones: Prostitution and Liberation in Asia and the United States (Brock and Thistlethwaite), 104
Catholic Church, as hub for communal fellowship and mutual support, 69–71
Catholicism
  among Asian Americans, 64–74
  missionary influence on, for Asian Americans, 67
Catholics, Vietnamese, 56

Catholic theologians, 105–6
Cayton, Horace R., 92
Celtic worldview, 158
Chafetz, Janet Saltzman, 69
Chan, Simon, 171
Chan, Sucheng, 43
Chang, Jonah, 92
Chawla, Amrik Singh, 48
Chin, Vincent, 47
Chinatowns, emergence of, in response to hostility, 26
Chinese American Citizens Alliance (CACA), 89
Chinese Americans
  curbing immigration of, 26
  Christianity of, 62–64
  demise of ethnic congregations for, 92
  early immigration of, to the United States, 20–28
  Evangelicalism among, 146–48, 151–52
  generations of, facing perpetual bachelorhood, 26
  immigration of, encouraged by Burlingame Treaty, 22
  integrating Chinese culture into Christianity, 63–64
  involvement of, in California Gold Rush, 20–21
  prejudice against, 22–24
  prized for their work ethic, 24
  as railroad laborers, 22, 24
  as scapegoats in late 1800s, 25
  treatment of, moving from discrimination to exclusion, 24–27
  viewed by European immigrants as rivals, 24
  in U.S. Catholic Church, 66
  working as unskilled farmhands after Gold Rush, 21–22
Chinese Exclusion Acts, 26–27, 28, 29–30
Chinese Exclusion Repeal Act of 1943 (Magnuson Act), 27
Chinese Protestant immigrants, experience of, compared with 1 Peter, 114–15
Chinese Six Companies, 89

Chinese Women and Christianity,
  1860–1927 (Kwok), 105
Cho, Seung-hui, 37
Chou Family Foundation, 155
Chow, Moses, 148
Christianity, Asianized forms of, 58
Chung Hyun Kyung, 103, 168
church, Ng's vision of, 96–97
Civil Liberties Act of 1988, 32
civil rights movement, 33, 45, 86, 125
Clemons, Charles, 128
Cleveland, Grover, 27
color-blind policies, 45–46, 51, 152
Commission on Wartime Relocation
  and Internment of Civilians
  (CWRIC), 32
Cone, James, 87, 93, 94
Confucianism
  ethical values of, 63–64
  influence of, on Ng, 98–99
Congregation of Mary, Queen, 72
Congregation of the Mother Co-
  Redemptrix, 72
contextual hermeneutics, 112–14
contextualization, 67, 78–80
contextual theology, 78–80, 167
Conversations: Asian American Evan-
  gelical Theologies in Formation,
  155
credibility, as element of common Asian
  American theology, 174–76
Crowe, Jerome, 80
cultural assimilation, 41, 42, 44, 51

Daoist worldview, 158
de Unamuno, Pedro, 20
devotional piety, among Asian
  American Catholics, 68–69
diasporic experiences, implications of,
  for hermeneutics, 114–15
Discovering the Bible in the Non-
  Biblical World (Kwok), 105
Displaced Persons Act of 1948 and
  1950, 32
double identity, 117
double rejection, of Asian Americans,
  113

Ebaugh, Helen Rose, 69
Eck, Diana, 57–58

empathy, suggested as element of
  common Asian American theology,
  166–68
enclave mentality, 138
engabachamiento (whitening), 46
Espina, Marina, 20
ethnic identity, complexity of, 51
Eucharistic Youth Society, 71
European ethnic churches, losing
  identity and culture, 75–76
European immigrants
  anti-Chinese agitation of, 25
  forming trade unions and political
    parties, 24, 25
  straight-line assimilation available to,
    42
European theologies, contrasted with
  contextual theologies, 79
Evangelical Christianity, 106–7
  among Chinese Americans, 56,
    146–48, 151–52
  constructing theology for Asian
    Americans, 157–61
  emergence of Asian American
    theologies, 154–57
  identity construction among Asian
    Americans, 148–49
  among Korean Americans, 145–46
  presence of, on university campuses,
    63
  rapid growth of, among Asian
    Americans, 144–45, 149, 151
  suggestions for Asian American
    theology of, 155–56, 160–61
  theologians of, struggling with
    ambiguity toward mainline
    Protestant colleagues, 154–55
  theological complacency of, 149–54,
    159–60
  theology of, overview, 143–44
Executive Order 9066 (Japanese
  American internment), 31–32

Faith Voices for the Common Good,
  103
Falling Down, 46–47
family, practice of, 140
feminist theologians, 102–5
Fernandez, Eleazar S., 47–48, 115

Filipino Americans
Catholic devotional piety of, 68
devotions' prominence among
Catholics, 68
immigration of, 20, 28, 30–31
predominantly Catholic, 58
presence of, in U.S. Catholic Church,
65–66
reasons for migrating, 66
*Flexible Citizenship: The Cultural
Location of Transnationality*
(Ong), 54–55
forever foreigners, 41, 44–45, 50–51,
141
*Forever Foreigners or Honorary
Whites? The Asian Ethnic Experience Today* (Tuan), 44–45,
153
Foskett, Mary, 116, 120, 168, 170
friendship evangelism, 149
Friendship Society, 88
Furrow, Buford, 47
Fuzhounese Chinese, transnationalism
of, 54–55, 56

Geary Act, 27
generational differences, influence of,
on biblical interpretation, 119
Gentlemen's Agreement, 29–30
Gih, Andrew, 148
glass ceiling, 38
Goldman, Ari L., xi
*Grace of Sophia: A Korean North
American Women's Christology*
(Kim), 83
Guanyin, 103
Guest, Kenneth, 54–55, 56
Guillermo, Emil, 48
Gutiérrez, Gustavo, 137
Gyory, Andrew, 25

Ha, Thao, 56
Hall, Douglas J., 78
Hall, George W., 23
han, 101
hapa identity, 116, 119–20
Hart-Celler Act of 1965, 33–34, 54, 76
hate crimes, anti-Asian, 47–48
Hayes, Rutherford B., 26
Hearn, Lafcadio, 20

hermeneutics
and implications of diasporic and
postcolonial experiences, 114–15
identity constructions and, 115–20
hermeneutics of hyphenation, 112–13
hermeneutics of suspicion, 137
Hertig, Young Lee, 45–46, 107,
138–40, 157–59
heterogeneity, 116
holistic spirituality, of Asian American
Christians, 73
Hollinger, David A., 50–51
honorary whites, 141
Hopkins, Dwight N., 87
Hsu, Francis, 43
huiguan, 88
Humanitarian Operations program, 35
Hurh, Won Moo, 38–39, 42, 43–44,
61
hybridity, 116

identity
bifurcated, by being Asian American
woman, 104
formation of, 117–18
moving beyond idealized and
essentialized notions of, 170–71
Ileto, Joseph, 47–48
immigrants, first from England,
identifying selves as Christian,
123
immigration
after World War II, 32–33
growing wave of, since 1960s, 33–34
quotas for, 27, 30, 31, 33
Immigration Act of 1917, 30
Immigration Act of 1924, 30, 31
Immigration and Nationality Act of
1952, 32, 123
Immigration and Nationality Act of
1965, 33–34
inculturation, for Asian American
Catholics, 67–68
independence movements, 88
Indian Americans
difficulty of, integrating into
American churches, 60–61
in U.S. Catholic Church, 66
Indian Citizenship Act of 1924, 123

individualism, Ng rejecting Western
preference for, 97
Indochinese immigration, 34–35
Institute for Leadership Development,
100
Institute for the Study of Asian Amer-
ican Christianity (ISAAC), 100,
106, 107, 155, 156–57
Intercollegiate Chinese for Social Action
(ICSA), 89, 90
intercultural theology, for Asian
American Catholics, 67–68
interstitial living, 116
InterVarsity Christian Fellowship,
144–45
Introducing Asian Feminist Theology
(Kwok), 105
Irvin, Dale, 171

Jacobson, Matthew Frye, 123
Japan, agreeing to voluntary restraint of
immigration to the United States,
29
Japanese Americans
advice for, on assimilation, 135
early immigration to the United
States, history of, 28
internment of, 31–32, 135
racist and discriminatory treatment
of, 29–30
in U.S. Catholic Church, 66
Japanese American Citizens' League
(JACL), 89
Japanese Exclusion Act, 30
Jeung, Russell, 148–49
Johnson, Lyndon B., 33, 86
Johnson-Reed Act, 30, 31
Jordan, Winthrop D., 123
*Journeys by Heart: A Christology of
Erotic Power* (Brock), 83, 104
Jue, Jeffrey, 154, 155–56

Kagawa, Joy, 132–33
Kearney, Dennis, 25
kenjinkai, 88
Kim, Eunjoo Mary, 116, 117–18
Kim, Grace Ji-Sun, 83
Kim, Jung Ha, 58
Kim, Kwang Chung, 38–39, 43–44, 61
Kim, Rebecca, 144–45

Kim, Uriah Yong-Hwan, 116–17
King, Martin Luther, Jr., 86, 87
kinship, practice of, 140
koinonia, 97–98
Korean American Christianity, 61–62
weakness of immigrant church, 138
Korean Americans
call for race reconciliation, 138–40
churches of, providing social
functions for, 61–62
Evangelicalism among, 145–46
experience of, Min's description, 106
immigration to the United States,
history of, 28–29
inability of, to attain structural
assimilation, 43–44
predominantly Protestant, 58
racist and discriminatory treatment
of, 29–30
role of, in Los Angeles riots, 40
in U.S. Catholic Church, 66
Kuan, Jeffrey Kah-Jin, 110
Kwok Pui-Lan, 104–5, 168

L2 Foundation, 155–56
Lazarus, Emma, 27
Lee, Deborah, 140
Lee, Jung Young, 83, 91, 94–95, 134,
154, 168
Lee, Robert G., 46–47
Lee, Sang Hyun, 60, 91, 168
Legion of Mary, 71
Levitt, Peggy, 53–54, 70–71
liberation theology, 94
Lie, John, 52–53, 75
Liew, Tat-siong Benny, 51, 108
Lim, Paul Chang-Ha, 154
liminality, 118, 169
Little Saigons, 35
Liu, Eric, 49–50
Lively, Anne O., 92
Long Depression (1873–96), 24–25
Loo, Jim, 47
López, Ian, 127
Los Angeles riots (1992), 40, 101, 138
Lovers of the Holy Cross, 72
Loving v. Virginia, 122
Lowe, Lisa, 2

Luce-Celler Act of 1946, 32
Luzon Indians, 20

Malcolm X, 86, 87
marginality, 95, 112–13, 116, 118, 169
affirming, 134–35
centered on memory and
imagination, 135–38
as center of life-giving creativity,
134
double, of Asian American women,
102
as humanizing experience, 135
theologies of, 134–38
*Marginality: Key to Multicultural
Theology* (Lee), 95
martyrdom, heritage of, in Asian
church, 74
Matsuoka, Fumitaka, 133, 168
McCarran-Walter Act, 32, 33, 123
McLaren, Peter, 46
megachurch movement, 143–44
Meiji Restoration, 28
Menace II Society, 46–47
Mexican American Students
Confederation (MASC), 90
middle minority image, as divide-
and-conquer technique of the
dominant elite, 39–40
middle-agent minority, 39
migration
Asian American Catholic experiences
of, 66–67
paradigm shift in, 163
Min, Anselm Kyungsuk, 106
Min, Pyong Gap, 61–62, 63
Mineta, Norman, 27
Minjung theology, 103
model minority, 141, 146
image of, used to absolve whites from
racism against Asian Americans,
39
myth of, 37–39
scandal of the thinking of, 149–54
status of, path to, 41
Morikawa, Jitsuo, 91
Moy, Russell G., 114–15
multicultural parish, 66
mutual aid societies, 88

Nagano, Paul M., 91, 134–35
narrative theology, 98
National Committee of Negro
Churchmen (NCNC), 86
National Council for Japanese
American Redress (NCJAR),
32
National Federation of Asian American
United Methodists (NFAAUM),
92
National Origins Act, 30
National Survey of Religious
Identification, xi
*Nations Unbound: Transnational
Projects, Postcolonial Predica-
ments, and Deterritorialized
Nation-States* (Basch et al.), 52
Native Sons of the Golden State, 89
Naturalization Act of 1790, 123
neoconservative movement
approach of, to racism in society, 45
influence of, against affirmative
action policies, 152
"New Colossus" (Lazarus), 27
*New Religious America, A: How a
"Christian Country" Has Become
the World's Most Religiously
Diverse Nation* (Eck), 57–58
*New Spiritual Homes: Religion and
Asian Americans* (Yoo), 58
Ng, Chiong Hui (Shoki Coe), 78
Ng, David, 91, 95–99
Ngan, Lai-Ling Elizabeth, 112
Nisei (second-generation Japanese), 89
Noll, Mark, 150

Ohio Conference of the Methodist
Church, 95, 134
Okihiro, Gary, 141
Omi, Michael, 1, 46, 122
Ong, Aihwa, 53, 54
Orderly Departure Program (UNHCR),
35
Orientalism
in mainstream United States, xi
overcoming, 141–42
Ozawa, Takao, 128–29

Pacific, Asian, and North American
    Asian Women in Theology and
    Ministry (PANAAWTM), 100,
    102
Pacific and Asian American Center for
    Theology and Strategies, 94
Pacific Islander, U.S., population
    profiles, 10–11
Pacific Japanese Provisional Conference,
    92
parachurch organizations, 71, 144–45
Park, Andrew Sung, 40, 83, 101, 154
Park, Hyung, 61
Park, Robert E., 141
Parks, Rosa, 86
*Pastoral Acre of Immigrants from the
    Philippines* (USCCB), 65
Pelikan, Jaroslav, 171–72
People v. Hall, 23–24
personal parish, 66
Phan, Peter C., 67, 68, 72, 77–78,
    83–84, 105–6, 135–38
Philippine American College Endeavor
    (PACE), 89, 90
Philippine Independence Act of 1934,
    31
plastic surgery, to change Asian
    features, 42
plurality, 116
Polish Peasant in Europe and America
    (Thomas and Znaniecki), 53
politics of exclusion and inclusion, 115
popular devotions, popularity of, for
    Asian American Catholics, 68–69
postcolonial experiences, implications
    of, for hermeneutics, 114–15
*Postcolonial Imagination and Feminist
    Theology* (Kwok), 105
*Postethnic America: Beyond Mul-
    ticulturalism* (Hollinger),
    50
Poston Relocation Center, 93
prejudice, in contemporary United
    States, 131–33
Presbyterian Church, dilemma of,
    related to Korean American
    members, 60
Proposition 209 (1995 California Civil
    Rights Initiative), 45–46, 138

*Proverbs of Ashes: Violence, Redemp-
    tive Suffering, and the Search
    for What Saves Us* (Brock and
    Parker), 104
public school segregation, in San
    Francisco, 29
*Purpose-Driven Life: What on Earth
    Am I Here For?* (Warren), 144

Qing Dynasty (China), 21

race
    as dynamic sociohistorical category,
        123–25
    as juridical concept, 127–31
    understanding, 121–25
race reconciliation, 154
    twin challenges of, 140
    yinism in, 139–40
*Racial Formation in the United States:
    From the 1960s to the 1990s* (Omi
    and Winant), 46, 122
racial inferiority, Chinese accused of,
    22–24
racial prerequisite cases, 127–31
racial separation, offensive to God, 153
racism
    ambivalence about, for Asian Amer-
        ican Evangelical Christians,
        152–53
    Asian American experiences of,
        45–48
    Asian American theological responses
        to, 133–34
    overcoming, 141–42
    responses to, 138–42
redaction criticism, 113
reform movements, 88
Refugee Relief Act of 1953, 32
*Religions in Asian America: Building
    Faith Communities* (Min), 63
reproduction, inherited vs. constructed,
    119–20
Rietz, Henry Morisada, 116, 119–20,
    168, 170
Rising Sun, 46–47
Roberts, J. Deotis, 93
Roosevelt, Franklin D., 31
Roque, Frank, 48

saigu, 40
Saint Malo settlement, 20
San Francisco School Incident of 1907, 29
San Francisco State College, shutdown of, 90
Sano, Roy Isao, 91, 93–94, 113–14
Sarrazin, Brian, 103
Saxton, Alexander, 126
Scandal of the Evangelical Mind (Noll), 150
Schiller, Nina Glick, 52
Second Vatican Council, 91
Shih, Torrey, 148
Shin, Eui Hang, 61
Shinto, William Mamoru, 91
signs of the times, reading, as element of common Asian American theology, 168
Sikh American community, abuse against, 48
Snyder Act, 123
Society of Asian North American Christianity Studies (SANACS), 100, 157
Sodhi, Balbir Singh, 48
solidarity of others, 106
Song, C. S., 154
Srole, Leo, 74
Stanford, Leland, 24
Statue of Liberty, dedication of, 27
stereotyping, in contemporary United States, 131–33
stories, Ng as proponent of, 98
straight-line assimilation, 41–43
structural assimilation, 41–44, 51, 132
Struggle to Be the Sun Again: Introducing Asian Women's Theology (Chung), 103
Study of Pacific and Asian North American Religion (PANA), 100
Suh, Sharon A., 75
Sung, John, 148
Sutherland, George, 128–31
Suzuki, Lester E., 92
syncretism, charges of, against Chinese American Christians, 64
systematic theologies, of Asian Americans, 82–83
Szanton-Blanc, Cristina, 52

Takaki, Robert, 43
Takao Ozawa v. United States, 127, 128–29
talk story (talking story), 140
territorial parish, 66
Theologies of Asian Americans and Pacific Peoples: A Reader (Sano), 94
theologizing, vertical and horizontal dimensions of, 175
theology, contextuality in, 78
Theology of Change, A: A Christian Concept of God in Eastern Perspective (Lee), 83, 95
Third World Liberation Front, 90
Third World Strike, 90
Thomas, William Isaac, 53
Tomasi, Silvano M., 74
traditioning, as element of common Asian American theology, 171–73
tradition-maintenance, moving away from, 171
transnationalism, 52–56
Trinity in an Asian Perspective (Lee), 83, 95
Tsai, Christiana, 148
Tseng, Timothy, 106–7, 141–42, 147–48, 150–54, 156, 168
Tuan, Mia, 44–45, 50, 141, 153
tuanqi, 97–98
tuen kai, 97–98
Tydings-McDuffie Act, 31

Umemoto, Karen, 90
United Methodist Church, 92
United Nations High Commission for Refugees (UNHCR), 35
United States
    first legislation of, barring specific ethnic group, 26
    projected population, by race and Hispanic origin, 12–13
United States Conference of Catholic Bishops (USCCB), 64–65, 73, 74
United States v. Balsara, 130
United States v. Bhagat Singh Thind, 127, 129–31
United States v. Dolla, 130

Vietnamese Americans
  devotional piety among Catholics, 69
  experience of, as immigrants, 135–38
  immigration to the United States,
    history of, 34–35, 66
  importance of Catholic parish in
    communities of, 70
  presence of, in U.S. Catholic Church,
    65–66
  significant contribution of, to priestly
    and religious vocations, 72
  theology of, 68
Vietnamese Dominican Sisters, 72
vocations, priestly and religious, growth
    among Asian Americans, 72
Volf, Miroslav, 153
Voting Rights Act of 1965, 86

Wan, Enoch, 83
Wan, Sze-Kar, 109, 112–13
Wang, L. Ling-Chi, 89
Wang, Thomas, 148
War Brides Act of 1945, 32
Warner, William Lloyd, 74
Warren, Earl, 122
Warren, Rick, 144
WASPs (white Anglo-Saxon Protes-
    tants), as racial and ethnic class,
    124–25
Watchman Nee, 148

*Ways of Being, Ways of Reading: Asian
    American Biblical Interpretation*
    (Foskett and Kuan, eds.), 109
white Americans, granted free pass
    against Chinese Americans, 23–24
whiteness, 46
  as racial identity, 123–25
white privilege, 51, 127
Williams, Raymond Brady, 58, 60–61
Wilmore, Gayraud S., 93, 94
Wilson, Woodrow, 30
Winant, Howard, 1, 46, 122
Woo, Wesley S., 91
Workingmen's Party, 25
*Wounded Heart of God: The Asian
    Concept of Han and the Christian
    Doctrine of Sin* (Park), 83

Yamada, Frank, 116, 118–19
Yang, Fenggang, 56, 63, 146–47
Year of the Dragon, 46–47
Yee, Gale A., 110–12
Yellow Peril, 25, 46–47, 141
yinism, in race reconciliation, 139–40
Yinist theology, 158–59
Yong, Amos, 107, 159–61, 171
Yoo, David, 58
Youxue Zhengdaohui, 115

Znaniecki, Florian, 53